‘Professor Fried and her co-contributors have produced a book with significant implications for the fields of compliance, regulation, organizational behavior, corporate governance, and applied business ethics. The book reviews taxonomies and case studies to help us understand how and why deviance from standards occurs in organizations. Most helpful for research into large-scale corporate wrongdoing, the book closes with a discussion of how their findings should shape our thinking about individual versus corporate liability, civil, and criminal penalties for such behavior. I recommend the book to anyone looking for insight into these questions.’

J. S. Nelson, Professor of Law (Business Ethics), Villanova Law & Business Schools, Villanova University

‘Why do organizations deviate from standards? Are there good and bad organizational reasons for deviations beyond individual misbehaviour? You can find answers to these questions in this intellectually stimulating book that is full of critical reflection and fascinating empirical insights, for example about attentive deviance, over-conformity, non-regulated, and illegitimate deviance within software developing organizations.’

Günther Ortmann, Professor of Leadership, Witten/Herdecke University, formerly Helmut Schmidt University Hamburg

‘Standards are intended and expected to be repeatedly or continuously used by a substantial number of the parties for whom they are meant. However, this use is not self-evident. Standards may be ignored, unconsciously or consciously, but this book highlights another phenomenon: stakeholders may deviate from standards – again unconsciously or consciously. This book provides a thorough analysis of such deviations using in-depth case studies, revealing that different categories of deviations apply. Some of these were touched on in previous research but this is the first real study of them, making this book a great addition to the body of knowledge of standardisation, relevant for both the academic community and practitioners.’

Henk de Vries, Professor of Standardisation Management, Rotterdam School of Management, Erasmus University and President of European Academy for Standardisation EURAS

Understanding Deviance in a World of Standards

Edited by

ANDREA FRIED

OXFORD
UNIVERSITY PRESS

OXFORD
UNIVERSITY PRESS

Great Clarendon Street, Oxford, OX2 6DP,
United Kingdom

Oxford University Press is a department of the University of Oxford.
It furthers the University's objective of excellence in research, scholarship,
and education by publishing worldwide. Oxford is a registered trade mark of
Oxford University Press in the UK and in certain other countries

First Edition published in 2020

Published in the United States of America by Oxford University Press
198 Madison Avenue, New York, NY 10016, United States of America

British Library Cataloguing in Publication Data
Data available

Library of Congress Control Number: 2019945435

ISBN 978–0–19–883388–8

DOI: 10.1093/oso/9780198833888.001.0001

Preface

In Latin, the term *personare* stands for translucency. I found this exciting, i.e. what role a person would like to play in the external aspect of personality. The painting shows different faces of the same self that appears in different ways. It shows sides, what one was, is or could be and, furthermore, exaggerations, transformations, expansions and downsides of being human. It is ultimately about the absurdity of human behaviour, the play with roles, even falling out of the role. In the painting, I printed the same face on the canvas, almost like a wallpaper pattern... and then I painted it over, thus, alienated the same face. It is always the stencil (the silkscreen) that one sees through in the faces as a kind of standard and then there are the over-paintings, the deviations.

Undine Bandelin about her painting
Von Angesicht zu Angesicht (2015), basis for the book cover.

Not without intention, the title of the book refers to *A World of Standards*, a book authored by Nils Brunsson and Bengt Jacobsson and published by the same publisher almost two decades ago. The book gave inspiration for the research programme *Dangerous and Beneficial Drifts of Standards in the Modern Working Environment* (DaDriS) which I have been directing since 2010, today based at the Friedrich Schiller University Jena, Germany. Funded a second time by the German research council (DFG) (FR 2892/3-1), DaDriS highlights an important aspect of modern organizations in industrialized as well as developing countries: the appearance of standards as an expression of global form of rule setting and regulation and as a general tendency to minimize risk which coincides with auditing and control processes. The book represents the main outcome of our investigations between 2015 and 2019.

I am grateful for the thoughtful discussions of DaDriS's previously presented papers which paved the way for this book: for instance, at the Critical Management Studies Division Scholarly Program of the Academy of Management Annual Meetings in 2016 in Anaheim, CA and 2017 in Atlanta; at the European Group of Organization Studies conference with the sub-theme

The Power of Organizational Ethnography in Naples in 2016 organized by Juliette Koning and Jana Costas; at the European Academy of Management conference with the strategic interest group Innovation and Standardization in Glasgow in 2017 organized by Matts Kärreman, Magnus Johansson, Geerten Van de Kaa, Henk de Vries, Knut Blind, and Kai Jakobs; and at the 10th Critical Management Studies conference in Liverpool in 2017, where Arvind Singhal, Sarah Langer, and myself organized a stream on Deviance in Management and Organization Studies.

I warmly remember fruitful discussions with colleagues from Norway, South Africa, and Sweden, in particular with Erik Bjurström, David Coldwell, and Agnieta Pretorius and participants of the Annual Doctoral Workshop in the business administration division, but also during the collaborative research seminar series at the Management and Engineering Department, Linköping University, Sweden. Further, the workshop that Arvind Singhal gave on Positive Deviance in Linköping in December 2016 prepared the ground 'to flip' some taken-for-granted assumptions about organizational deviance. Moreover, DaDriS's PhD candidates received useful comments and gained experiences during numerous research colloquiums under the chair of Peter Walgenbach at the Friedrich Schiller University Jena, Germany. Peter Walgenbach also provided valuable feedback on an earlier version of the book's case studies.

Colleagues at the Friedrich Schiller University Jena, notably Chancellor Klaus Bartholmé, Head of Personnel Department, Uta Bock, and Stefan Ipach from the Service Centre for Research and Transfer, did an incredibly intense 14-day job in hosting DaDriS in April 2015. I am most grateful to Markus Rettenmayr as chair and Sandra Langner as administrator from the Otto Schott Institute of Materials Research (OSIM) based at the university for offering both the facilities and administrative support, and especially Markus Rettenmayr's enormous trust and belief in the whole undertaking.

DaDriS research assistants Martin Drüe, Martin Graef, and Claudia Krahl did an amazing job not only in providing technical support for compiling this book but also spending long hours transcribing our interview recordings.

True scientific funding bodies provide freedom and support for researchers to follow their inspiration. I appreciate that the DFG provided this opportunity, even across national borders.

The three companies that served as empirical partners for the case studies of this book did this with passion, offering their time and trust in the DaDriS project. It was a pleasure to gain insights into their daily work.

I appreciate the collaboration with all the contributors in this book; it has been an exciting journey. I also thank the editorial team of Oxford University Press for their guidance and support.

It is my deep hope that the insights on deviance in a world of standards offered in this book will provide ground for further conceptual and empirical research.

Andrea Fried

Jena and Linköping
July 2019

Contents

PART III. EXPLAINING ORGANIZATIONAL DEVIANCE FROM STANDARDS

List of Figures

List of Tables

List of Boxes

List of Abbreviations

AC	alternating current electricity flow
ANSI	American National Standards Institute
BSI	British Standards Institution
CCS	Combined Charging System
CENELEC	European Committee for Electrotechnical Standardization
DC	direct current electricity flow
DGUV	Institute for Occupational Safety and Health of the German Social Accident Insurance
DIN	Deutsche Institut für Normung
FAA	US Federal Aviation Administration
FDA	Food and Drug Administration
GSM	Global System for Mobile Communications
IMS	integrated management system
ISO	International Organization for Standardization
ITU	International Telecommunication Union
LTE	long-term evolution, standard for wireless broadband communication
RAMS	reliability, availability, maintainability, and safety
SOP	standard operating procedure
TFS	team foundation server
UN	United Nations

List of Contributors

Andrea Fried is Associate Professor in Business Administration at the Linköping University, Sweden and director of the DFG research project Dangerous and Beneficial Drifts of Standards in the Modern Working Environment at the Otto Schott Institute of Materials Research, Friedrich Schiller University Jena, Germany.

Ronny Gey is a doctoral candidate at the Friedrich Schiller University Jena, Faculty of Economics and Business Administration, and a research librarian at Leipzig University, Germany.

Besma Glaa, PhD, is a senior lecturer at the Service Research Center, Karlstad University, as well as working in Business Administration at Linköping University, Sweden.

Diana Karadzhova-Beyer, PhD, is a sociologist and post-doctoral researcher in the DFG research project Dangerous and Beneficial Drifts of Standards in the Modern Working Environment at the Otto Schott Institute of Materials Research, Friedrich Schiller University Jena, Germany.

Sarah Langer is a doctoral candidate at the Friedrich Schiller University Jena, Faculty of Economics and Business Administration, and a researcher in the DFG research project Dangerous and Beneficial Drifts of Standards in the Modern Working Environment at the Otto Schott Institute of Materials Research, Friedrich Schiller University Jena, Germany.

Arvind Singhal is the Samuel Shirley and Edna Holt Marston Endowed Professor of Communication at the University of Texas at El Paso, and William J. Clinton Distinguished Fellow at the Clinton School of Public Service, Little Rock, Arkansas, USA, as well as Distinguished Professor 2 in the Faculty of Business Administration, Inland Norway University of Applied Sciences, Norway.

Peter Walgenbach is Professor of Organization, Leadership, and Human Resource Management at the Friedrich Schiller University Jena, Germany.

1

Introduction to Deviance in a World of Standards

Andrea Fried and Besma Glaa

National standardization bodies such as the British Standards Institution (BSI), the American National Standards Institute (ANSI), and the Deutsche Institut für Normung (DIN) (German Institute for Standardization) and other international standardization bodies have established standards as important regulatory instruments that promote global trade and innovation, efficiency, and quality, helping to protect the economy, environment, and society. Standards have become widespread. For instance, the International Organization for Standardization (ISO)—responsible for the ISO 9000 and other international management standards—reports that in 2015 more than 1,5 million ISO standards certificates were issued worldwide (www.iso.org).

The intentions with which standards are being created and the number of certificates issued worldwide are impressive. By enabling a 'systematic reproduction and consistency' of processes and products (Ortmann 2010: 208), standards contribute, for instance, to a safe, reliable, and good quality of services and technologies. They allow the modularization of technologies and services. Advantages of modular design can be seen in aircraft to the extent that there are certain parts of the aircraft that can be tested, added, or even removed without affecting the rest of it. Thus, standards allow, for example, fast, independent innovations in the supply chain while keeping development, testing and production costs low. In addition, the currently accepted status of technologies and services is inscribed in standards.

However, where necessary, standards or specific standard requirements are adapted or renewed to new technological achievements, processes or services when they become obsolete. Disruptive innovations such as autonomous vehicle technologies, genetic scissors, and block chain financial services technologies are some recent examples where new standards still need to be developed to support high levels of safe, reliable, and ethically acceptable quality (Wiegmann et al. 2017). The Combined Charging System (CCS),

Andrea Fried and Besma Glaa, *Introduction to Deviance in a World of Standards* In: *Understanding Deviance in a World of Standards*. Edited by: Andrea Fried, Oxford University Press (2020). © Oxford University Press.
DOI: 10.1093/oso/9780198833888.003.0001

standardized in IEC 62196-3 and SAE J1772 as a uniform standard throughout Europe, was recently developed in collaboration with leading automobile manufacturers (e.g. BMW, Mercedes-Benz, Ford, and Volkswagen) in order to provide a charging standard for electric vehicles. Compared to Tesla's charging system, which is exclusive to its clients, CCS is a double plug that has the advantage of charging both alternating current (AC) and direct current (DC) electricity flow. Such new standards can increase the number of suitable spots where drivers can recharge their cars. The deviation from existing standards and the creation of new standards thus not only contributes to the dissemination of innovations, but also supports the achievement of environmental goals such as the reduction of CO_2 emissions in the European Union (see for example Directive 2014/94/EU of the European Parliament and of the Council on the deployment of alternative fuels infrastructure).

In contrast, critical deviations from standards have been reported in many sectors, including the textile, automobile, and aviation industries. For example, the textile industry neglected standards for health, fire, and building safety, leading to the use of extremely inferior material to build the Rana Plaza complex in Bangladesh—resulting in its collapse in 2013 where more than 1,100 people perished (*BBC News*, 10 May 2013). Volkswagen admitted in September 2015 that 11 million diesel-engine cars were equipped with software that manipulated the emission test results for the US American market. Hans-Dieter Pötsch, head of Volkswagen's supervisory board, claimed at the first open news conference following these revelations that within his company 'there was a tolerance for breaking the rules' (*The New York Times*, 10 December 2015). In a similar vein, the Boeing Company faced software problems, causing two tragic air disasters in 2018 and 2019. In addition to strong competition from Airbus, these problems seem to be due to the close relationship between Boeing and the US Federal Aviation Administration (FAA). A decade ago, the FAA began to allow Boeing to do more self-certification. A former Boeing consultant stated, 'it's like putting children in charge of the sweet shop' and suggested that Boeing has not been held responsible enough to meet aviation standards (*The Economist*, 23 March 2019).

As these phenomena demonstrate, such intentional deviations from standards by organizations can either contribute to or challenge quality, human health, safety, consumer trust, and environmental protection. Therefore, it becomes important to investigate the innovative, criminal and further reasons behind organizations' deviance from standards. The authors of this book argue that the sole existence of standards and their positive rating or certification does not necessarily reflect the quality of their organizational implementation.

To understand deviance from standards, it is therefore highly relevant to investigate organizations as recipients of standards and to better understand their actual dealing with standards.

The book explicitly answers the question *why organizations deviate from standards.* It provides a rather unique theoretical approach and empirical explanations for deviance in organizations that go beyond an understanding of individual misbehaviour where single persons (senior managers, middle managers, employees) are held responsible for deviations in organizations. The book explores the organizational conditions and contradictions under which different types of deviance in organizations occur and explains the responsibility of organizations when deviating from standards. Such improved understanding can help various actors, for instance, legal experts and authorities to better understand the reasons of standard deviations in organizations. And it could support customers or clients who need to take organizational deviance into account when making decisions on investments or other strategic decisions, or when buying certified products and services.

The next section positions *Understanding Deviance in a World of Standards* in the current literature on standards and standardization.

1.1 The Current Discourse on Standards and our View of it

Standardization research uses in many cases the terms standard and standardization interchangeably. Some studies, however, refer explicitly to the terms' interconnectedness but also to their differences. Timmermans and Epstein (2010: 69) argue that standards and standardization have the same aim, which is 'to render the world equivalent across cultures, time, and geography'. Similarly, Wright et al. (2012: 653) suggest that 'standards and standardization refer to rules which imply similarity, uniformity and continuity of behavior, actions or beliefs'. Timmermans and Epstein (2010: 71) add that 'standards and standardization typically imply one another, which means that we need greater nuance to understand their implications for a world significantly shaped by both'. These scholars agree that the concept of standardization needs to be investigated in connection to standards and vice versa.

1.1.1 Distinguishing Standards and Standardization

To do so, Brunsson and Jacobsson (2000a) distinguish analytically what standards are and what standardization is. Standards are a 'specific kind of rules', whereas standardization encompasses 'the production of such rules' (Brunsson & Jacobsson 2000a: 15). Loconto and Demortain (2017: 384) add that an 'approach to standardization that limits itself to the setting of the standard would be incomplete'. In their view, standardization also encompasses the 'active use of a standard' and the 'reinvention of rules and reallocation of responsibilities for implementing those rules' (Loconto & Demortain 2017: 384). Standardization targets 'uniformities across time and space, through the generation of agreed-upon rules' (Timmermans & Epstein 2010: 71; see also Wright et al. 2012).

Brunsson et al. identify three different but interrelated categories of standardization: the standardization by organizations; standardization as a form of organization; and standardization of organizations (Brunsson et al. 2012: 619f.). The first category, *standardization by organizations*, describes standards as produced by formal organizations and concerns the 'entities that produce, revise and diffuse standards'. What Loconto and Demortain (2017) describe similarly as *standards in the making* refers likewise to the process of creating standards and to the outcomes of negotiations between interested actors for constructing these standards.

The second category, *standardization as a form of organization*, defines standardization as 'a way of organizing society' (Brunsson et al. 2012: 620). In the same manner, Loconto and Demortain (2017) define *standards in circulation*, where they refer to the diffusion of standards and their dissemination in diverse places and sociocultural contexts (see also Engwall 2000). They add that these circulations may create new versions and interpretations of the same standard. Therefore 'the process of circulation can both redeliver diversity in standard practices and reduce diversity as practices converge to form a new or revised standard, only to be reopened again' (Loconto & Demortain 2017: 386).

The third category, *standardization of organizations*, concerns the question how organizations are affected by standards. Organizations 'adopt' standards which were created previously elsewhere in the environment of the organization. This type of standardization describes *standards in action* and is about applying standards by users (Loconto & Demortain 2017). Of interest here is how organizational structures and practices are shaped by standards and how the multiple ways of standard enactment can look like.

Just like Brunsson et al., Loconto and Demortain, and others, contributors to this book distinguish standards from standardization. However, their theoretical and empirical efforts clearly concentrate on the *standardization of organizations* and focus on how standards are applied in organizations.

1.1.2 Definition of Standards

Several definitions of standards can be found in the literature. Brunsson et al. identify three key characteristics of standards: they state that standards are a specific type of rule (as described above), formally voluntary, and for common use (Brunsson et al. 2012, see also Blind 2004; Rasche 2010; Rasche & Seidl 2019). Brunsson et al. link the three characteristics and define a standard 'as a rule for common and voluntary use, decided by one or several people or organizations' (Brunsson et al. 2012: 616). In the same vein, Wright et al. (2012: 652) define standards as 'externally-determined rules' adopted by organizations voluntarily to align their activities with other organizations, for instance, in regard to product design, quality, or financial reporting.

Other scholars have mentioned the effect of standards and their mediating role between different parties. For instance, Spivak and Brenner (2001: 16) define a standard as 'a uniform set of measures, agreements, conditions, or specifications between parties (buyer–user, manufacturer–user, government–industry, or government governed, etc.)'. Likewise, Borum and Hansen (2000) stress the role of standards as coordinator and controller of both the activities and actors involved. Accordingly, standards may be used to control disagreeing interests and create an agreement between the various actors (cf. Botzem & Quack 2006; Cyert & March 1963; Nelson & Winter 1982). Similarily, Brunsson and Jacobsson (2000a: 16) argue that 'standards facilitate co-ordination and communication', 'make a complex world simpler and... provide optimal or at least good solutions, policies or products'. Thus, standards have been associated with the concept of uniformity and similarity and define proper behaviour (Brunsson & Jacobsson 2000b).

Additionally, David and Greenstein (1990: 4) have provided a definition that considers standards as 'a set of technical specifications that can be adhered to by a producer, either tacitly, or in accord with some formal agreement, or in conformity with explicit regulatory authority'. This definition adds something about the origin of standards. Standards can result from state regulation or industry self-regulation, or can indirectly emerge as quasi-standards through a wide diffusion of technology on the market (Wiegman 2019) (see also *de facto standards* in section 1.1.3).

In this book, authors take a closer look at standards that are a result of industry self-regulation and state regulation—thus, the formalized appearance of standards. Standards are first of all externally determined rules. Close to the definition proposed by Brunsson and Jacobsson (2000a), contributors to this book understand *standards* as documents established by consensus and approved by an identifiable author, for instance, a standardization body such as ISO, United States Food and Drug Administration (FDA), or DIN (see also Beck & Walgenbach 2005; Bénézech et al. 2001; Sandholtz 2012). From standards, the authors distinguish and investigate in this book, however, *internal standard documents*, which arise with the users' recursive interaction with standards (Fried et al. 2013). Internal standard documents are often called *standard operating procedures* (Ortmann 2015, see also Naveh & Marcus 2005), or more colloquially 'standard bibles' by practitioners (Gey & Fried 2018).

1.1.3 Categories of Standards

Standards have been categorized based on numerous distinctions serving different purposes. Three types of standards have been proposed by Brunsson and Jacobsson (2000a): standards about being something, about having something, or about doing something. The first type are *standards about being something* that serve to classify things or actors. Examples are standards for measuring and statistical standards. The distinction between *de jure standards* and *de facto standards* is another categorization, which can be classified here (e.g. Borraz 2007; Brunsson et al. 2012; Chiesa et al. 2002; Farrell & Saloner 1988; Funk 2002). *De jure* standards are written documents 'establishing technical specifications for goods, services, or processes, resulting from a consensus, and whose application is voluntary' (Borraz 2007: 57). This type of standards concerns standards that are disseminated by governmental agencies or legislative bodies in agreement with regulatory authority, and standards issued by independent organizations such as ISO (Brunsson et al. 2012). Examples of *de jure* standards include the Global System for Mobile Communications (GSM) protocol in telecommunications, the medical devices law, and the German railway regulation act. In contrast, *de facto standards* 'result from a unilateral act and emerge through the mediation of market processes' (Borraz 2007: 57). Examples are standards for the software and hardware architecture of personal computers. For this book, this widely cited distinction between *de jure* and *de facto* standards is of lower relevance insofar that it mainly covers *standardization by organizations*—thus, where the standards are being made before they enter the organization (Brunsson et al. 2012). However, the organizations investigated in this book must implement *de jure* standards since all of them develop software for safety-critical hardware environments (see also Langer et al. 2020a).

The second type of standards is about things that we should have. *Standards about having something* can, for instance, refer to a strategic plan, compliant technology, or a quality system that an organization should have. Brunsson et al. 2012 call these standards *outcome standards*, as they concentrate on the presence of measurable and visibly discernible outcomes. Beyond this, a distinction between *technical standards* and *non-technical standards* has been offered (Brunsson et al. 2012). Known as 'compatibility' or 'interface' standards (David & Greenstein 1990), technical standards are defined as 'codified specifications about components and their relational attributes' (Garud & Kumaraswamy 1993: 353; see also Reinecke et al. 2012). Thus, technical standards could be subsumed under *outcome standards* or *standards about having something*, but are not investigated in this book.

The third type of standards, *standards about doing something*, refers to how standards can apply to different processes, such as how organizations should behave or how to design a product that can be manufactured and offered for sale. Brunsson et al. also call this type *process standards*. Process standards 'regulate processes within and between organizations (e.g. safety processes) without predetermining any specific outcomes' (Brunsson et al. 2012: 616). Today, the audited objects of standards are above all mainly the internal organizational processes and not their results, i.e., the organization's products or services themselves (Power 1997). Process standards are created to answer the need for, for example, organizational accountability, control, and legitimacy internally and externally. They have a massive influence on customer and investment decisions nowadays since they minimize financial risks through global rule setting. Process standards are standards that specify how organizations should 'behave'. With it, a standard sets a norm about what a proper organizational behaviour is: in particular, 'how organizational processes should be designed and controlled' (Brunsson & Jacobsson 2000a: 4). Empirically, authors in this book have seen that standards in particular in software-developing organizations include aspects of process standards and outcome standards. However, what they are interested in is how standards shape the structure and interaction of organizations. For this reason, this book places theoretically and empirically an emphasis on the processual impact of standards on software development, and, thus, on what standards do in organizations (Brunsson & Jacobsson 2000a).

1.1.4 Dynamics of Standards

Lately, researchers have begun to consider standards and standardization as a dynamic phenomenon and shown an interest in the several dynamics associated with the processes of standardization (e.g. Brunsson et al. 2012; Egyedi &

Blind 2008). Damtew and Aanestad (2012) investigated, for instance, the tension between the notion of stability and sameness allied with the nature of standardization as well as the need for flexibility and adaptation when implementing standards in practice. The authors distinguish 'fixed and flexible elements of standards' and highlight that for applying organizations it becomes challenging to handle both rigour implementation and context-specific adjustment (Damtew & Aanestad 2012: 27; see also Jacobsson & Sahlin-Andersson 2006; Timmermans & Epstein 2010). The fact that these authors refer also to flexible elements of standards points to another important discussion that standardization researchers have conducted.

1.1.5 Standards and their 'Use Mode'

By distinguishing standards and internal standard documents as described above, the authors of the book support the perspective that usually a drift occurs 'between the institutional template [here, the standard] and the exigencies of daily life' (Barley 1986: 80). The internal standard document results from an enactment of the actual standard when users and specialists in organizations continuously learn to discover and exploit features, affordances, and potentials of standards in the daily stream of interventions, tinkering, and improvizations (Ciborra 2002; Ortmann 2010; Weick 1995). Thus, the standard created and provided, for instance, by a standardization body and the standard *in use* within an organization necessarily differ.

For this reason, authors in this book are particularly interested in the use mode of standards while distinguishing it from the design mode (following Orlikowski 1992). The *design mode of standards* describes standardization by organizations—that is, by standardization bodies or other regulatory authorities (Brunsson et al. 2012). Research on the design mode encompasses at least two perspectives. On the one hand, researchers ask how standards come into being, how standardisation bodies function, are set up and organized, and how they convince potential stakeholders to certify their organizations (e.g. Casadesús et al. 2008; Furusten 2000; Marimon & Casadesús 2009; Walgenbach 2000). In addition, questions of democracy, corruption and the emergence of industry clusters in standardization processes are researched (e.g. De Souza e Silva 2009; Ruwet 2011; Venard 2009). On the other hand, researchers contribute to the development of procedural models like the V-model (Ruparelia 2010; see also Langer et al. 2020b) or the Scrum approach to give advice and 'translate' standards for practitioners.

Investigating the *use mode of standards* is, however, closely connected to standardization of organizations (Brunsson et al. 2012). For example, previous empirical studies have found that companies are often considered more innovative and more leadership-competent than non-certified companies. This is discussed as problematic since the effects of the bureaucratic rationalization on the non-routine and knowledge work activities through standards are not deterministic and show a wide range of potential results (Beck & Walgenbach 2005; Fried et al. 2013; Staw & Epstein 2000). Hence, the same standard can be 'simultaneously mock, coercive, and enabling' (Adler 2005: 401; see also Adler & Borys 1996; Boiral 2003; Wouters & Wilderom 2008).

Further empirical studies provide additional evidence for this. For instance, the long-term quantitative study on the implementation of ISO 9000s standards in the paint and photography industry shows a 'crowding out effect' on innovative activities after implementing a total quality management regime (Benner & Tushman 2002). Complementary results are provided by Beck and Walgenbach who conclude that the likelihood of adopting ISO 9000s standards in organizations with a non-routine, highly customized production is reduced (Beck & Walgenbach 2005). Thus, it means that standards do not bring automatically more innovations or better managerial competence to an organization. It is the members of the organization who enact standards in one way or the other. This non-automatism turns the use mode of standards into an interesting and important field of investigation and is illuminated in this book.

To date, the use mode literature on standards is chiefly shaped by the research on the ISO 9000s and ISO 14000s process quality standards that culminated in the early 2000s (e.g. Boiral 2003; Niazi et al. 2005; Zeng et al. 2007). Here, research on the use mode has been done concerning the functioning of standards as a form of regulation as well as a code of corporate governance (e.g. Power 2007; Seidl 2007; Wieland 2005). This is also addressed when investigating institutional isomorphisms to understand similarities of the processes or structure among organizations after implementing a certain standard (e.g. Benders et al. 2006; see also DiMaggio & Powell 1983). Focusing on isomorphic pressures, however, implies that standards are mainly a phenomenon of homogenization of modern working environments, hiding local interpretations (Boiral 2003; Timmermans & Epstein 2010). In contrast, this book, however, strengthens the perspective that a standard is something flexible and 'creates significant opportunities for localized adaptation or "translation" but also for shirking and avoiding' (Djelic & den Hond 2014: 69). The authors of the book agree that standards are locally and socially constructed when people encounter a standard and use it in their daily work. That standards are locally and socially constructed implies that an objective state of standard compliance does not exist. For this reason, it becomes even more interesting and important to investigate the organizations' enactment of standards, as well as their deviations from standards.

1.1.6 Standard Enactment in Organizations

To explore further the social construction of standards theoretically, we refer to the concept of *enactment*. Weick describes enactment as a process in which people bring structures and events into existence and swing them into action (Weick 1988). An enacted standard is in our definition the 'residuum of changes produced by enactment' and emphasizes that 'what is left after a process cannot be ignored or left out of account because it has potential significance' (Weick 1988: 307). The enactment of standards does not happen accidently. Instead, it is an 'orderly, material, social construction that is subject to multiple interpretations' (Weick 1988: 307).

Utilizing this concept and referring to structuration theory in this book, we believe that standards are enacted when they show characteristics in the following three dimensions: structural dimension, material dimension, and action dimension. The *structural dimension* reminds us that standards once enacted constitute sense and define rights and responsibilities. They clarify which actions are deviant or legitimated and which are consequently sanctioned or rewarded within an organization. Standards unfold self-sustaining authoritative effects (e.g. a sequential path of a project execution process) and allocative effects through the assignment of organizational resources to standardization activities (e.g. to quality managers or to regulatory affairs units) and standardized processes (e.g. due to the need for additional resources for increased documentation efforts) (Giddens 1984). They are for organizations, thus, of political and economic appearance. Enacted standards show also a *material dimension*. Standards are adapted and written down in the form of documents. This dimension represents the materialized moments of enactment and include interpretative schemes (e.g. role descriptions of software developers in view of standards for software process improvement, assignments of economic value), administrative and economic resources of power (e.g. quality appraisals/standard certification, distributed responsibilities and facilities), and social norms (e.g. company visions about meaning of quality, customers, innovation) (following Becker 2003; Giddens 1984). The *action dimension* mirrors how organizational members refer to the material and structural dimension of standards in their daily practices. With reference to standards, organizational members consequently change communication, power and social norms in organizations.

1.1.7 Deviance from Standards in Organizations

Standards produce structures and impact on interactions that do not exist before people decide to implement them (following Giddens 1984). Thus, the social construction of standards does not end with their creation by standardization bodies. Organizational members enact standards by shaping their structural, material, and action dimensions according to their specific context. But organizational members also reflect on the organizational conditions and contradictions of standard enactment and assess the intended as well as unintended consequences of standards on their daily activities. Depending on the results of this reflection, organizational members deviate from standards through pragmatic action and situated improvisation in various ways.

1.2 Structure of the Book

The authors of this book share a common interest in developing the organizational perspective on deviance, both in general as an emerging topic in management and organization studies and in view of standards in organizations as an exciting phenomenon to investigate. Overall, it is important to hold that the ten chapters of *Understanding Deviance in a World of Standards* are strongly integrated. The chapters were written in different author constellations, but all chapters are based on each other. Our recommendation for readers is to read them preferably one after the other.

The book consists of three main parts. Part I contains the theoretical and methodological framework for the empirical studies on organizational deviance from standards. Andrea Fried and Arvind Singhal review in chapter 2 functionalist as well as interactionist approaches to deviance and conclude seven lessons learned. They highlight which novel research questions arise when taking a second-order perspective on organizational deviance. Fried and Singhal furthermore define organizational deviance more precisely by distinguishing it according to its descriptive aspect, its normative aspect and its sanctioning aspect to facilitate its operationalization. They formulate six assignments for developing the concept of organizational deviance.

The review on deviance prepares the ground for the next chapter. In chapter 3, Andrea Fried and Peter Walgenbach develop a structurationist framework for exploring organizational deviance from standards empirically. They identify standards as modalities of action which trigger rules of interpretation, claim allocative and authoritative resources, and furthermore cause rules of sanctions. In their view, how standards are enacted as modalities of action can yield different asymmetries and contradictions, which lead again to different types of organizational deviance. This theoretical framework lays the foundation for the empirical studies presented in part II.

In chapter 4, Sarah Langer, Ronny Gey, and Diana Karadzhova-Beyer introduce the qualitative research design for the case studies that are presented in the third part of the book. The empirical investigations of organizational deviance from standards are designed as focused ethnography. The chapter explains in detail how the case studies were accomplished. But it can also serve as a starting point for potential replication studies or studies that can be set up to prove the empirical findings of the book quantitatively.

Part II builds theoretically and methodically on the first part of the book and explores organizational deviance from standards by studying three different cases of standard enactment in software-developing organizations. Sarah Langer and Andrea Fried introduce this part with an overview of which deviations from standards the investigated organizations carried out.

The reasons why each organization deviates in a different way and to varying degrees are explained thereafter in three case studies in chapters 5, 6, and 7. Each case study is structured in the same manner: first, the case introduction provides general information about market conditions, the investigated software-development projects, the company's standard landscape, and the realm of empirical investigations. This is followed by thorough descriptions and rich empirical evidence of how standards shape interpretative schemes and social norms, as well as their claim for additional facilities for software development. An analysis of the asymmetries and contradictions that occur between these standard-induced interpretative schemes, social norms, and facilities explains a specific type of organizational deviance from standards and finalizes each case study.

In chapter 5, Ronny Gey, Sarah Langer, and Andrea Fried describe a software-developing project of the crane manufacturer CraneSolutions which is confronted with a situation where no standards are directly suitable for their niche products. They analyse how the organization enacts standards appropriately but deviates from them notwithstanding. The asymmetries that emerge during standard enactment at CraneSolutions can be described as productive. The authors call this type attentive deviance from standards.

Chapter 6 written by Ronny Gey, Sarah Langer, and Andrea Fried presents the MedTech case study. It analyses a case from software development in the medical technology industry where standards have shaped development processes for a long time and resulted in a constraining impact. MedTech deviates just temporarily when, for instance, standardizing bodies change or enforce standard requirements. When these changes in standard requirements are detected, it adjusts its standard operating procedures accordingly. This leads, however, to organizational inertia—productive asymmetries and contradictions in standard enactment are hardly found. This type of deviance is called over-conformity to standards.

In chapter 7, Sarah Langer, Ronny Gey, Diana Karadzhova-Beyer, and Andrea Fried discover organizational deviance from standards at MetroEngineers, a service engineering company for trains. Their explanations for organizational deviance are in particular of interest since software development takes place in the less regulated standard landscape of China. Organizational deviations from standards are in this case hardly sanctioned. This contributes to several asymmetries and contradictions MetroEngineers need to cope with during standard enactment. In the end, standards are not adequately enacted in this company; this type is called non-regulated deviance from standards.

Part III offers the theoretical desideratum of the book. Introduced by Andrea Fried and Sarah Langer, it explains in three chapters why organizations deviate from standards. In chapter 8, Andrea Fried and Sarah Langer develop a typology including four types of organizational deviance from standards: attentive deviance, over-conformity, non-regulated deviance, and illegitimate deviance from standards. The basis of the typology is a cross-case comparison of cases in chapters 5, 6, and 7 where the authors explain which organizational conditions and contradictions in standard enactment make a certain type of organizational deviance likely. The fourth type of organizational deviance from standards, illegitimate deviance, is logically deduced from our insights on the three empirical cases.

In chapter 9, Sarah Langer and Andrea Fried discuss the aspect of social agency during standard enactment. They suggest that how organizational members monitor standard enactment and deviations from standards influences the exploratory character as well as the exploitative character of organizational processes. By identifying reflexive, diagnostic, self, and inadequate ways of monitoring, the standard–innovation nexus can be explained in a novel way. The chapter finishes with propositions for further research.

Chapter 10 encompasses concluding remarks about the responsibility of organizations when deviating from standards. Based on the empirical findings and theoretical contributions of the book, Andrea Fried reflects on effective compliance management systems in organizations but also on the crucial role of external control and sanctioning mechanism for standard deviations. She describes the limits of organizational self-regulation and discusses the topical question of whether national legislations should also take account of organizational liability in the event of criminal deviations from standards in addition to individual liability.

References

Adler, P. S. 2005. The evolving object of software development. *Organization*, 12, 401–35.

Adler, P. S. & Borys, B. 1996. Two types of bureaucracy: enabling and coercive. *Administrative Science Quarterly*, 41, 61–89.

Barley, S. R. 1986. Technology as an occasion for structuring: evidence from observations of CT scanners and the social order of radiology departments. *Administrative Science Quarterly*, 31, 78–108.

Beck, N. & Walgenbach, P. 2005. Technical efficiency or adaptation to institutionalized expectations? The adoption of ISO 9000 standards in the German mechanical engineering industry. *Organization Studies*, 26, 841–66.

Becker, A. 2003. *Controlling als reflexive Steuerung von Organisationen*. Stuttgart: Schaeffer-Poeschel.

Benders, J., Batenburg, R. & van der Blonk, H. 2006. Sticking to standards; technical and other isomorphic pressures in deploying ERP-systems. *Information & Management*, 43, 194–203.

BéNézech, D., Lambert, G., Lanoux, B., Lerch, C. & Loos-Baroin, J. 2001. Completion of knowledge codification: an illustration through the ISO 9000 standards implementation process. *Research Policy*, 30, 1395–407.

Benner, M. J. & Tushman, M. 2002. Process management and technological innovation: a longitudinal study of the photography and paint industries. *Administrative Science Quarterly*, 47, 676–706.

Blind, K. 2004. *The Economics of Standards: Theory, Evidence, Policy*. Cheltenham: Edward Elgar.

Boiral, O. 2003. ISO 9000: outside the iron cage. *Organization Science*, 14, 720–37.

Borraz, O. 2007. Governing standards: the rise of standardization processes in France and in the EU. *Governance: An International Journal of Policy, Administration, and Institutions*, 20, 57–84.

Borum, F. & Hansen, H. F. 2000. The local construction and enactment of standards for research evaluation: the case of the Copenhagen business school. *Evaluation*, 6, 281–99.

Brunsson, N. & Jacobsson, B. 2000a. The contemporary expansion of standardization. *In*: Brunsson, N. & Jacobsson, B. (eds) *A World of Standards*. Oxford: Oxford University Press.

Brunsson, N. & Jacobsson, B. 2000b. Following standards. *In*: Brunsson, N. & Jacobsson, B. (eds) *A World of Standards*. Oxford: Oxford University Press.

Brunsson, N., Rasche, A. & Seidl, D. 2012. The dynamics of standardization: three perspectives on standards in organization studies. *Organization Studies*, 33, 613–32.

Casadesús, M., Marimon, F. & Heras, I. 2008. ISO 14001 diffusion after the success of the ISO 9001 model. *Journal of Cleaner Production*, 16, 1741–54.

Chiesa, V., Manzini, R. & Toletti, G. 2002. Standard-setting processes: evidence from two case studies. *R & D Management*, 32, 431–50.

Ciborra, C. 2002. *The Labyrinths of Information*. Oxford: Oxford University Press.

Cyert, R. M. & March, J. G. 1963. *A Behavioral Theory of the Firm*. Englewood Cliffs: Prentice Hall.

Damtew, Z. A. & Aanestad, M. 2012. Benefits of local knowledge in shaping standards: a case study from community health service and information systems in Ethiopia. *Scandinavian Journal of Information Systems*, 24, 27–50.

David, P. & Greenstein, S. 1990. The economics of compatibility standards: an introduction to recent research. *Economics of Innovation and New Technology*, 1, 3–41.

De Souza E. Silva, A. 2009. Hybrid reality and location-based gaming: redefining mobility and game spaces in urban environments. *Simulation & Gaming*, 40, 404–24.

Dimaggio, P. J. & Powell, W. W. 1983. The iron cage revisited: institutional isomorphism and collective rationality in organizational fields. *American Sociological Review*, 48, 147–60.

Djelic, M. L. & Den Hond, F. 2014. Introduction: multiplicity and plurality in the world of standards. Symposium on multiplicity and plurality in the world of standards. *Business and Politics*, 16, 67–77.

Egyedi, T. & Blind, K. (eds) 2008. *The Dynamics of Standards*. Cheltenham: Edward Elgar.

Farrell, J. & Saloner, G. 1988. Coordination through committees and markets. *The RAND Journal of Economics*, 19, 235–52.

Fried, A., Gey, R., Pretorius, A. & Günther, L. 2013. Decoupling from standards—process management and technical innovation in software development organisations. *International Journal of Innovation Management*, 17.

Funk, P. 2002. Induced innovation revisited. *Economica*, 69, 155–71.

Furusten, S. 2000. The knowledge base of standards. *In*: Brunsson, N. & Jacobsson, B. (eds) *A World of Standards*. Oxford: Oxford University Press.

Garud, R. & Kumaraswamy, A. 1993. Changing competitive dynamics in network industries: an exploration of Sun Microsystems' open systems strategy. *Strategic Management Journal*, 14, 351–69.

Gey, R. & Fried, A. 2018. Metastructuring for standards: how organizations respond to the multiplicity of standards. *In*: Jakobs, K. (ed.) *Corporate and Global Standardization Initiatives in Contemporary Society*. Pennsylvania: IGI Global.

Giddens, A. 1984. *The Constitution of Society*. Cambridge: Polity Press.

Langer, S., Gey, R., Karadzhova-Beyer, D. & Fried, A. 2020a. Deregulated deviance from standards at MetroEngineers. *In*: Fried, A. (ed.) *Understanding Deviance in a World of Standards*. Oxford: Oxford University Press.

Langer, S., Gey, R. & Karadzhova-Beyer, D. 2020b. Investigating Organizational deviance from standards in-depth. *In*: Fried, A. (ed.) *Understanding Deviance in a World of Standards*. Oxford: Oxford University Press.

Loconto, A. M. & Demortain, D. 2017. Standardization as spaces of diversity. *Engaging Science, Technology, and Society*, 3, 382–92.

Marimon, F. & Casadesús, M. 2009. ISO 9000 and ISO 14000 standards: a projection model for the decline phase. *Total Quality Management and Business Excellence*, 20, 1–21.

Naveh, E. & Marcus, A. 2005. Achieving competitive advantage through implementing a replicable management standard: installing and using ISO 9000. *Journal of Operations Management*, 24, 1–26.

Nelson, R. R. & Winter, S. G. 1982. *An Evolutionary Theory of Economic Change*. Cambridge, MA: Belknap Press.

Niazi, M., Wilson, D. & Zowghi, D. 2005. A maturity model for the implementation of software process improvement. An empirical study. *Journal of Systems and Software*, 74, 155–72.

Orlikowski, W. J. 1992. The duality of technology. Rethinking the concept of technology in organizations. *Organization Science*, 3, 398–427.

Ortmann, G. 2010. On drifting rules and standards. *Scandinavian Journal of Management*, 26, 204–14.

Ortmann, G. 2015. *Organisation und Moral. Die dunkle Seite*. Weilerswist: Velbrück.

Power, M. 1997. *The Audit Society. Rituals of Verification*. Oxford: Oxford University Press.

Power, M. 2007. *Organized Uncertainty. Designing a World of Risk Management*. Oxford: Oxford University Press.

Rasche, A. 2010. The limits of corporate responsibility standards. *Business Ethics: A European Review*, 19, 280–91.

Reinecke, J., Manning, S. & von Hagen, O. 2012. The emergence of a standards market: multiplicity of sustainability standards in the global coffee industry. *Organization Studies*, 33, 789–812.

Ruparelia, N. B. 2010. Software development lifecycle models. *SIGSOFT Software Engineering Notes*, 35, 8–13.

Ruwet, C. 2011. Towards a democratization of standards development? Internal dynamics of ISO in the context of globalization. *New Global Studies*, 5, Article 1.

Sandholtz, K. W. 2012. Making standards stick: a theory of coupled vs. decoupled compliance. *Organization Studies*, 33, 655–79.

Seidl, D. 2007. Standard setting and following in corporate governance: an observation-theoretical study of the effectiveness of governance codes. *Organization*, 14, 705–27.

Spivak, S. M. & Brenner, F. C. 2001. *Standardization Essentials: Principles & Practice*. New York: Marcel Dekker.

Staw, B. M. & Epstein, L. D. 2000. What bandwagons bring: effects of popular management techniques on corporate performance, reputation, and CEO pay. *Administrative Science Quarterly*, 45, 523–56.

Timmermans, S. & Epstein, S. 2010. A world of standards but not a standard world: toward a sociology of standards and standardization. *Annual Review of Sociology*, 36, 69–89.

Venard, B. 2009. Organizational isomorphism and corruption: an empirical research in Russia. *Journal of Business Ethics*, 89, 59–76.

Walgenbach, P. 2000. *Die Normgerechte Organisation. Eine Studie über die Entstehung, Verbreitung und Nutzung der DIN EN ISO 9000er Normenreihe*. Stuttgart: Schäffer-Poeschel.

Weick, K. E. 1988. Enacted sensemaking in crisis situations. *Journal of Management Studies*, 25, 305–17.

Weick, K. E. 1995. *Sensemaking in Organizations*. Thousand Oaks: Sage.

Wieland, J. 2005. Corporate governance, values management, and standards: a European perspective. *Business & Society*, 44, 74–93.

Wouters, M. & Wilderom, C. 2008. Developing performance-measurement systems as enabling formalization: a longitudinal field study of a logistics department. *Accounting, Organizations and Society*, 33, 488–516.

Wright, C., Sturdy, A. & Wylie, N. 2012. Management innovation through standardization: consultants as standardizers of organizational practice. *Research Policy*, 41, 652–62.

Zeng, S. X., Shi, J. J. & Lou, G. X. 2007. A synergetic model for implementing an integrated management system: an empirical study in China. *Journal of Cleaner Production*, 15, 1760–7.

Botzem, S. & Quack, S. 2006. Contested rules and shifting boundaries: international standard-setting in accounting. *In:* Djelic, M. L. & Sahlin-Andersson, K. (eds.) *Transnational governance—institutional dynamics of regulation.* Cambridge: Cambridge University Press.

Engwall, L. 2000. The globalisation of management: standardisation processes in management with an illustration from Scandinavia. *Zeitschrift für Betriebswirtschaft,* 70, 1–22.

Jacobsson, B. & Sahlin-Andersson, K. 2006. Dynamics of soft regulations. *In:* Djelic, M. L. & Sahlin Andersson, K. (eds.) *Transnational governance-institutional dynamics of regulation.* Cambridge: Cambridge University Press.

Rasche, A. & Seidl, D. 2019. Standards between partial and complete organization. *In:* Ahrne, G. & Brunsson, N. (eds.) *Organization outside organizations: the abundance of partial organization in social life.* Cambridge: Cambridge University Press.

Wiegmann, P. M. 2019. *Managing innovation and standards: a case in the European heating industry,* Cham, Palgrave Macmillan.

Wiegmann, P. M., de Vries, H. J. & Blind, K. 2017. Multi-mode standardisation: a critical review and a research agenda. *Research Policy,* 46, 1370–1386.

PART I
FRAMING ORGANIZATIONAL DEVIANCE FROM STANDARDS

Framing organizational deviance from standards provides as part I the theoretical and methodological fundamentals of the book.

Understanding Deviance in a World of Standards, Andrea Fried, Oxford University Press (2020).

DOI: 10.1093/oso/9780198833888.001.0001

2

A Second-Order Observation of Organizational Deviance

Andrea Fried and Arvind Singhal

The purpose of this chapter is to review organizational deviance from two different, incommensurable scientific paradigms—the functionalist and interactionist. In the functionalist perspective, organizational deviance is viewed as being objectively manifest, whereas in interactionist studies deviance is understood as being subjectively problematic (Anderson 2014; Downes & Rock 2011; Rubington & Weinberg 1970, 2016). In assessing the underlying assumptions of these two perspectives—both shared and contested—we propose a novel theoretical formulation for organizational deviance. We refer to this proposed formulation as a second-order observation of organizational deviance.

Deviance has been theorized as 'a breach of a socially acceptable standard' (Anderson 2014: 3), arising from 'an act, person, situation, or event as a departure from social norms' (Rubington & Weinberg 1970: v). Deviance can arise either from informal relations or from formal established standards (Rubington & Weinberg 2016). As deviance is from accepted standards, its assessment lies in the eye of the beholder (Giddens et al. 2013). Usually, deviance from an established standard, or non-conformity, is punished and conformity and compliance are rewarded (Giddens et al. 2013).

In the discipline of sociology, while some aspects of the deviance discourse have seen an intellectual revival (e.g. anomie theory, symbolic interactionism), the 'rate of intellectual innovation' on deviance scholarship is declining (Downes & Rock 2011: xii). In contrast, in management and organization studies, especially in the second half of the last century, interest in research on deviance has been increasing (Power 1997).

While a substantial body of literature focuses on the causes and consequences of deviance (see, for instance, reviews by Griffin et al. 1998; Robinson & Greenberg 1998; Warren 2003), we take a different path in the present

Andrea Fried and Arvind Singhal, *A Second-Order Observation of Organizational Deviance* In: *Understanding Deviance in a World of Standards*. Edited by: Andrea Fried, Oxford University Press (2020). © Oxford University Press. DOI: 10.1093/oso/9780198833888.003.0002 chapter. We begin by introducing the reader to the functionalist perspective on deviance, delineating its key characteristics and theoretical strands. An assessment is made of how the functionalist perspective has been applied in management and organization studies. Next, we introduce the reader to the interactionist perspective, followed by a section that contrasts and compares the two perspectives and ends with a critical reflection. We conclude by distilling seven key lessons in proposing and charting a new agenda to investigate organizational deviance in a world of established standards.

2.1 First-Order Observations of Deviance—The Functionalist Perspective

The central assumption of the functionalist perspective is that a referent—a point of comparison—exists by which deviation can be measured (Durkheim 1982). Thus, deviance is viewed as an objective fact based on what is statistically *normal* and how an act, a person, a situation, or an event differs from its statistically normative appearance (Anderson 2014: 36). Managing deviance is accomplished as *first-order cybernetics* (von Foerster 1984). Thus, the observer, a researcher or manager, is viewed as an 'external' agent who objectively discovers, assesses, and manages deviance (Beyes 2005).

The functionalist perspective on deviance is characterized by three sets of assumptions (Rubington & Weinberg 1970). First, consensus exists on what constitutes a social norm in a specific social group. Second, deviance is unwanted and undesirable and calls for legal or social punishments. Third, these punishments reaffirm for the group what falls outside of social norms, reinforcing the need for compliance. Typical research questions include who or what is deviant, how does deviance occur, what are the conditions under which deviance arises (Rubington & Weinberg 1970), when does deviance hinder stability in a population (Erikson 1962), and how does a society normalize deviance (Moynihan 1992). Key proponents of the functionalist perspective of deviance in sociology include Durkheim (1964), Erikson (1962), and Merton (1938).

Traditional management research of the functionalist kind tends to focus on this negative, undesirable, and malfunctioning aspect of deviance. Deviance is conceptualized as an act of norm or rule violation, and investigations focus on individual motivations or conditions for norm-breaking behaviour. The prevailing assumption is that deviance not only violates established norms, but also leads to negative consequences for the organization, requiring social control by management, often through education or sanctions (Bryant & Higgins 2010; Kidwell & Martin 2005; Linstead et al. 2014). Functionalist studies view deviance as 'problematic behaviour' or 'misbehaviour' (Bennett & Robinson 2000; Bordia et al. 2008; Lau et al. 2003; Lawrence & Robinson 2007; Marcus & Schuler 2004; Robinson & Bennett 1995; Warren 2003; quoted from Linstead et al. 2014). Consequently, the management of organizational deviance serves in this case as the practical response to misbehaviour (Kidwell & Martin 2005).

Other authors reinforce the value of management control of deviance. Vaughan (1999) developed a theoretical concept of organizational deviance building on Merton's (1938) idea of unanticipated consequences when purposive social action is undertaken. She defined organizational deviance as 'an event, activity, or circumstance, occurring in and/or produced by a formal organization, that deviates from both formal design goals and normative standards or expectations, either in the fact of its occurrence or in its consequences, and produces a suboptimal outcome' (Vaughan 1999: 274). She systematically analysed what led to the production of suboptimal outcomes at NASA when the US space shuttle Challenger exploded soon after take-off in January 1986. She argued that organizational deviance is often a predictable and recurring product of socially organized systems, identifying how power, rules, and culture cause 'routine nonconformity'—that is, the systematic production of deviance in the form of mistakes, misconducts, and disasters.

Another stream of research investigating the 'dark side' of organizational deviance is embedded in the neo-institutional discourse (Bromley & Powell 2012; Lounsbury 2008; Meyer & Rowan 1977; Powell & DiMaggio 1991). Here, researchers ask how organizations react to the so-called hypernorms, for instance, international accounting or quality standards (Aguilera et al. 2018). If these hypernorms are perceived as oppressive, organizations tend to deviate. Deviations are described here as decoupling (Bromley & Powell 2012; MacLean and Benham 2010; see also Fried et al. 2013) or as wrongdoing from the referent of hypernorms (Palmer 2017).

In their study on white-collar crime, Monahan and Quinn (2006) argued for a neo-institutional analysis of organizational deviance. In contrast to the idea that deviance within organizations is a product of individual choices or behaviours, they illustrated 'how deviance is produced by organizations when the organization decouples structure from action' (Monahan & Quinn 2006: 366). For instance, in an organizational environment with conflicting norms, workers more easily cross the line into deviance. In the neo-institutional view, 'deviance is the dirty secret of decoupled organizations' (Monahan &

Quinn 2006: 378) and a response to environmental pressures (e.g. pressure to be compliant with safety protocols or rules of financial bookkeeping).

MacLean and Benham (2010) confirm that decoupling compliance activities from actual core business activities can lead to a 'legitimacy façade' that facilitates institutional misconduct and potentially a loss of external legitimacy in organizations. Such was observed to be the case when certification audits were carried out of how organizations implemented safety standards in software development (Fried 2010). To prevent such institutional misconduct, the value orientation of organizational members is crucial for realising an effective legal–ethical compliance programme 'such as willingness to report bad news, organizational commitment, ethical awareness, and observed unethical behavior' (MacLean & Benham 2010: 1516). In turn, decoupling has a negative impact on the perception of internal legitimacy of compliance programmes, a negative effect on the organizational members' willingness to contribute, and an affirmative effect on organizational deviance. For this reason, the authors suggest that deviant behaviour can be reduced by incorporating 'compliance into their ongoing, day-to-day, core processes, such as training, monitoring, and discipline' (MacLean & Benham 2010: 1517).

Similarly, Palmer relates deviance to organizational wrongdoing that is intentional that include 'behavior(s) that violates ethical principles, social norms, organizational rules and protocols, industry or professional guidelines, and civil or criminal laws' (Palmer 2017: 739). From an institutional point of view, Palmer states how institutions curtail, countenance, stimulate, or sustain organizational wrongdoing, how they shape the extent and form of wrongdoing, and how they encourage wrongdoers (Palmer 2017). He concludes, from his review of institutionalist studies on organizational wrongdoing, that scholars 'should pay more attention to the ways in which institutions draw the line separating right from wrong in particular times and places' (Palmer 2017: 753).

In a different vein, we also see a positive turn in management and organization studies to recognize the value of distributed innovativeness and situated deviance, to honour the 'odd' agent of variation, and frame deviant behaviour as something vital to continued learning, innovation, and organizational survival (Lundmark & Westelius 2012; Singhal & Bjurström 2015). Lounsbury (2008) argues, for instance, how variation and deviation can create the conditions for organizations to innovate new beneficial practices. More recently, scholars have developed the positive deviance concept to describe how groups in business, healthcare, education, and social settings identify and adopt behaviours that lead to better outcomes compared to their peers (Pascale & Sternin 2005; Singhal et al. 2010). In the positive organizational scholarship movement, positive deviance refers to 'intentional behaviors that significantly depart from the norms of a referent group in honorable ways' (Spreitzer & Sonenshein 2004). Thus, positive deviance pays attention to exceptional deviations within a certain population. It puts an emphasis on the individual rationality of actors and their space of action within a certain context in the search for agency and innovativeness (Singhal & Bjurström 2015).

There are also approaches to deviance in the recent management literature which simultaneously consider its dysfunctional *and* positive effects. Warren (2003) developed the concept of constructive and destructive deviance in organizations, proposing that deviance can be associated with both 'desirable as well as undesirable behavior(s)' of employees (Warren 2003: 622). She argued that a coherent framework should incorporate both positive and negative aspects of deviance by explicitly stating the normative standards of functionalist views as well as reference group norms in interactionist accounts.

Drawing on institutional theory, Aguilera et al. (2018) emphasized the entrepreneurial quality of organizational deviance—both as over-conformity and under-conformity. Some organizations have an entrepreneurial identity where it is 'more likely to adopt over-conforming or under-conforming governance practices that deviate from established norms and practices' (Aguilera et al. 2018: 87). There are two entrepreneurial directions representing either social or commercial motives. Both motives are applied to over-conformity and under-conformity with dominant governance logics. The resulting typology identifies commercial mavericks, commercial rate-busters, social rebels, and social angels as four different deviance types. These types understand organizational deviance as a result of the 'national governance context [e.g. accounting standards, stock market regulations] that "sets the stage" for defining normative expectations'. The entrepreneurial identity of the organization, however, defines its over-conformity or under-conformity with these governance logics (Aguilera et al. 2018: 101).

In summary, research on deviance utilizing a functionalist perspective provides important lessons for the readers of this book. Most importantly, organizations tend to deviate from established standards of the institutionalized environment when these are perceived as being inappropriate in their specific context. Further, deviance has potentially positive as well as negative outcomes depending on how the different reference groups socially construct their understanding. Importantly, research on deviance in a functionalist perspective requires a statistically valid identification of the deviant act, person, situation, or event, i.e. an empirical departure from the norm or average (Becker 1963)—for the better or the worse. But often there exists a lack of statistical agreement on these norms. What objectively constitutes as positive or negative deviance is not so clear-cut (Anderson 2014; Rubington & Weinberg 2016) as social norms are often not static or overall valid. By defining deviance in an interactionist perspective and addressing the 'observing observer', these issues can, however, be addressed.

2.2 Second-Order Observations of Deviance—The Interactionist Perspective

While widely absent in management and organization studies, the interactionist perspective dominates the study of sociological phenomena. The interactionist perspective does not treat deviance as an objective entity, but one that results from a social interaction in which an act, a person, a situation, or an event is constructed as deviant. Researching and managing deviance is understood as *second-order cybernetics* (von Foerster 1984). Thus, the observation—accomplished by a researcher—is not independent from the observer whose attributes influence his/her descriptions. In essence, the observer's self-reflection of his/her own role in discovering, assessing, and managing deviance is part of the mix (Beyes 2005).

In contrast to functionalism, interactionist studies scrutinize the perception of deviance and make it a subject of study. Typical research questions in the interactionist perspective include what positive and negative traits and values are associated with deviance, how deviance is reasoned, and how an actor might react when designated as deviant (Rubington & Weinberg 1970). Instead of understanding deviance by the quality or the character of a person, symbolic interactionism turns the individual *perception* (Rubington & Weinberg 1970) and *social construction* of deviance (Anderson 2014) into a matter of investigation. Thus, in the interactionist perspective, deviance does not come into being until it is created as a response in a social interaction. In this respect, the interactionist perspective shifts its focus from the identification of the various kinds of deviance (as would be the concern of the functionalist perspective), to an understanding of deviance as subjectively problematic (Downes & Rock 2011).

In sociological scholarship, two related interactionist streams—'symbolic interactionism' and 'phenomenology'—are important to explicate in our discussion of deviance. *Symbolic interactionism* is interested in and concerned with the processes through which events and conditions, artefacts, people, and other factors achieve meaning—becoming objects of social orientation.

Symbolic interactionism views deviance 'among other things, [as] a consequence of the responses of others' (Becker 1963: 8) to an event, an artefact, people, or similar. In Becker's labelling theory on 'outsiders', 'social groups create deviance by making the rules whose infraction constitutes deviance, and by applying those rules to particular people and labeling them as outsiders' (Becker 1963: 9). The labelling theory reflects deviance not as the actual quality of an act or a person, but rather as a consequence of the application of rules and sanctions. That is, the definition of deviance is constructed in and through social processes.

In the symbolic interactionism tradition, Bryant and Higgins view deviance as 'a product of situations being defined in particular ways and individuals become deviant as a consequence of being labelled so by others' (Bryant & Higgins 2010: 253). Thus, researchers on deviance are not interested in what is labelled as deviant behaviour but rather in how norms are interactively constructed. According to Bryant and Higgins (2010: 269) the capacity to label behaviour as deviant (or not) highlights the significance of power relations within organizational studies of deviance. For instance, managers hold power to label certain employee behaviours as deviant (Bryant & Higgins 2010: 250). Here the 'rule enforcer' (Becker 1963) delineates a starting point for the analysis of deviant behaviour. Heckert and Heckert (2002) describe the labelling theory as 'reactivist' due to its focus on dynamics of reactions and evaluations of the other—an individual, group, or a social community. They developed an integrative typology of deviance emphasizing the contextual and situational nature of deviance. That is, definitions of the same behaviour and its evaluations vary across social groups and time.

The *phenomenological view* of deviance focuses on the common-sense reasoning of deviance in daily life (Berger 1973; Garfinkel 1967; Goffman 1963; Schütz 1962). In modern working environments, 'bureaucratically organized agencies are increasingly invested with social control functions, the activities of such agencies...generate as well as maintain definitions of deviance and produce populations of deviants' (Kitsuse & Cicourel 1963: 139). In the end, 'deviance is evidence of a moral diversity which others would repress in the name of an oppressive uniformity' (Downes & Rock 2011: 210).

According to the phenomenological view, research on deviance should investigate the businesses of 'identifying, classifying, managing, and reporting deviant events in everyday life' (Downes & Rock 2011: 219). For instance, Greve et al. (2010) put social-control agents at the centre of interest who identify and classify deviance and assess, report, and manage resulting misconduct. Social-control agents represent 'a collectivity and that can impose sanctions on that collectivity's behalf' (Greve et al. 2010: 56). Examples of social-control agents include international standardization bodies, states, and professional associations. The authors' way of observing deviance from a second-order perspective becomes obvious when they suggest investigating deviance in relative terms—thus simply investigating the behaviour that 'qualifies as misconduct when social-control agents consider it to be such' (Greve et al. 2010: 92). This is a crucial step for the investigation of deviance. It departs from first-order observations that analyse deviance and misconduct in absolute terms (Greve et al. 2010). By raising interest in social-control agents instead of the deviants themselves, Greve and others avoid making the claim that deviance and misconduct depends on 'a researcher-defined standard, perhaps informed by the work of philosophers or theologians' (Greve et al. 2010: 92). Research questions they suggest relate, for instance, to the degree of consensus among social-control agents when evaluating deviance and misconduct.

In summary, unlike in the functionalist perspective, research on deviance employing second-order observations does not address statistically valid identification of a deviant act, person, situation, or event. Rather, researchers who become second-order observers raise interest in how knowledgeable agents (Giddens 1984; see also Fried & Walgenbach 2020) socially construct and judge deviations. Thus, in investigating organizational deviations from established standards, we, in this book, became second-order observers. The organizations we investigated were the ones who judged what constituted deviations from standards and how these deviations were assessed. Empirical investigations of applying a second-order observation are few and far between—whether investigating compliance with or deviance from established standards. Therefore, we recognize the need to examine deviance and misconduct on an organizational level. In this quest, the present book does not try to understand deviations of single organizational members but rather is interested in the interplay of organizational structures and interactions that give rise to deviations from established standards.

2.3 Lessons Learned for Studying Organizational Deviance from Standards

In previous sections, we introduced two ways of researching deviance—functionalism and interactionism—as incommensurables (Kuhn 1962) in terms of their scientific paradigm, and resulting theories, research methods, and assumptions (see Table 2.1).

Table 2.1 A comparison of functionalist and interactionist perspectives on deviance

Perspectives on deviance	**Functionalist perspective**	**Interactionist perspective**
Scientific paradigm	Critical realism	Social constructivism
Identifying deviance	Deviance is statistically provable (holism). Social norms are static and overall valid	Deviance is socially constructed (contingency). Social norms are socially constructed, variable, not predictable, and differ in time and population
Role of researchers and managers	Observers (first-order cybernetics)	Observing observers (second-order cybernetics)
Assessing the consequences of deviance	Older approaches provide absolute assessments (positive/negative) and do not specify for whom deviance is functional. Newer approaches see the assessment of deviance in the eyes of the beholder and provide, for example, extensive cost and benefit analyses	The assessment is either an identification of who labels (positive/negative) whom for what, or it observes the observer of deviance and leaves the assessment (positive/negative) of deviance to the field
Typical research questions	What/who is (statistically) normal? How does deviance occur? Which conditions contribute to deviance?	How is deviance defined by different actors? How is deviance reasoned? How does an actor react after being treated as deviant?
Research methods	Quantitative methods, mixed methods	Qualitative methods, in particular ethnography
Social actor	Individuum, passive	Individuum, passive
Limitations regarding...	• the question of why individuals, groups, or organizations become deviant • structural reasons for deviations and power dynamics	• the question of why individuals, groups, or organizations become deviant • structural reasons for deviations and power dynamics

2.3.1 A Comparison of Functionalist and Interactionist Perspectives on Deviance

The functionalist perspective on deviance is rooted in the scientific paradigm of critical rationalism (Popper 1974), whereas the interactionist perspective is grounded in social constructivism (Berger & Luckmann 1966). The perspective chosen impacts how deviant acts, persons, situations, or events are identified and assessed, which research methods are (not) used, and which research questions are (not) asked.

There are at least seven lessons learned that undergird both the functionalist and the interactionist perspective on organizational deviance. They hold important implications for researching *organizational* deviance in the field of standardization (see section 2.4).

(1) Assessing deviance means to judge an act, a person, a situation, or an event. In sociology, as in other fields like management and organization studies, a central concern is the assessment of negative and positive consequences of deviance. Some functionalists treat deviance mainly as something dysfunctional or as a temporary irregularity to cope with conflicting norms (e.g. Monahan & Quinn 2006; Vaughan 1999; Warren 2003). Deviance is understood as norm violation that needs to be corrected and aligned (Heckert & Heckert 2002). Other authors point out that the narrow and negative perspective on deviance fundamentally valorizes the social desirability of 'the most likely case, scenario, or outcome for most of the people' (Singhal & Bjurström 2015: 5). Lounsbury criticises, for instance, the dark-side approach (Vaughan 1996) for putting deviance as 'a rational mimicry on the surface' (Lounsbury 2008: 350), noting that deviant behaviour might be done by knowledgeable, performance-oriented managers. Singhal and Bjurström argue that a solely negative perspective would limit the problem-solving potential of empirical research in which positive deviants, 'the unusual, the implausible, and exceptional are routinely ignored' (Singhal & Bjurström 2015: 6). Thus, to identify positive deviants recognizes the reflexivity and innovativeness of agents, their agency and space to act 'otherwise', and the importance of finding variant institutional solutions (ibid.).

Overall, challenges remain in delineating absolute norms and assessing deviance from them as being universally valid in content and across time. If deviance is analysed as something statistically provable (characterized as a holistic view in Downes and Rock (2011)), researchers risk to 'treat workplace norms as unproblematic and relatively stable objects of knowledge' (Bryant & Higgins 2010: 250). In our view, deviance needs to be described 'in all its complexity, so that there is no division between "good" poor people and "bad" poor people, legal and illegal or any such false dichotomy' (Duneier et al. 2000: 1562).

(2) Deviance by itself is a problematic concept when defined in dualistic terms. As shown in Figure 2.1, the main distinctions are often drawn between positive and negative deviance and between deviance and compliance.

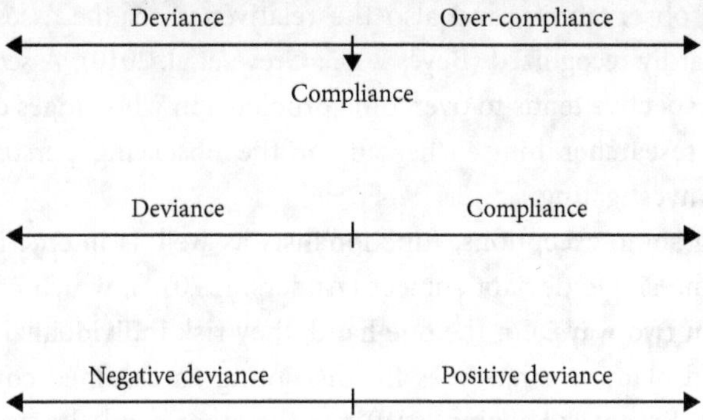

Figure 2.1 Examples of the common deviance dualisms

We see this as a linguistic impoverishment that can severely limit what we see when investigating organizational deviance. From a social constructivist perspective, rules, standards, norms, regulations, and the like are enacted, i.e. interpreted and realised in a context-specific way (Fried & Glaa 2020). Thus, organizations always deviate. In this context, the term *compliance* becomes a blurred concept. Compliance as an organization-independent concept does not exist in a social-constructivist reading. It can only serve as a proxy for the general commitment to social norms, standards, etc. (see also Fried & Langer 2020; Fried & Walgenbach 2020).

(3) Deviance encompasses three different aspects that must be distinguished analytically: (a) the description of a deviation, (b) the assessment of it, and (c) the sanction following a deviation. This is often mixed in the discourse on deviance and complicates the comprehensibility of typologies for deviance (e.g. Heckert & Heckert 2002; Robinson & Bennett 1995).

(4) It is crucial to disclose who judges what constitutes deviance, i.e. who identifies it as being positive or negative. Identifying deviance can serve a useful function, especially when extensive cost and benefit analyses are carried out for assessing 'sociological balance sheets' (Downes & Rock 2011). Interactionists, on the other hand, realise that deviance cannot be something positive or negative in absolute terms, and thus they focus primarily 'on the mechanism underlying group members' reactions to people who deviate from prescriptive norms' (Levine & Marques 2016: 3). Phenomenologists emphasize the role of the observer in this labelling process (Kitsuse & Cicourel 1963), arguing that researchers should leave the assessment of deviance—whether positive or negative—to empiricists and take on the role of a second-order observer (Luhmann 2000). Thus far, in research on deviance the possibility of

second-order observations, and also the relativeness of the assessments of deviance, is hardly recognized (Beyes 2005; Greve et al. 2010). A second-order observer's perspective tends to overcome problems in who judges deviance—whether the researcher himself/herself, or the observing person that the researcher is investigating.

(5) Barring some exceptions, functionalists as well as interactionists pay attention to the single deviant subject (Anderson 2014), which can become problematic in two ways. On the one hand, they risk individualizing deviant behaviour and blaming employees for disrupting an assumed consensus in organizations (Bryant & Higgins 2010). On the other hand, deviants are seen as 'passive nonentity' and are treated 'like sheep or robots' (Downes & Rock 2011: 193 and 90), devoid of subjective experiences. They embody the risk to view deviants as having no agency for redemption or alleviation. Thus, management and organization studies should highlight the role of social agency—the notion of the knowledgeable agent. Instead of investigating deviance as an experience or responsibility of an individual actor, we suggest investigating deviance as 'social practices ordered across time and space' (Giddens 1984: 2).

(6) The literature on deviance has not yet focused much on why organizations are likely to deviate from norms and adopt non-compliant practices (Aguilera et al. 2018). In order to better understand interventions in organizational processes, research should ask why deviance occurs, and why some organizations become deviant and others not.

(7) Deviance is an act of power (Anderson 2014) but rarely investigated in this regard (Bryant & Higgins 2010). Researchers on deviance do not tend to investigate the role that structural, institutional, or power concepts can play in human interaction. Identifying structural, institutional, and power-related aspects could help create a better understanding of why some organizations are more likely to deviate than others.

In the next section, we propose where research on deviance in management and organization studies should be headed.

2.4 In Conclusion: New Directions for Studying Organizational Deviance

To overcome the theoretical and conceptual problems discussed in the previous sections, we propose new directions for research on organizational deviance.

(1) We propose the concept of the 'second-order observer' (Luhmann 2000; Roberts 1993; von Foerster 1984)—that is, researchers should take on the position of an observer of the observers of deviance. In this view, a researcher should be the observer of the assessor/observer of deviance and not the assessor/observer of deviance himself/herself. Importantly, this proposed shift to understand researchers as 'second-order observers' has important consequences for the type of research questions that are raised in investigating organizational deviance.

(2) We categorize organizational deviance analytically (see Figure 2.2) into three aspects (applied in Gey et al. 2020a, 2020b; Langer et al. 2020b) to facilitate its operationalization and to address what is meant exactly when the empirical field describes deviations. The three aspects of organizational deviance are:

- the *descriptive aspect*, where an observer states deviation as a fact; every point in the circular continuum characterizes a deviation (e.g. deviation from development milestones);
- the *normative aspect*, where an observer assesses the deviation with respect to a compliance point of reference (e.g. standard requirements);
- the *sanctioning aspect*, where an observer relates the assessment to the negative and positive consequences of deviation (e.g. no certification of software).

(3) We call for thick descriptions of organizational life and a proactive 'loss of [normative] authority on science's side' (Beyes 2005: 457) in the discourse of deviance in management and organization studies. The notion of the 'second-order observer' with its call for thick descriptions of organizational

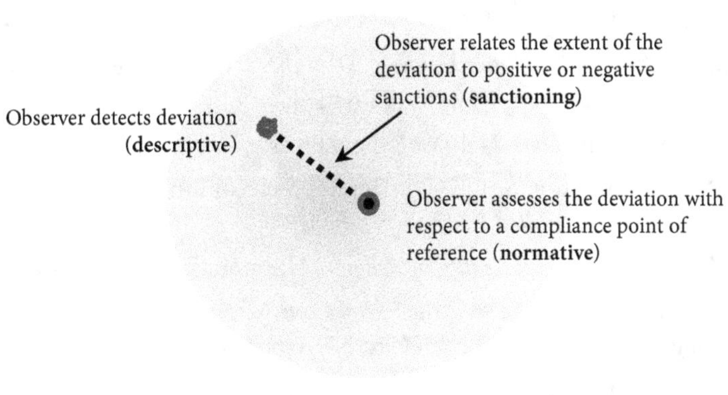

Figure 2.2 Analytical aspects of deviance

deviance leads consequently (4) to a phenomenological perspective on deviance that asks for a common-sense reasoning of deviance by organizations. We go beyond the investigation and explanation of individual deviance and take the deviants, and thus organizational members' perspective, to find out under which organizational circumstances they become deviant and 'what value, positive or negative, do they place on the facts of deviance' (Rubington & Weinberg 1970: 3.

To this end, (5) we utilize Giddens' structuration theory for the conceptualization and analysis of organizational deviance (Giddens 1984). Structuration theory views actors as knowledgeable, reflexive agents who not only develop rules but also deviate from them. At the interplay of standards as facilities (domination), standards as interpretative schemes (signification), and standards as social norms (legitimation), we propose a new formulation of the concept of *organizational deviance*.

While it is important to inventory the breaches of accepted social norms, it is also important to 'understand the types of things' norms and standards regulate (Anderson 2014: 4). By describing the interplay of legitimation, signification, and domination, (6) we reveal contradictions (Giddens 1979; Papa et al. 1995; Putnam et al. 2016) that deviance 'requires in order to exist as a social phenomenon' (Rubington & Weinberg 1970: 1). The explanation of inherent contradictions of an organization reveals the reasons for its deviance from normative functioning.

References

Aguilera, R. V., Judge, W. Q., & Terjesen, S. A. 2018. Corporate governance deviance. *Academy of Management Review*, 43.

Anderson, T. L. 2014. *Understanding Deviance. Connecting Classical and Contemporary Perspectives*. New York: Routledge.

Becker, H. S. 1963. *Outsiders*. New York: Free Press.

Bennett, R. J. & Robinson, S. L. 2000. Development of a measure of workplace deviance. *Journal of Applied Psychology*, 85, 349–60.

Berger, P. L. 1973. *The Social Reality of Religion*. Harmondsworth: Penguin Books.

Berger, P. L. & Luckmann, T. 1966. *The Social Construction of Reality: A Treatise in the Sociology of Knowledge*. Garden City, NY: Doubleday.

Beyes, T. P. 2005. Observing observers. Von Foerster, Luhmann, and management thinking. *Kybernetes*, 34, 448–59.

Bordia, P., Restubog, S. L. D., & Tang, R. L. 2008. When employees strike back: investigating mediating mechanisms between psychological contract breach and workplace deviance. *Journal of Applied Psychology*, 93, 1104–17.

Bromley, P. & Powell, W. W. 2012. From smoke and mirrors to walking the talk: decoupling in the contemporary world. *Academy of Management Annals*, 6, 1–48.

Bryant, M. & Higgins, V. 2010. Self-confessed troublemakers: an interactionist view of deviance during organizational change. *Human Relations*, 63, 249–77.

Downes, D. & Rock, P. 2011. *Understanding Deviance. A Guide to the Sociology of Crime and Rule-Breaking*. Oxford: Oxford University Press.

Duneier, M., Carter, O., & Hasan, H. 2000. *Sidewalk*. London: Farrar Straus and Giroux.

Durkheim, É. 1964. *The Rules of Sociological Method*. London: Collier-Macmillan.

Durkheim, É. 1982. Rules for the distinction of the normal from the pathological. *In:* Lukes, S. (ed.) *The Rules of sociological method. Contemporary social theory.* London: Palgrave.

Erikson, K. T. 1962. Notes on the sociology of deviance. *Social Problems*, 9, 307–14.

Fried, A. 2010. Performance measurement systems and their relation to strategic learning: a case study in a software-developing organization. *Critical Perspectives on Accounting*, 21, 118–33.

Fried, A. & Glaa, B. 2020. Introduction to research on standards. *In:* Fried, A. (ed.) *Deviance in a World of Standards.* Oxford: Oxford University Press.

Fried, A. & Langer, S. 2020. Typology of organizational deviance from standards. *In:* Fried, A. (ed.) *Understanding Deviance in a World of Standards.* Oxford: Oxford University Press.

Fried, A. & Walgenbach, P. 2020. Theoretical framework to explore organizational deviance from standards. *In:* Fried, A. (ed.) *Understanding Deviance in a World of Standards.* Oxford: Oxford University Press.

Fried, A., Gey, R., Pretorius, A., & Günther, L. 2013. Decoupling from standards—process management and technical innovation in software development organisations. *International Journal of Innovation Management*, 17.

Garfinkel, H. 1967. *Studies in Ethnomethodology*. Englewood Cliffs, NJ: Prentice Hall.

Gey, R., Langer, S. & Fried, A. 2020a. Attentive deviance from standards at CraneSolutions. *In:* Fried, A. (ed.) *Understanding Deviance in World of Standards.* Oxford: Oxford University Press.

Gey, R., Langer, S., & Fried, A. 2020b. Over-conformity with standards at MedTech. *In:* Fried, A. (ed.) *Understanding Deviance in a World of Standards.* Oxford: Oxford University Press.

Giddens, A. 1979. *Central Problems in Social Theory. Action, Structure and Contradiction in Social Analysis*. Houndmills: Macmillan.

Giddens, A. 1984. *The Constitution of Society. Outline of the Theory of Structuration*. Cambridge: Polity Press.

Giddens, A., Duneier, M., Appelbaum, R. P., & Carr, D. 2013. *Essentials of Sociology with 10 Readings*. New York: Norton Custom.

Goffman, E. 1963. *Behavior in Public Places: Notes on the Social Organization of Gatherings*. New York: Free Press.

Greve, H. R., Palmer, D., & Pozner, J.-E. 2010. Organizations gone wild: the causes, processes, and consequences of organizational misconduct. *Academy of Management Annals*, 4, 53–107.

Griffin, R. W., O'leary-Kelly, A., & Collins, J. 1998. Dysfunctional work behaviors in organization. *In:* Cooper, C. L. & Rousseau, D. M. (eds) *Trends in Organizational Behavior*. Chichester: Wiley.

Heckert, A. & Heckert, D. M. 2002. A new typology of deviance: integrating normative and reactivist definitions of deviance. *Deviant Behavior*, 23, 449–79.

Kidwell, R. E. & Martin, C. L. 2005. *Managing Organizational Deviance*. Thousand Oaks: Sage Publications.

Kitsuse, J. & Cicourel, A. 1963. A note on the uses of official statistics. *Social Problems*, 11, 131–9.

Kuhn, T. S. 1962. *The Structure of Scientific Revolutions*. Chicago: University of Chicago Press.

Langer, S., Gey, R., Karadzhova-Beyer, D., & Fried, A. 2020b. Deregulated deviance from standards at MetroEngineers. *In:* Fried, A. (ed.) *Understanding Deviance in a World of Standards*. Oxford: Oxford University Press.

Lau, V. C. S., Au, W. T., & Ho, J. M. C. 2003. A qualitative and quantitative review of antecedents of counterproductive behavior in organizations. *Journal of Business and Psychology*, 18, 73–99.

Lawrence, T. B. & Robinson, S. L. 2007. Ain't misbehavin: workplace deviance as organizational resistance. *Journal of Management*, 33, 378–94.

Levine, J. M. & Marques, J. M. 2016. Norm violators as threats and opportunities: the many faces of deviance in groups. *Group Processes & Intergroup Relations*, 19, 545–52.

Linstead, S., Maréchal, G., & Griffin, R. W. 2014. Theorizing and researching the dark side of organization. *Organization Studies*, 35, 165–88.

Lounsbury, M. 2008. Institutional rationality and practice variation: new directions in the institutional analysis of practice. *Accounting, Organizations and Society*, 33, 349–61.

Luhmann, N. 2000. *Organisation und Entscheidung*. Wiesbaden: Opladen.

Lundmark, E. & Westelius, A. 2012. Exploring entrepreneurship as misbehavior. *In:* Barnes, A. & Taksa, L. (eds) *Rethinking Misbehavior and Resistance in Organizations*. Bingley, UK: Emerald Group Publishing.

Maclean, T. L. & Benham, M. 2010. The dangers of decoupling: the relationship between compliance programs, legitimacy perceptions, and institutionalized misconduct. *Academy of Management Journal*, 53, 1499–520.

Marcus, B. & Schuler, H. 2004. Antecedents of counterproductive behavior at work: a general perspective. *Journal of Applied Psychology*, 89, 647–60.

Merton, R. 1938. Social structure and anomie. *American Sociological Review*, 3, 672–82.

Meyer, J. W. & Rowan, B. 1977. Institutionalized organizations: formal structure as myth and ceremony. *American Journal of Sociology*, 83, 340–63.

Monahan, S. C. & Quinn, B. A. 2006. Beyond 'bad apples' and 'weak leaders': toward a neo-institutional explanation of organizational deviance. *Theoretical Criminology*, 10, 361–85.

Moynihan, D. 1992. Defining deviance down. *American Scholar*, 62, 17–30.

Palmer, D. 2017. Institutions, institutional theory and organizational wrongdoing. *In:* Greenwood, R., Oliver, C., Lawrence, T. B., & Meyer, R. E. (eds) *The SAGE Handbook of Organizational Institutionalism*, 2nd edn. Los Angeles: SAGE.

Papa, M. J., Auwal, M. A., & Singhal, A. 1995. Dialectic of control and emancipation in organizing for social change: a multitheoretic study of the Grameen Bank in Bangladesh. *Communication Theory*, 5, 189–23.

Pascale, R. T. & Sternin, J. 2005. Your company's secret change agents. *Harvard Business Review*, May, 1–10.

Popper, K. 1974. *Objektive Erkenntnis*. Hamburg: Hoffmann und Campe.

Powell, W. W. & Dimaggio, P. J. (eds) 1991. *The New Institutionalism in Organizational Analysis*. Chicago: University of Chicago Press.

Power, M. 1997. *The Audit Society. Rituals of Verification*. Oxford: Oxford University Press.

Putnam, L. L., Fairhurst, G. T., & Banghart, S. 2016. Contradictions, dialectics, and paradoxes in organizations: a constitutive approach. *Academy of Management Annals*, 10, 65–171.

Roberts, D. 1993. Die Paradoxie der Form in der Literatur. *In:* Baecker, D. (ed.) *Probleme der Form*. Frankfurt: Suhrkamp.

Robinson, S. & Greenberg, J. 1998. Employees behaving badly: dimensions, determinants and dilemmas in the study of workplace deviance. *In:* Cooper, C. & Rousseau, D. (eds) *Trends in Organizational Behavior*. Chichester: Wiley.

Robinson, S. L. & Bennett, R. J. 1995. A typology of deviant workplace behaviors: a multidimensional scaling study. *Academy of Management Journal*, 38, 555–72.

Rubington, E. & Weinberg, M. S. 1970. *Deviance: The Interactionist Perspective. Text and Readings in the Sociology of Deviance*. Toronto: Macmillan.

Rubington, E. & Weinberg, M. S. 2016. *Deviance: The Interactionist Perspective*. Milton Park: Routledge.

Schütz, A. 1962. Common-sense and scientific interpretation of human action. *In:* Schutz, A. (ed.) *Collected Papers I. Phaenomenologica*. Dordrecht: Springer.

Singhal, A. & Bjurström, E. 2015. Reframing the practice of social research: solving complex problems by valuing positive deviation. *International Journal of Communication and Social Research*, 3.

Singhal, A., Bruscell, P., & Lindberg, C. 2010. *Inviting Everyone: Healing Healthcare Through Positive Deviance*. Bordentown, NJ: Plexus.

Spreitzer, G. M. & Sonenshein, S. 2004. Toward the construct definition of positive deviance. *American Behavioral Scientist*, 47, 828–47.

Vaughan, D. 1996. *The Challenger Launch Decision*. Chicago: University of Chicago Press.

Vaughan, D. 1999. The dark side of organizations: mistake, misconduct, and disaster. *Annual Review of Sociology*, 25, 271–305.

Von Foerster, H. 1984. Principles of self-organization in a socio-managerial context. *In:* Ulrich, H. & Probst, G. J. B. (eds) *Self-Organization and Management of Social Systems*. Berlin: Springer.

Warren, D. E. 2003. Constructive and destructive deviance in organizations. *Academy of Management Review*, 28, 622–32.

3

Structurationist Framework to Explore Organizational Deviance from Standards

Andrea Fried and Peter Walgenbach

In this chapter, we develop a heuristic framework and analytical questions to explore deviance from standards in organizations. Structuration theory (Giddens 1984) seems to be a fruitful theoretical approach to grasp the institutional aspects as well as aspects of agency in standards enactment (Tempel & Walgenbach 2007).

To explain organizational deviance in more detail (section 3.2), we utilize three concepts that are central to structuration theory—the 'duality of structure', the 'stratification model', and the 'dialectic of control' (section 3.1). In doing so, we go beyond the literature that is concerned with the explanation of individual deviance and investigate the institutional circumstances that lead to deviation from standards in organizations. By applying structuration theory, we theorize deviance neither as an experience or a responsibility of an individual actor nor as a 'form of societal totality', but as 'social practices ordered across time and space' (Giddens 1984: 2) on the micro-level of and between organizations.

3.1 Standards through the Lens of Structuration Theory

3.1.1 The Dialectic of Control: Enactment of Standards by Knowledgeable Agents

Modern societies change fast not least because the modern capitalist enterprise extends 'its multinational activities beyond the bounds of a single country' and because 'the wide scope of contemporary organizations brings them into contradiction with so many other systems of activity' (Whittington 1992: 696). Globally effective standards are a good example of how contemporary

Andrea Fried and Peter Walgenbach, *Structurationist Framework to Explore Organizational Deviance from Standards* In: *Understanding Deviance in a World of Standards*. Edited by: Andrea Fried, Oxford University Press (2020).

DOI: 10.1093/oso/9780198833888.003.0003

organizations are challenged by other systems of activity, e.g. through nation states and internationally acting standardization bodies.

We endorse what Giddens once described as the dialectic of control: 'to be a human agent is to have power, to be able to "make a difference" in the world.... The most seemingly "powerless" individuals are able to mobilize resources whereby they carve out "spaces of control" in respect of their day-to-day lives' (Giddens 1982: 197). Recognizing the dialectic of control, we acknowledge the actors' pivotal role in our empirical investigations, who know best the daily practices and challenges of standards enactment. Actors are *knowledgeable agents* who enact standards by creating, modifying, or manipulating contextually bound rules, which are induced by standards. It is they who use standards as powerful resources in foreseen or unforeseen ways. Organizational members have the power to deviate from standards due to their access to alternative, sometimes contradictory structural principles from other social contexts (Whittington 1992). As Giddens writes: 'structure [here a standard] has no existence independent of the knowledge that agents have about what they do in their day-to-day activity' (Giddens 1984: 26). Hence, the enactment of global standards is always contextually bound and characterized by the tension between dependency on globally effective regulations and autonomous, local strategies of individual actors, e.g. in organizing software development (Beck & Walgenbach 2005; Djelic & den Hond 2014; Fried et al. 2013; Gey & Fried 2018; in more general terms: Sydow & Windeler 1997).

3.1.2 The Stratification Model: Unintended Consequences of Standard Enactment

The second central concept of structuration theory builds on the dialectic of control and the belief that not all agency is intentionally controlled. For example, members of software developing processes participating in a 'dialectic of control', on the one hand, engage in social agency that may be characterized as a 'temporally embedded process of social engagement, informed by... a "projective" capacity to imagine alternative possibilities... and a "practical-evaluative" capacity to contextualize past habits and future projects' (Emirbayer & Mische 1998: 962). On the other hand, the knowledgeability of these actors is context-bound and socially embedded (Giddens 1984). With regard to the enactment of standards, this implies that organizational members are only able to foresee to a certain extent the efforts they need to make in order to comply with the requirements of a standard and satisfy the explicit and implicit expectations of auditors (e.g. Fried 2010). They may also underestimate standards' unintended, coercive consequences, for instance, for their own and others' job satisfaction or for organizational innovation (e.g. Adler & Borys 1996).

To cope with organizational challenges such as software development, members of organizations are continuously engaged in the reflexive monitoring of their actions. The process of reflexive monitoring of actions is illustrated in the *stratification model* (Giddens 1979). This model is premised on the distinction of three strata of the actors' knowledgeability (see also Fried 2003; Sydow & Windeler 1997). Beside *subconscious motives*, which actors have hardly ever any access to, Giddens distinguishes practical and discursive consciousness. The *practical consciousness* summarizes the knowledge that actors implicitly apply in view of the social circumstances and conditions of their own and others' actions. An implicit application of knowledge means that actors do not provide information about the motives they have for a certain action; intentions for actions are taken for granted, and thus not discursively motivated or scrutinized. Actions that issue from the practical consciousness of actors reveal regularities and appear as routines. In other words, the practical consciousness is the cognitive capability of an actor of connecting actions to other actors facilitating social practices (Giddens 1984). Related to standards, this means that standards are considerably enacted, and thus shape the organizational practices, such as the routines of software development and hardware production. These practices are hardly scrutinized by those whose daily work is affected by them.

According to Giddens, practical consciousness can in principle also be made explicit, since actors are able to disclose and reflect on the causes of their actions (Giddens 1984). Hence, they can transfer implicit knowledge into *discursive consciousness*. In crisis or problematic situations, actors transfer implicit knowledge from practical into discursive consciousness, especially when actors find themselves forced to express reasons and normative justifications (Cohen 1989). The discursive consciousness thus includes knowledge that actors discursively use. For instance, standards are discussed in view of their meaning and practicality, as well as with regard to their benefits for the organization when they are adopted or implemented or when their importance is scrutinized by the stakeholders concerned. Both levels of consciousness are not entirely separated stocks of knowledge. However, practical and discursive consciousness differ in their actual accessibility: 'between discursive and practical consciousness there is no bar; there are only the differences between what can be said and what is simply done' (Giddens 1984: 7). This implies that social practices are based on relatively little discursively used knowledge (Becker 1996).

The *stratification model* addresses routinized, recursive actions and the practical consciousness of actors (Giddens 1979). The model describes recursive actions as a precondition for actors to connect to their own and others' past actions and to refer to one another. The practical consciousness enables, for instance, software developers to remember development processes without contesting the procedure or the standards inducing them. Once part of the practical consciousness, standards leave memory traces and represent structures cognitively.

According to the stratification model, actors rationalize their actions by following motivational impulses unconsciously to some extent, but also by providing reasons for their actions discursively (motivation of action) (Giddens 1984). By rationalizing actions, actors 'maintain a continuing "theoretical understanding" of the grounds of their activity' (Giddens 1984: 5). As part of the reflexive monitoring and control of their action, actors observe the context and consequences of their actions and those of other actors (see also Cohen 1989) while collating context and consequences with the primary intention of their actions. This may result either in a rationalization of their actions or in a modification of the actor's intentions (Giddens 1984).

The fact that actions are rationalized and accomplished deliberately does not mean that actors always have clarity about all possible conditions and consequences of their actions a priori. Although actors are skilled and reflexive human beings, they have only a limited capacity for receiving and processing information (see also Becker 1996). Their knowledge about conditions and consequences of actions is limited; thus their knowledgeability is *bounded*. Giddens therefore distinguishes between intended and unintended consequences as well as unacknowledged and known conditions of actions (Giddens 1984). Unintended consequences of actions result from bounded knowledgeability and the fact that these conditions are affected by contingent factors (like, for instance, new regulatory requirements or disruptive innovations shaking the market) and the results of other actors' actions. Furthermore, consequences of action have an effect on the conditions of future actions. Unintended consequences of action remain unrecognized and are frequently not perceived as future conditions of action. For these reasons, Giddens concludes that the conditions of actions are only manageable to a certain degree. With this causal connection between unknowledgeable conditions of action and unintended consequences of action, Giddens explains the reproduction of social systems as a *homeostatic causal loop* (see Giddens 1984).

When complying to or deviating from standards, organizational members are confronted with the homeostatic causal loop of the enactment of standards.

When organizational members, for instance, propose internal documents referring to standards, and thus formalize *inter alia* development and production processes, they reach a certain result regarding product and process safety, but they may also trigger unintended effects such as, for instance, a lower usability of the product. The intended as well as unintended consequences of the enactment of standards form the basis for prospective actions. Besides its action-oriented and cognitive dimension, standard enactment is 'also an expression of structural properties in ongoing social processes' (Sydow & Windeler 1997: 464). These dimensions of the enactment of standards can be explained in more detail by the *duality of structure*—the third central concept of the structuration theory.

3.1.3 The Duality of Structure: Standards as Modalities of Action

No attempt has been made by Giddens to conceptualize the notion of standards and to formulate the relationship between standards and organizations. By using structuration theory, we propose that standards are one kind of structural property for those organizations that enact them. That is, standards embody and hence are instantiations of some of the rules and resources constituting the structure of an organization. The details of the structurational model of standards are explicated in the following sections.

Inspired by the 'duality of structure' (Giddens 1984), we have already identified three roles standards can play in chapter 1 of the book. Once standards are enacted and become *modalities of action*, they serve as interpretative schemes, facilities, and social norms shaping an organization's structure and interactions. At the same time, standards are an integral part of the practical consciousness of organizational members. Organizational members are aware of their impact on rules and resources as well as interpret and use standards accordingly.

Following the concept of the 'duality of structure', Figure 3.1 shows how standards are embedded in the structure of and the interactions in organizations.

Taking a structurationist view, standards become effective when they shape organizational *rules* (Ortmann 2010) and *resources* of interaction in organizations (Sydow & Windeler 1997; Walgenbach 1999). As organizational *rules*, standards provide meaning for organizational members and deliver a reference frame for sanctions when organizational members deviate from them. Rules refer, on the one hand, to the constitution of meaning (signification)

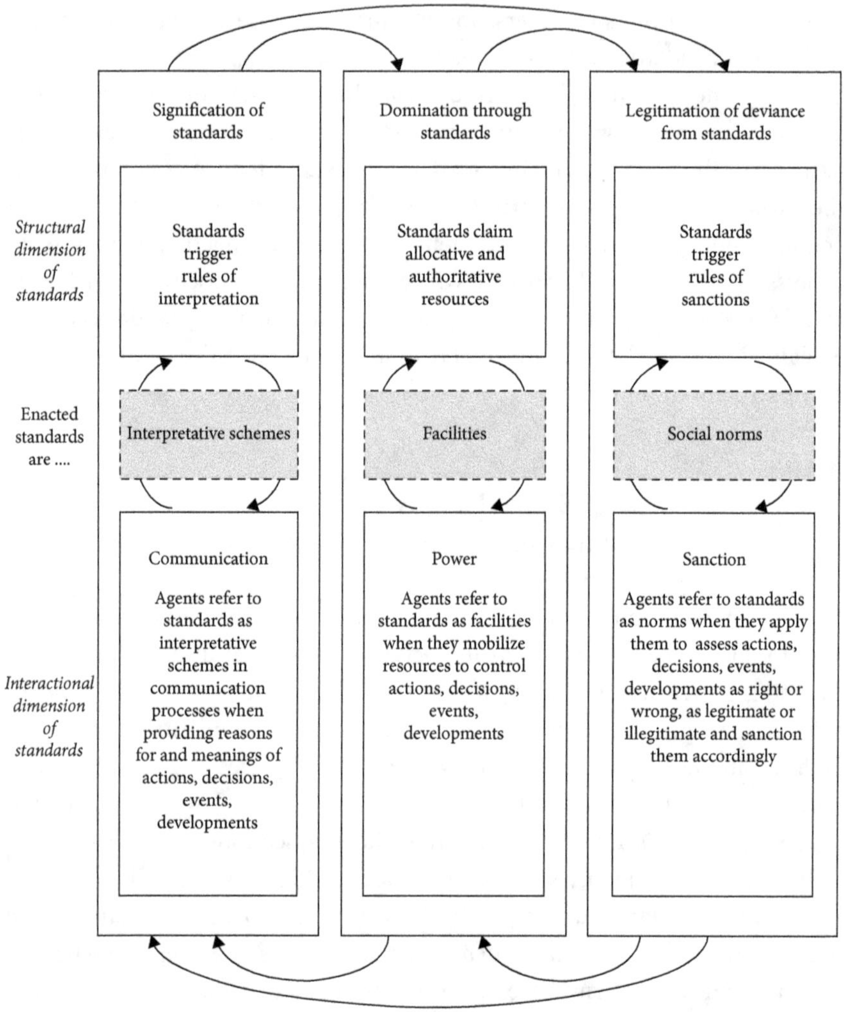

Figure 3.1 Standards as modalities of action (for the general model see Ortmann et al. 2000)

and, on the other hand, to the sanctioning of social behavior (legitimation) (Giddens 1984). As *resources* (Giddens 1984), standards coordinate organizational actors in time and space; they unfold power since they allow command over material objects, processes, and persons. Standards are modalities of action which shape rules and form resources for organizational practices. This way, they can enable as well as constrain organizational practices.

The three structurationist themes of the social world—legitimation, domination, and signification—are addressed when standards are perceived and subsequently discussed in organizations as relevant until they achieve a taken-for-granted nature. In the notions of structuration theory, this implies the discussion of the signification of standards, the domination through standards and situations in which complying with or deviating from the standards appears to be legitimate (see Figure 3.1). The analytical framework provided by Giddens allows exploring how signification, domination, and legitimation interact during the enactment of standards to understand how standards affect organizational practices.

Before we introduce organizational deviance from standards from a structurationist viewpoint in section 3.2, the three structurationist themes and their vertical connection, i.e. the linkages between the structural as well as the interactional dimension of standards, are described below.

3.1.3.1 Standards as Interpretative Schemes

Standards enfold signification when they are accepted as interpretative schemes (see figure 3.1) in organizational practices. In a structural dimension, signification encompasses the rules of interpretation which provide sense, offer rationales for behaviour, decisions, events, and developments, and add meaning to the engagement in standards. For instance, organizational members can agree on the idea that compliance to standards is a precondition to get access to a certain market or are important in order to ensure the quality of a product. Thus, rules of interpretation 'have a recursive and practical formulae…of how to go on in social practices' and 'provide a potential for what could be done and how it could be done over a range of contexts and occasions' (Sydow & Windeler 1997: 465). Giddens' rules of interpretations are 'codified rules of interpretation' (Giddens 1984: 21) and appear in organizational practices, for instance, in the form of internal standard documents or standard operating procedures (Ortmann 2015; see also chapter 1 of this book).

Human actors 'enact' their environment by bringing structures into existence and by setting them in action (Weick 1988). 'The product of enactment is not an accident….Instead, it is an orderly, material, social construction that is subject to multiple interpretations. Enacted environments contain real objects such as reactors, pipes, and valves [or in the context of this book: e.g. internal standard documents]. The existence of these objects is not questioned, but their significance, meaning, and content is' (Weick 1988: 307). During the enactment of standards, shared cognitive schemata about the signification of standards are discursively developed and become part of the practical consciousness of organizational members.

In the studies presented in this book, the signification of standards becomes manifest when organizational members of software development report on the meaning of standards in interviews or when they discuss, for instance, standard-related questions with clients or interact in software design meetings with the quality manager of their organization. Hence, in an interactional dimension, standards are referenced in daily communication. Standards are interpreted and reinterpreted while organizational members continually produce and reproduce their interpretations of these standards, but they are by no means made explicit or scrutinized in every organization or in every interaction to the same extent. As practical consciousness, they shape organizational practices, for instance, in view of the planning and documentation of the software development process (Fried 2010). The more standards are taken for granted and the more effective they provide meaning to organizational members, the less standards are part of the daily discourse. Meanings can arise from different interpretative frames and may be, for instance, of technical, business, ethical, regulatory, or administrative nature (see also Suddaby & Greenwood 2005; Tenbrunsel & Messick 1999).

In this book, we analyse the signification of standards and identify which accounts actors produce during the enactment of standards. On the one hand, we refer to *belief-driven processes of sensemaking* (Weick 1995) that evolve during the enactment of standards: 'sensemaking can begin with beliefs and take the form of arguing and expecting' (Weick 1995: 135). The *argument* to engage in standard enactment refers to 'concrete experience and more general concepts' (Weick 1995: 170). In view of standards, software developers address, for instance, their community of practice and the arguments they draw upon when they emphasize advantages of standards like quality improvements or assurance of technical interfaces. Furthermore, while making sense, certain *expectations* are addressed. Sensemaking as expecting relates to 'foresight, strategic planning, prediction, and extrapolation' (Weick 1995: 134). 'Expectations can serve as strong filters that their formation and activation are crucial for sensemaking' (Weick 1995: 146). As described in a similar way in the stratification model (Giddens 1984), through reflexive monitoring the expectation and the event, action, decision, and development itself can be adjusted due to unexpected consequences: 'when events seem to diverge from expectations, both the expectation and the event itself can be adjusted' (Weick 1995: 147). Both sensemaking as arguing as well as expecting are represented in the signification of standards.

On the other hand, when analysing the signification of standards, we study 'different actors' sensemaking behaviours' (Maitlis 2005: 22). Thus, when investigating processes of software development, we not only disclose which accounts of signification actors generate but also identify the interrelated activities among different stakeholders engaged in a project beyond the software development activities. The necessity also to take stakeholders beyond the actual software development into account can be illustrated by recent fraud cases in industry. Nelson, for instance, describes the role of Volkswagen's middle management when deviating from standards as crucial for the emissions-control fraud: 'especially in a command-and-control culture like VW's, it is "very unlikely" that even a "group of engineers could have taken the risk of modifying the software without approval at a high level of management" ' (Nelson 2019; citing Ewing, *supra* note 284).

For this reason, we depict not only signification of standards expressed by software developers but also the influence of leaders (middle or senior management) and other actors (e.g. clients or customers, suppliers, auditors, hardware developing activities of a software developing project) on sensemaking around standards. Maitlis (2005) suggests different forms of organizational sensemaking. She distinguishes these forms according to the level of sensegiving by leaders as well as the level of sensegiving by other actors. The different communicating activities in view of the signification of standards are also considered when the three case studies of the book are analysed and compared.

In the case studies that we present in chapters 5, 6 and 7, we picturize the meanings produced by software developing actors during the enactment of standards. At the same time, we analyse the interaction of different actors' sensemaking behaviours and its impact on the sensemaking for the enactment of standards. The main analytical question for analysing the standards as interpretative schemes is: Which sense do standards generate in software developing organizations? This question also includes the following aspects:

- Which meanings do organizational members communicate to reason their engagement in standard enactment?
- Which interpretative frames are addressed in view of standards from their point of view?
- What sense do further internal and external actors give to standards?

3.1.3.2 Standards as Facilities

While creating interpretative schemes for standards, actors also enact standards as *facilities* (means of power) to which they have access to in their context (see Figure 3.1; Giddens 1984): through these facilities, agents 'powerfully transform the interaction sequences and at the same time reproduce structures of domination' (Sydow & Windeler 1997: 464). Other authors have mentioned this dimension of standards. Backhouse et al. (2006: 413) focus, for instance, on power-related aspects but also examine 'the interaction of external contingencies, powerful agents, resources, and meaning' during the creation of *de jure* standards. Structures of domination are just analytically distinguishable from structures of signification and need to be investigated conjointly with structures of legitimation (Giddens 1984).

According to Giddens, power is accomplished through the availability of resources and their effective mobilization (Giddens 1984). Resources 'indicate capacities human agents may be able to use for achieving their purposes of social interaction' (Sydow & Windeler 1997: 465). Actors generate 'certain typical forms of resources...within discursively mobilized forms of information flow' (Giddens 1984: 203) and create sense and identity among their members. The asymmetrical distribution of resources among the various actors involved, and thus among those who supervise and control and those who are supervised and controlled, is of fundamental importance to understand organizational deviance from standards (Sydow & Windeler 1997). For instance, customers expect certification of the product they buy but do not consider that standard-compliant product development requires higher investment in the quality assurance of product development processes and that this again affects the price the customer has to pay for the product. The same applies to the internal provision of resources: to enfold the power of standards and to ensure, for instance, product safety, organizations need to create new roles such as the one of a safety manager or have to institutionalize an internal regulatory affairs unit.

The two examples picturize how power can be accomplished from a structuration theory's point of view. Power, here, is defined as *transformative capacity* by which knowledgeable agents transform the social and material world (Orlikowski 1992: 405; see also Roberts & Scapens 1985). It is facilitated by organizational resources that organizational members activate, for instance, to help standards become relevant and transform software developing processes. When organizational members refer to the transformative capacity, they usually do this by assessing the necessity, availability, and impact of resources.

There exist two kinds of resources. *Allocative* resources enable human domination over objects, goods, or material phenomena. Giddens adds here that 'some forms of allocative resources (such as raw materials, land, etc.) might seem to have a "real existence" in a way which I have claimed that structural properties as a whole do not' (Giddens 1984: 33). *Authoritative* resources are non-material sources of power resulting in the domination of some actors over others, i.e. command over the coordination of the activity of human agents. Authoritative resources refer to the transformative capacity allowing actors to control other persons or actors—for instance, by referring to employment contracts or job descriptions. These authoritative resources may also be supported by other means of power, such as the formal structure of organizations or the allocation of production factors.

Structures of domination exist due to an 'asymmetry of authoritative and allocative resources' (Orlikowski 1992: 405). When the asymmetry of authoritative and allocative resources is confirmed in daily interactions of organizational members, the 'existing structure of domination is reaffirmed' (Orlikowski 1992: 405). If an organization remains attached to a certain resource asymmetry, it might hamper a prospective enactment of standards. By mobilizing resources instead, organizational members can change the existing asymmetry of resources to the advantage of standard enactment.

The main analytical question for analysing standards as facilities is: Being a resource itself, which power do standards unfold in software developing organizations? This question also includes the following aspects:

- Which allocative and authoritative resources for standard enactment are reported from the software developing organizations?
- How do organizational members assess the transformative capacity of allocative and authoritative resources during standard enactment?

3.1.3.3 Standards as Social Norms

Once standards are continuously enacted, they become social norms. As such they constitute rules 'governing legitimate or "appropriate" conduct. Interaction in organizations does not occur blindly but is guided by the application of normative sanctions' (Orlikowski 1992: 405). This means that the structures of social systems also consist—besides the rules of signification expressed in interpretative schemas—of rules for sanctioning social action (legitimation). Thus, organizational members sanction by subordinating their own and other's actions to social norms and evaluate them based on these norms (Ortmann et al. 2000). Sanctions may be positive or negative (Giddens 1993). This way, they substantiate the normative order of organizations (Ortmann et al. 2000). Organizational members regulate behaviour when they refer in their practice of software development, for instance, to standards as their norms for a good, reliable development process.

Organizational members 'apply norms which in their view are apt to the particular situation for articulating and sustaining what they consider as wright or wrong, legitimate or not legitimate in organizational contexts. And, as in the case of the other dimensions, they thereby reproduce structures of legitimation' (Sydow & Windeler 1997: 464–5). Knowledgeable, performance-oriented software developing personnel eventually show compliant, deviant, or repair behaviour (Fried 2017) reasoned by different frames of legitimation. Justifications to comply with, to deviate from, or to repair, and thus to negotiate standards as social norms, can be of administrative, business, technical, ethical, and regulatory origin.

There is an intersection of interpretative schemes and social norms: to be 'accountable for one's activities is both to explicate the reasons for them and to supply the normative grounds whereby they may be "justified"' (Giddens 1984: 30). Standards as 'formal codes of conduct usually express some sort of claimed symmetry between the rights and obligations, the one being the justification of the other' (Giddens 1984: 30). As stated by Giddens (1984), often such symmetry does not exist in practice; related sanctions are rather an expression of asymmetries between rights and obligations, and thus interpretative schemes and social norms.

Besides the belief-driven processes of sensemaking that take place when interpretative schemes emerge in the form of expectations about or argumentations for standards, *action-driven processes of sensemaking* occur (Weick 1995). Organizational members manipulate or commit themselves to social norms when they legitimize compliance to and deviance from standards in action-driven processes of sensemaking. Weick (1995) states that *commitment* to social norms aims at binding actions to efficiency while reducing flexibility, learning, and adaption at the same time. Thus, committed organizational members 'consider only a few options, highlight only positive features of an alternative' to create 'enthusiasm and [this] increases the effort expended to carry out a decision', including motivational consequences (Weick 1995: 161f).

In contrast, *manipulation* aims at intervening, creating, and influencing the environment to enrich meaning, for instance, when software developers deviate from standards to get their development work done. Sensemaking through manipulation creates 'an environment that people can then comprehend and manage' and people then 'create sensible niches for themselves' (Weick 1995: 165f). Manipulation has 'a basic entrepreneurial quality' (Weick 1995: 166). The frames to legitimate commitment or manipulation can be of *technical* (e.g. usability), *business* (e.g. financial reason, contract), *ethical* (e.g. human life, environment), *regulatory* (e.g. external, standardization bodies), or *administrative* (e.g. roles, procedures, bonuses) origin.

Social norms provide grounds to reward (*positive sanctions*) or punish (*negative sanctions*) behaviour when in organizations certain actions, decisions, events, or developments are assessed as right or wrong, as legitimate or illegitimate (O'Reilly & Puffer 1989). According to Tenbrunsel and Messick (1999), sanctioning systems also influence the type of legitimation frame that is chosen. This means, in the context of this book, that the existence and strength of sanctions influence how commitment to or manipulation of social norms, and thus standards, are legitimized. Tenbrunsel and Messick state that in the case where *no sanctioning system* exists in an organization, the ethical aspects of decision-making are preferably considered. A *weak sanctioning system* is characterized by a low probability of detecting manipulations combined with the expectation of small fines if manipulations are detected anyhow. In this case, organizational members argue with business aspects when they comply or deviate from social norms compared to a situation when no sanctions are present and ethical aspects of decision-making are considered; this means that weak sanctioning systems prompt 'a perception that the decision concerns the costs' and often produce undesirable behaviours (Tenbrunsel & Messick 1999: 697).

Strong sanctioning systems appear as systems where deviance from social norms has a high probability of being detected, followed by high fines, but are distinguished by the absence of feedback (Tenbrunsel & Messick 1999). They produce desirable behaviours when it comes to compliance with social norms but are mainly legitimized by an 'economically rational course of action', whereas at the same time a 'decrease [in] the extent to which ethical considerations are taken into account' is observable (Tenbrunsel & Messick 1999: 704). This can consequently mean that software developers comply with standards for business reasons when they expect strong sanctions, but they do not comply in this case because they consider it as a moral or ethical obligation to do so. The main analytical question for analysing standards as social norms is: Which legitimations for deviations from standards evolve in software developing organizations? The following aspects point to this question:

- Which forms of deviation from standards are described by organizational members?
- Which reasons for deviations from standards are provided by organizational members?
- How do organizational members sanction deviations from standards?
- How do organizational members attribute responsibility for deviations from standards?

The next section identifies how we position organizational deviance from standards through the lens of structuration theory.

3.2 Organizational Deviance from Standards

As outlined above, the objective of this chapter is to present a theoretical framework that allows to analyse and understand why organizations deviate from standards. Section 3.1 and Figure 3.1 provided ground for this. We now link the three concepts—the 'dialectic of control', the 'stratification model', and the 'duality of structure'—in order to explore in subsequent chapters organizational deviance from standards empirically.

Studying organizational deviance can shed light on social order in general but can also unveil contradictory patterns that organizational 'deviance requires in order to exist as a social phenomenon' (Rubington & Weinberg 1970: 1). For the definition of contradictions we follow Giddens who states: 'I mean by "contradiction" the existence of two structural principles within a societal system, whereby each depends upon the other but at the same time negates it.... Societal totalities are *structured in contradiction* involving the fusion and exclusion of opposites' (Giddens 1981: 231; italics in original). Thus, 'system contradiction distinctions are not just opposites, or the "poles" of two dimensions. The conceptualization... is a more dialectical one' (Giddens 1979: 144). This means that even if they have opposing dimensions, contradictions can be managed in different ways (see also Fairhurst et al. 2002; Putnam et al. 2016; Seo et al. 2004) because 'actors are always knowledgeable about the structural framework within which their conduct is carried on' (Giddens 1979: 144).

Giddens (1979) distinguishes primary and secondary contradictions. The *primary contradiction* is characteristic for the system reproduction of society and describes the nature of the system. Fairhurst et al. (2002: 507) describe, for instance, that in a situation of downsizing an organization, organizations struggle with the contradiction 'between profit and people'; they enlarge profits and efficiency but, at the same time, risk losing the institutional memory by laying off people. *Secondary contradictions* are those contradictions that 'are brought about through the existence of primary contradictions, and which are in some sense a result of them' (Giddens 1979: 143). Standards requirements can, for example, demand, on the one hand, additional expenses for reliable development processes that decrease profits in the short run. On the other hand, standards may enhance the safety of end-users, i.e. employees, patients, or passengers. So, need for human safety and increasing cost for standard-compliant development can be considered as contradictory. However, as described above, organizational members as knowledgeable agents may, for instance, choose either to fuse societal needs like human safety and economic objectives in one way or the other or to manage them as opposites at each other's expense.

As Ortmann et al. (2000) state, in many respects, it is one of the most exciting questions in organization theory what the relationship between the structurationist dimensions of signification, legitimation, and domination is. By focusing on this relationship in the context of this book and led by the central research question (why organizations deviate from standards), we aim to identify the contradictions and asymmetries that might appear during the enactment of standards in organizations. In the horizontal dimension of our theoretical framework (see Figure 3.1), we ask about potential *contradictions* between standards as interpretative schemes, standards as facilities, and standards as social norms in a specific organizational setting. For example, standards can be given a high degree of relevance in an organization. However, this does not necessarily mean that sufficient resources are made available to implement them properly. The contradiction that organizational members perceive may be the need to meet customers' or senior management's expectations for standard certification while facing a lack of allocative or authoritative resources for standard enactment.

Furthermore, we will analyse the vertical dimension of our theoretical framework (see Figure 3.1), i.e., the contradictions that might appear as *asymmetries* between the structural and interactional dimension of standards. Standards do not unfold the desired effects when their structural dimension is insufficiently developed, hence when they are not satisfactorily institutionalized. In this case, they do not trigger rules of interpretation in an appropriate way, do not claim sufficient allocative and authoritative resources, or barely shape rules of sanctions which would, however, be necessary to become effective in organizational practices. Standards are part of the discursive consciousness (Giddens 1984), and it needs ongoing argumentation for making them significant (following Weick 1995).

In turn, standards do not unfold the anticipated effects when the interactional dimension is underemphasized. That means the impact of standards on organizational practices is not contested. Rather, it is taken for granted: the enabling but also the constraining effects of standards on organizational communication and also the mobilization of resources do not need further active legitimation. Neither the extent of standard fulfilment nor the once introduced sanctions for deviance from standards are longer scrutinized.

Standards are part of the practical consciousness of organizational members (Giddens 1984); there are clear expectations regarding their signification for the organization (following Weick 1995). Especially when they cause conflicts due to unintended consequences, contradictions, and asymmetries, the enactment of standards needs to be managed by the involved organizational members (e.g. Fairhurst et al. 2002). Organizational deviance in its various types of appearance is one way to manage standards. As Weick (1995) puts it, organizational deviance is 'a basic entrepreneurial quality' of knowledgeable agents to create, modify, or manipulate standard requirements to create an environment they can comprehend and manage.

In summary, structuration theory provides us with grounds for answering the question why organizations deviate from standards. It allows us to reveal contradictory patterns that in consequence may lead to different types of deviance from standards.

References

Adler, P. S. & Borys, B. 1996. Two types of bureaucracy: enabling and coercive. *Administrative Science Quarterly*, 41, 61–89.

Backhouse, J., Hsu, C. W., & Silva, L. 2006. Circuits of power in creating de jure standards: shaping an international information systems security standard. *MIS Quarterly*, 30, 413–38.

Beck, N. & Walgenbach, P. 2005. Technical efficiency or adaptation to institutionalized expectations? The adoption of ISO 9000 standards in the German mechanical engineering industry. *Organization Studies*, 26, 841–66.

Becker, A. 1996. *Rationalität strategischer Entscheidungsprozesse: ein strukturationstheoretisches Konzept*. Wiesbaden: DUV.

Cohen, I. J. 1989. *Structuration Theory. Anthony Giddens and the Constitution of Social Life*. Houndsmills: Palgrave Macmillan.

Djelic, M. L. & Den Hond, F. 2014. Introduction: multiplicity and plurality in the world of standards. Symposium on multiplicity and plurality in the world of standards. *Business and Politics*, 16, 67–77.

Emirbayer, M. & Mische, A. 1998. What is agency? *American Journal of Sociology*, 103, 962–1023.

Fairhurst, G. T., Cooren, F., & Cahill, D. J. 2002. Discursiveness, contradiction, and unintended consequences in successive downsizings. *Management Communication Quarterly*, 15, 501–40.

Fried, A. 2003. *Wissensmanagement aus konstruktivistischer Perspektive. Die Doppelte Dualität von Wissen in Organisationen*. Frankfurt am Main: Peter Lang.

Fried, A. 2010. Performance measurement systems and their relation to strategic learning: a case study in a software-developing organization. *Critical Perspectives on Accounting*, 21, 118–33.

Fried, A. 2017. Terminological distinctions of 'control': a review of the implications for management control research in the context of innovation. *Journal of Management Control*, 28, 5–40.

Fried, A., Gey, R., Pretorius, A., & Günther, L. 2013. Decoupling from standards—process management and technical innovation in software development organisations. *International Journal of Innovation Management*, 17.

Gey, R. & Fried, A. 2018. Metastructuring for standards: how organizations respond to the multiplicity of standards. *In:* Jakobs, K. (ed.) *Corporate and Global Standardization Initiatives in Contemporary Society.* Hershey, PA: IGI Global.

Giddens, A. 1979. *Central Problems in Social Theory. Action, Structure and Contradiction in Social Analysis*. Houndmills: Palgrave.

Giddens, A. 1981. *A Contemporary Critique of Historical Materialism,* London: Macmillan.

Giddens, A. 1982. *Profiles and Critiques in Social Theory,* London: Palgrave.

Giddens, A. 1984. The constitution of society. Outline of the theory of structuration. Cambridge: Polity Press.

Giddens, A. 1993. *New Rules of Sociological Method. A Positive Critique of Interpretative Sociologies*. Cambridge: Polity Press.

Maitlis, S. 2005. The social processes of organizational sensemaking. *Academy of Management Journal*, 48, 21–49.

Nelson, J. 2019. Disclosure driven crime. *UC Davis Law Review*, 52.

O'reilly Iii, C. A. & Puffer, S. M. 1989. The impact of rewards and punishments in a social context: a laboratory and field experiment. *Journal of Occupational Psychology*, 62, 41–53.

Orlikowski, W. J. 1992. The duality of technology. Rethinking the concept of technology in organizations. *Organization Science*, 3, 398–427.

Ortmann, G. 2010. On drifting rules and standards. *Scandinavian Journal of Management*, 26, 204–14.

Ortmann, G. 2015. *Organisation und Moral. Die dunkle Seite*. Weilerswist: Velbrück.

Ortmann, G., Sydow, J., & Türk, K. 2000. *Theorien der Organisation. Die Rückkehr der Gesellschaft*. Wiesbaden: Westdeutscher Verlag.

Putnam, L. L., Fairhurst, G. T., & Banghart, S. 2016. Contradictions, dialectics, and paradoxes in organizations: a constitutive approach. *Academy of Management Annals*, 10, 65–171.

Roberts, J. & Scapens, R. W. 1985. Accounting systems and systems of accountability—understanding accounting practices in their organizational contexts. *Accounting, Organizations & Society*, 10, 443–56.

Rubington, E. & Weinberg, M. S. 1970. *Deviance: The Interactionist Perspective. Text and Readings in the Sociology of Deviance*. Toronto: Macmillan.

Seo, M., Putnam, L. L., & Bartunek, J. M. 2004. Dualities and tensions of planned organizational change. *In:* Poole, M. S. & Van De Ven, A. (eds) *Handbook of Organizational Change and Innovation*. Oxford: Oxford University Press.

Suddaby, R. & Greenwood, R. 2005. Rhetorical strategies of legitimacy. *Administrative Science Quarterly*, 50, 35–67.

Sydow, J. & Windeler, A. 1997. Managing inter-firm networks: a structurationist perspective. *In:* Bryant, C. G. A. & Jary, D. (eds) *Anthony Giddens: Critical Assessments*. London: Routledge.

Tempel, A. & Walgenbach, P. 2007. Global standardization of organizational forms and management practices? What new institutionalism and the business-systems approach can learn from each other. *Journal of Management Studies*, 44, 1–24.

Tenbrunsel, A. E. & Messick, D. M. 1999. Sanctioning systems, decision frames, and cooperation. *Administrative Science Quarterly*, 44, 684–707.

Walgenbach, P. 1999. Giddens' Theorie der Strukturierung. *In:* Kieser, A. (ed.) *Organisationstheorien*, 3rd edn. Stuttgart: Kohlhammer.

Weick, K. E. 1988. Enacted sensemaking in crisis situations. *Journal of Management Studies*, 25, 305–17.

Weick, K. E. 1995. *Sensemaking in Organizations*. Thousand Oaks: SAGE.

Whittington, R. 1992. Putting Giddens into action: social systems and managerial agency. *Journal of Management Studies*, 29, 693–712.

4

Investigating Organizational Deviance from Standards in Depth

Sarah Langer, Ronny Gey, and Diana Karadzhova-Beyer

This chapter describes the methodological approach of our research on organizational deviance from standards. First, the research design is described with regard to some empirical premises we set; thereafter our research strategy of a focused ethnography is illustrated, and the sampling is explained in detail. Finally, we describe the chosen methods of data gathering and the process of data analysis which is structured by the operationalization of key theoretical elements. A conclusion is drawn at the end of the chapter by highlighting some lessons learned for future research.

4.1 Empirical Premises

Since the *enactment of standards* has not been investigated in depth so far, we developed an empirical research design to meet this challenge using the following premises described in sections 44.1.1 to 4.1.4.

4.1.1 Qualitative Research Design

We investigated standard enactment *in situ*, and examined organizational practices and practitioners' reproduction of these practices which allows them to use standards in daily activities. With the aim of gaining rich data, we decided on a qualitative research design to understand the practitioners' 'world of standards' (Brunsson & Jacobsson 2000).

Sarah Langer, Ronny Gey, and Diana Karadzhova-Beyer, *Investigating Organizational Deviance from Standards in Depth* In: *Understanding Deviance in a World of Standards*. Edited by: Andrea Fried, Oxford University Press (2020).
DOI: 10.1093/oso/9780198833888.003.0004

4.1.2 Focus on Software Developing Projects as Sites of Standard Enactment

To understand the challenges of standard enactment, we focused on the question how organizational members enact standards in software development projects and why they deviate from them. Moreover, Ladner puts it aptly for the challenge of ethnographic research in corporate fields: 'today's corporate touchstone is the "project"' (Ladner 2014: 41). In software development, standards are mainly enacted as a set of several single standards which companies need to comply with (Gey & Fried 2018). When discussing 'standards' and 'organizational deviance from standards' in the book, we refer to this set of standards.

4.1.3 A Qualitative Design of Multiple Methods for Virtual Working Environments

Taking software development literally means to understand it as a virtual form of work. Due to the essentially virtual appearance of the work process and results, software development is especially elusive in its character for empirical investigation. To meet this challenge, we applied complementing qualitative methods.

4.1.4 'Minimally Invasive' Research Design

Contemporary working conditions are characterized by short product development cycles and tight project budgets. Our case organizations requested a research design that would interfere with daily work as little as possible. At the same time, we were interested in gathering in-depth data with rich explanatory power. Thus, in the selection and use of data-gathering methods we tried to be 'minimally invasive', as one of the empirical partners from the medical field put it. The term refers to surgical techniques that limit the number and size of incisions needed during operations. This approach was guided by the empirical partners' needs and an understanding of the 'ritualistic nature of project management' (Ladner 2014: 44) with regular meetings and successive milestones.

4.2 Focused Ethnography

Based on these empirical premises, we decided for a *focused ethnography* as the research strategy. In line with Alvesson and Deetz (2000), we used the term ethnography for a research strategy that is typically broader and gives richer qualitative material than traditional research approaches. A classical ethnographic study involves a longer period of fieldwork trying to get close to an organization or group, relying on their accounts as well as on observations of a variety of naturally occurring events and gathering of further material such as documents (Alvesson & Deetz 2000). Ladner (2014) appreciates the most important reasons to use an ethnography for the corporate sector: to reveal and understand the participant's viewpoint. Ethnography is an '*in situ* method' (Ladner 2014: 17) which collects direct insights from contextual observation. However, a *focused ethnography* (Knoblauch 2005) deals with a specific problem in a distinct context and is especially appropriate when conducting applied research in highly fragmented and specialized fields of study like standard-compliant software development in corporate organizations.

With a focused ethnography, we also meet the challenge of exploratory research in the highly dynamic, virtual working environment by applying a mixed set of qualitative methods. We combined the following qualitative methods, which will be explained in more detail in section 4.4:

- participant observations;
- qualitative interviews;
- online logbook;
- gathering of official and internal documents;
- questionnaire.

Furthermore, we designed the *focused ethnography* to identify unique and common features across cases, encouraging theoretical reflections on the findings (Bryman & Bell 2011). We decided on an *alternative, interpretive approach* of focused ethnography (Piekkari et al. 2009) to produce rich, holistic, and detailed explanations in different situational contexts by using multiple methods of data collection. Embedded in this interpretive approach, we have chosen a *comparative case design* which relates and contrasts the findings derived from the three different software development units of high technology companies. As a case study strategy is concerned with the complexity and particular nature of each case (Bryman & Bell 2011), great importance is placed on the construction of the cases. This will be explained in detail in the following section.

4.3 Sampling

The decision for a unit of analysis is 'fundamentally an interpretive issue regarding judgement and choice' (Van Maanen et al. 1986: 5). We followed a *purposive sampling strategy* (Bryman & Bell 2011: 442) based on the empirical premises as stated above. Our sampling was guided by the following principles—we were interested in:

- hardware-related software development projects;
- middle to large sized companies;
- working in sectors such as transportation (aeronautics, automobile, and railway) or healthcare where customer safety is a critical factor; and
- working in sectors where process standard certifications are therefore mandatory.

These choices led us to the investigation of organizational members' efforts to comply with mandatory safety-critical standards. We believe that investigations in safety-critical environments where functional safety standards are mandatory deliver distinct results.

After searching corporate profiles that fit the sampling according to their online appearance, we approached these companies via mail and phone with information on the research project and offered a personal introduction to our research. Altogether, we approached forty-five organizations; not all of them eventually had software development integrated in product development but rather bought in software components. After preselecting the companies with in-house software development, we successfully won two companies out of the six we contacted in the medical technology sector and two engineering companies out of seven in the heavy industry sector. Not a single company from the twenty-six companies approached in the automobile sector could be won as an empirical partner. After one of the empirical partners from the medical technology sector did not get approval for collaboration, we finished the selection phase with three companies. Eventually, we investigated hardware-related software development projects at *CraneSolutions*, *MedTech*, and *MetroEngineers*, for several months—each of them from the beginning till the end. Each case is anonymized and presented in detail in part II of the book.

During our investigations, we had access to software development projects for new products or engineering services including quality or product management. We especially focused on the activities of the software development unit in each project. In a participative manner, we asked the responsible gatekeepers to select one or more projects for investigation which they regard as innovative and challenging regarding the prospective compliance with standards. As well as this, we encouraged them to look for software development projects that would give us the chance to investigate the course of the software development from start till end. In one company, we were asked to introduce our research at the workers' council for their approval. The workers' council suggested to investigate a second development project to create a larger sample, guaranteeing higher anonymity to the employees. This led to an extension of the sample to two development projects in this case company. However, from an empirical saturation point of view, we analysed both projects together as two examples of one case.

In summary, the gatekeepers of the case organizations identified the innovative character of the development project and, thus, motivated their selection as follows:

- **PMA project at CraneSolutions**—challenge to integrate a new control unit and to adopt the control software to meet new standard demands; development of a product with innovative functionalities tailored to the clients' needs.
- **Siberia project at MedTech**—Linux as new system software; challenge to reinnovate an old product; partly automated testing as innovation which could not be enforced in the end.
- **Fidelio project at MedTech**—challenge to develop a new software release for an already running diagnosis product.
- **BRT project at MetroEngineers**—organizational innovation due to the introduction of a software development process model (V-Model as in DIN EN 50126) to meet European Standards prospectively; development of an innovative product tailored to the clients' needs.

After empirical access to the cases was established, we followed what Glaser and Strauss (1967: 45) call a *theoretical sampling strategy:* jointly collecting, coding, and analysing data in order to develop theory as it emerges. In an iterative process we decided which first findings provide the basis for further investigations, such as continuing the participant observations, interviewing key persons again, or searching for further experts in the field. Correspondingly,

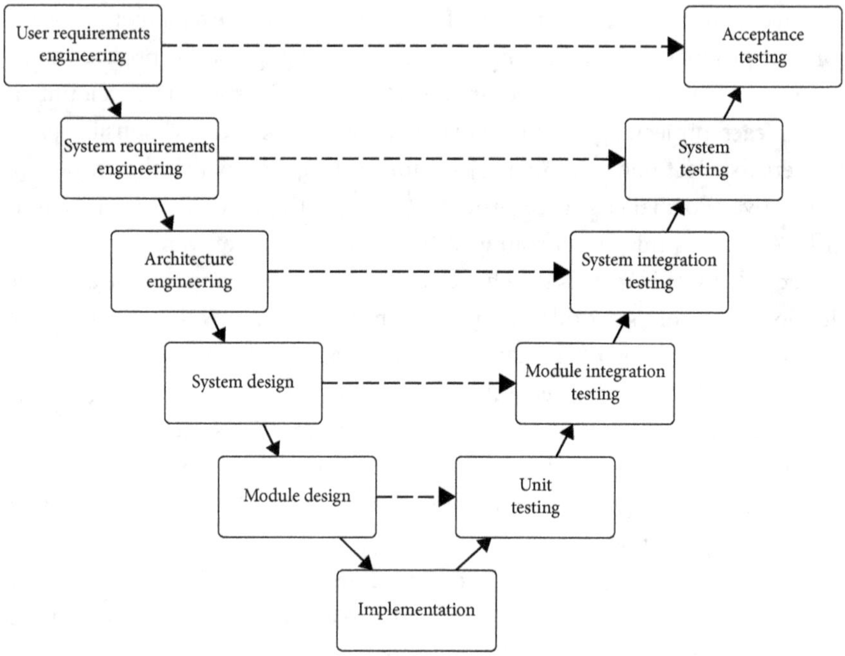

Figure 4.1 Simplified representation of the V-model

data gathering was guided by the idea of *theoretical saturation* (Strauss & Corbin 1997: 212). Since the access to the investigated three software development units took place consecutively, it allowed us to pay close attention to the saturated development of categories and their relationships for each case.

While investigating, we discovered that all three software development units had implemented or were implementing the same model for their software development processes. The V-Model (see Figure 4.1) as an approach of a (software) development process model (Ruparelia 2010) unites the three cases, even though they are grounded in different industrial sectors. The V-Model is a variation of the earlier waterfall model. On the left side of the V, along different phases (requirements engineering, architecture engineering, system design, and module design) requirements are decomposed into systems specifications which form the basis for the implementation into software code. This happens at the tip of the V. On the right side, each phase on the left side is associated with a respective phase of testing (unit testing, integration testing, system testing, user acceptance testing). Integration and verification of the different components leads to an assembly and implementation of the final product. The V-model is often used in very large projects, where different contractors and teams need to be coordinated (Ruparelia 2010). In Europe and especially in Germany, a variant of the V-model is commonly used which was first developed by the German Ministry of Defence. In a modified form, it was integrated into several industry standards (e.g. as advised in DIN EN 50128 for the railway sector, in IEC 60601-1 and IEC 62304 for the medical technology sector). Among other suggestions, it comprises an elaborate role concept with up to thirty-five different roles.

To sum up, we provide some major information on the sample of our comparative case design in Table 4.1. Several similarities, such as the V-Model as a comparable software development process model or the safety-critical

Table 4.1 Variables of the sample

	Software development at CraneSolutions	**Software development at MedTech**		**Software development at MetroEngineers**
Company information				
Headquartered in	Germany			
Geographical scope	Globally active company			
Size of company	Middle to large sized company			
Sector	Heavy industry			Heavy industry
	Crane sector	Medical technology sector		Rail sector
Investigated software development project				
Project name	PMA	Siberia	Fidelio	BRT
Employees in software development	5	6	14	7
Employees' profile	Highly qualified, mainly male project employees			
Project outcome	New engineering product	New engineering product	Engineering product with software update	New engineering product as service
Type of software developed	Hardware-related, embedded software			
Standards underlying software development				
Regulatory constraints	Safety critical development environment with rigid regulatory constraints			
Important standards	EN 13000, EN 13849, further anonymized standards	EN 13485, EN 14971, EN 62304, EN 60601, FDA Guidelines		EN 50126, EN 50128, EN 50129
Standard-related software development model	V-Model			

environment in middle to large companies, enable us to draw analytical comparisons for later theoretical reflections from the cross-case analysis. As well as this, the sample is typical for software development in general, with mainly male participants having enjoyed a highly qualified academic engineering education. In an attempt to offer rich explanations from the cross-case analysis of the sample, we can conclude a high theoretical generalizability for standard enactment in software units in middle to large companies working in safety-critical sectors.

4.4 Methods of Data Gathering

In this section we describe the five different methods of data gathering (field observations, qualitative interviews, online logbooks, documents, and questionnaire) which we used for the investigations in the three case companies. The temporality of each project is depicted in a separate timeline, where each interview, observation, or entry in the online logbook is marked on a horizontal timeline (PMA project of CraneSolutions: Figure 4.2; Siberia project of MedTech: Figure 4.3; Fidelio project of MedTech: Figure 4.4; and BRT project of MetroEngineers: Figure 4.5).

4.4.1 Field Observations

First, gathering data through observations is fundamental to ethnography (Gobo & Marciniak 2016). We consider field observations as a data-gathering method in which the observer's investigation takes place in the social situation itself. The researcher directly observes the phenomenon in its natural setting in a methodically planned manner to extract meaningful interpretations of the social world (Singleton & Bruce 2005). Observations differ in the extent of the researcher's active participation in the field. The researcher either can be completely immersed in the setting and can participate fully or is completely separated from the setting as a non-participant. In practice, we rarely encountered either of these extremes but rather characteristics of both (Schwartz & Schwartz 1955).

We characterize our field observations as overt, non-covered, passively participant, and complemented observation added to by irregular, personal inquiry options subsequent to the observations (Bryman 2004; Schwartz & Schwartz 1955). Hardly addressed in the daily development routines, we

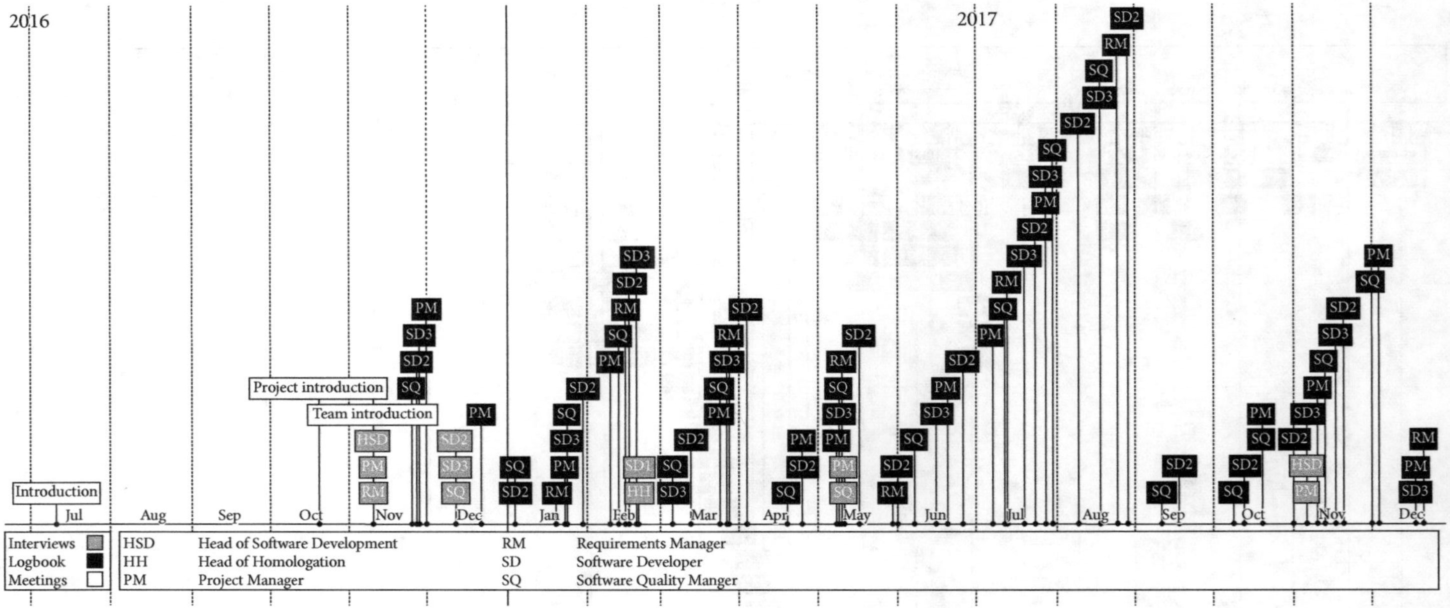

Figure 4.2 Timeline of empirical investigations at CraneSolutions' PMA project

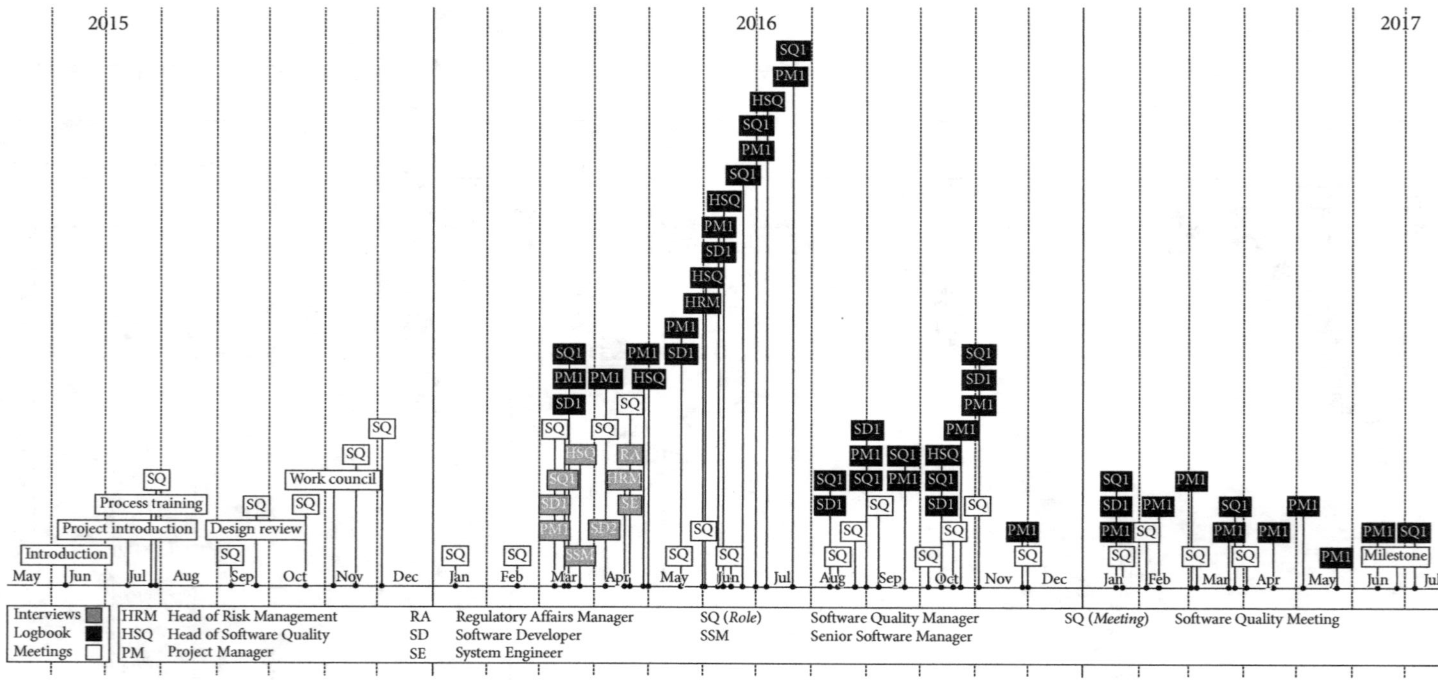

Figure 4.3 Timeline of empirical investigations at MedTech's Siberia project

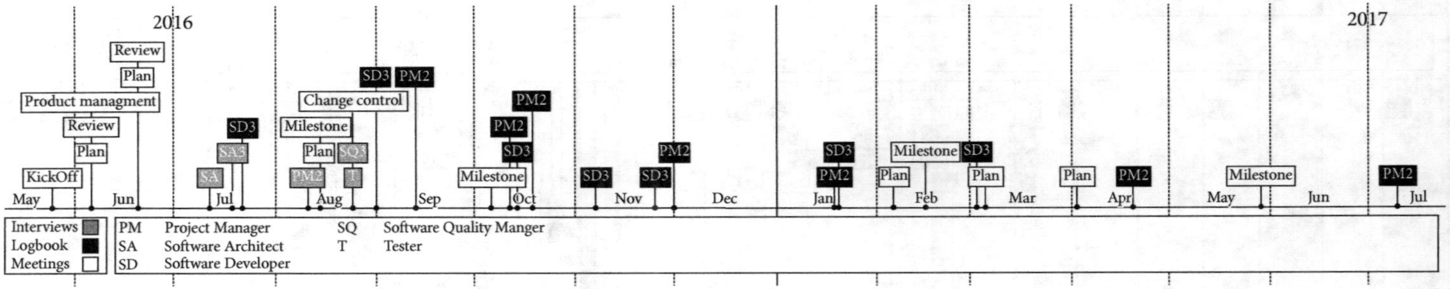

Figure 4.4 Timeline of empirical investigations at MedTech's Fidelio project

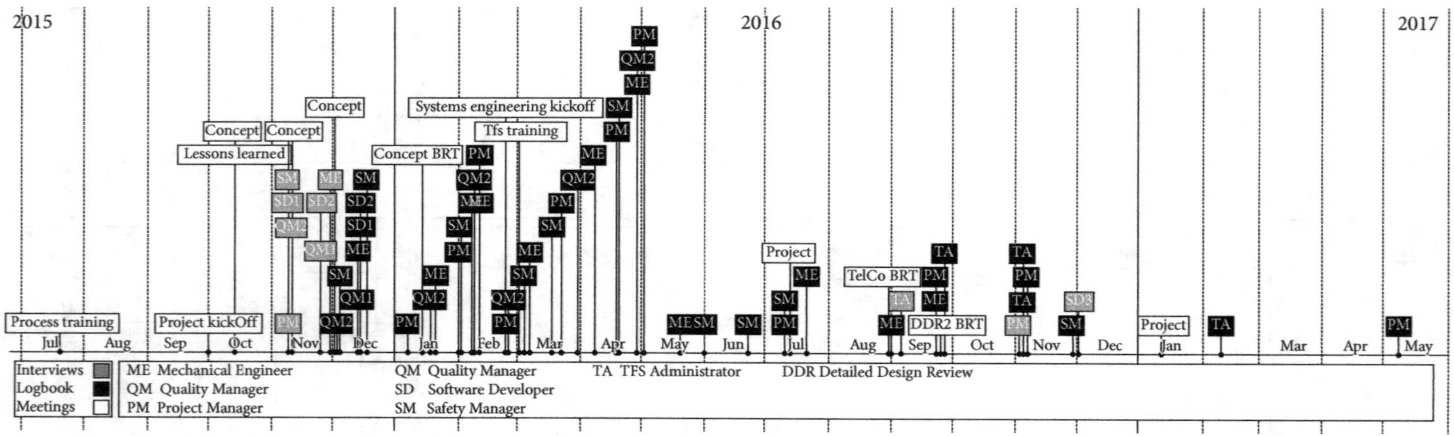

Figure 4.5 Timeline of empirical investigations at MetroEngineers' BRT project

observed project meetings where standard relevant topics are usually discussed. For access to these meetings, we asked the project managers of each case beforehand. We observed regular meetings with a defined frequency on a 2-week basis in the two MedTech development projects with at least one researcher present. As well as this, irregular meetings were scheduled at MedTech and MetroEngineers. Sometimes our contact person invited us to attend these meetings; sometimes we asked for invitation. The meetings were concerned with project milestones, quality, and design reviews or review meetings with the customer. At CraneSolutions there was no formal meeting routine. We addressed this lack of observational data with additional interviews throughout the software developing project.

During our observations the meeting participants were aware of our physical presence. However, we did not participate in the social interactions during the observed situations and events. Even though we tried to avoid any obstruction of the natural setting, our presence, the associated undertaking, and its goals were well known to the group members. We had eye contact with the group members and seldom would a member address us in a confirmatory fashion as if we were business consultants. After many observations, the project managers answered questions about the observation, allowing us to rectify misinterpretations or to understand peculiarities of the organization-specific language and context.

During our observations we took field notes, describing the observed interactions either as handwritten notes or digitally. In a post-processing step directly after the observation, each of the observing researchers transferred the notes to a standardized observation protocol (Emerson et al. 2011). We designed the protocol along the lines of our empirical focus on standard enactment and our theoretical approach—the structuration theory. We created a section for events/activities, behaviour, actors, and modalities of action where we described the different situations we encountered during observations. Further, we added contextual information like date, time, place, and participants, our own emotions about the field, and our potential to influence it. Moreover, we noted our first reflections on standard enactment and software development. We added further aspects such as appointments and to-do's, as well as organization-specific language, for instance, abbreviations, and keywords. The descriptions of our observations and the contextual information we collected were both referenced back in inquiries after the observations.

Considering the analysis of the material derived from the field observations, we first examined the observation protocols for important events containing descriptions of deviance and resources, and regarding the enactment of standards. Subsequently, we listed the selected events chronologically in a common MS Excel spreadsheet and supplemented them with additional information on the author of the field notes, the date of observation, and a brief description of the event type. We then coded the events, first with systematic open coding (Corbin & Strauss 1990) followed by a focused coding (Emerson et al. 2011). In the end, we selected the identified events for a qualitative content analysis (Mayring 2000).

4.4.2 Qualitative Interviews

Qualitative interviews were the second principal source of data for the empirical investigations. We applied a semi-structured type of interview in a face-to-face manner (Bryman 2004). With the interviews we obtained emotions, thoughts, and intentions of our participants and discovered their perspective of the social world (Patton 2002). In addition to the field observations, we obtained information on past events or events that we could not participate in.

The interviews were conducted in each company at the beginning of the development projects and were also an appropriate opportunity to get in contact with the field (Meuser & Nagel 2009). After we agreed on the general outline of our investigations with the project managers, we collectively identified all the project members. We selected those interview partners who were actively involved in the development of the software, in charge of the standard requirements and the certification process, or in further standard-related key roles. Consequently, we interviewed software engineers, software architects, quality managers, safety engineers, project managers, and managers of the software department. We contacted each participant by e-mail and later identified and contacted further participants to gain further significant information. At the end of our investigations, we conducted follow-up interviews with some of the participants of the first round. This was especially the case with *CraneSolutions* due to missing field observations.

The interviews lasted between 30 and 150 minutes, with an average length of 90 minutes. We conducted the interviews on-site, mostly in respective meeting rooms or personal offices, i.e. those of project managers. We conducted the interviews following an interview guide structured in four parts. After a brief introduction to our research project and an agreement on data anonymization, we asked the interviewees about their personal work experience, education, and their position in the organization and the development project. In the second part, we focused on the software development process in the organization and in the specific project, on the different roles involved, and the research and development in the organization. Third, we addressed the topic of standard enactment and organized the questions following a structuration theory point of view, for instance, standards and signification, standards and legitimation, as well as standards and domination (see Fried & Walgenbach 2020). We further added questions regarding standard modalities and reflexive governance. In a fourth part, we raised person- or organization-specific questions. However, we considered the interview process as flexible, allowing us to focus on interesting standard-related topics mentioned by the interviewee. Finally, we finished the interviews by introducing the participant to the online logbook method in order to increase the acceptance of this rather unusual method.

During the interviews we took notes. Thereafter, we wrote a short protocol of the interview situation. Every interview was tape-recorded and subsequently transcribed using the software tool easytranscript.[1] While transcribing, we followed basic transcription rules. One interviewee demanded to countercheck the transcribed interview several weeks after the interview and withdrew some of the interview parts in the end.

4.4.3 Online Logbook

Specially designed online logbooks was a third qualitative method we used for empirical investigations on standard enactment. We consider logbooks as a prestructured method for self-observations (Kunz 2015). Individuals document their daily routines; they explicate their individual practices, orientations, experiences, and knowledge on a regular basis. Logbook studies offer reflexive self-reports of individual observations and thus represent a special form of diary studies (Bolger et al. 2003). By the use of diary studies, the qualitative researcher overcomes the shortcomings of traditional qualitative methods such as interviews and observations: the retrospection problem, the space–time problem, and the memorization problem (Alaszewski 2006; Bolger et al. 2003; Roth 2015). Alaszewski (2006) puts the focus on hard-to-reach or hard-to-observe phenomena which can ideally be observed with diary methods in general and logbooks specifically.

The online logbooks had several purposes: one of the expected challenges in our focused ethnographic field study was the space–time problem. We

[1] http://www.e-werkzeug.eu/index.php/de/produkte/easytranscript

anticipated that the case organizations would not grant us regular access to their daily practices, for different reasons such as secrecy, disturbance of daily routines and time, and work exertion. Further, in order to study processes or temporal dynamics, the use of diary studies is explicitly suggested at times when change is likely to occur (Bolger et al. 2003). In order to identify project-disturbing events and to follow-up the project's progress in general, we chose the complementary online logbook method.

Since computer literacy was not an issue for our subjects, we chose to implement an *online* logbook based on the open source online survey tool LimeSurvey.[2] While deploying an online solution, we gained data that did not necessitate transcriptions and which could easily be exported into different file formats. After we had introduced each interviewee to the online logbook method during the interviews at the beginning of the empirical investigations, we invited all of them with a link to the online form provided via e-mail. We reminded them to fill out their logbooks every 3 weeks. In the online logbook, we asked the participants about three specific events (one was mandatory) within the previous 3 weeks which they regarded as the most important. They were asked to explain its importance and the advantageous and disadvantageous aspects of the event in respect of the development process. Finally, the participants could rate the current project progress regarding its goals and could comment on this rating. Finally, we asked the participants to provide feedback on the usage of the online logbook. On a 3-week basis, we exported the answers from the logbook into text files and analysed them regarding important events for our study. The return rate of the logbook entries differed among the different cases (CraneSolutions: 41 per cent, MedTech—Siberia: 22 per cent, MedTech—Fidelio: 19 per cent; MetroEngineers: 37 per cent) and varied substantially among the different project phases due to workload differences during the software development process.

For further analysis we compiled an MS Excel-file with all logbook entries in a chronological manner. We selected relevant entries which we analysed according to qualitative content analysis (Mayring 2000). In view of our analytical questions, we selected sequences that described events regarding the meaning of standards for the organization, standard-related resources, and deviations from standard requirements. The online logbook entries were also used to compile information on important events for the illustration of a project timeline for each case.

[2] https://www.limesurvey.org/

4.4.4 Documents

As a further source of data collection, we identified documents as the materialized products of communicated decisions and social relations in organizations (Froschauer 2009). The analysed documents functioned as supplementary sources complementing the principal data from field observations and qualitative interviews (Bowen 2009).

Of interest here was to analyse more the content of these documents and less their function and use (Prior 2016); they provided important context information about the organizations at the beginning of our investigations. The documents contained insights about the main products and processes and were provided by empirical partners throughout the investigations. Among others, these documents were organization charts of the projects, overviews of applicable standards, procedural documents, project plans, and documents on process trainings, lists of abbreviations, and even a bachelor thesis on the design and implementation of the software development process model. During the analysis process, they were an important source of reference on which the participants themselves often commented. Further, we gathered public documents via the website of the case organizations such as annual reports, product presentations, and marketing brochures.

4.4.5 Questionnaire

The fifth data-gathering method of our empirical investigations was a questionnaire with the intention to quantitatively supplement our qualitative data from the interviews and field observations. Applied to our research question, the aim of the questionnaire was to verify the changes we tracked along the standard enactment process of the case organizations. The changes we found during the field observations and in the constructions of the participants in the interviews were qualitative data by nature. For verification purposes, we reverted to quantitative data that could display similar changes. Practically, we wanted to know whether a statement such as 'standardization-related work increased heavily in the last few years' could be found in variables like employment figures or the amount of standardization-relevant internal documents. Furthermore, we used the questionnaire to complement information about the context of each case (e.g. the organization's size in terms of employees or turnover).

The questionnaire covered questions on the entire organization and specifically on the areas of standardization, research, and development as well as software development. For each area, we asked about employment data (development of roles and positions) and about documentation data (number of documents, the share of standard or software development relevant topics within these documents, and the development of these numbers over time). We asked the managers of the software development units to fill out the questionnaire. However, this turned out to be a highly complex task and we decided to personally guide the participants. Filling out the questionnaire turned into another interview situation with the software development managers, which we analysed later. During these sessions, we had to revise or abandon several questions due to unavailable company data. Further, the participants suggested additionally analying annual company reports concerning information on financial data, personnel, or patents. As advised by the software development manager at *CraneSolutions*, we consulted the accounting office to assess financial and employment figures. In the end, we conducted a content analysis of the questionnaires.

To give an overview of the data-gathering process we compiled a summary of methods per case organization and the data gathered in Table 4.2.

4.5 Process of Data Analysis

In general, our data analysis started with a coding process with the aid of the software tool NVivo, followed by a qualitative content analysis (Mayring 2000) based on our analytical questions (see Fried & Walgenbach 2020). During the analysis process we made use of *investigator triangulation* (Denzin 1970) to guarantee trustworthiness and intersubjective validity: two researchers per interview coded the interview data. The focused coding was done collectively by all researchers. After the coding the results were also discussed and summarized collectively to reach an agreement on our interpretations. Subsequently, we first describe the coding process and then present the analytical steps for each of the three different structurationist themes. The process of data analysis is summarized by an overview of the research and analytical questions in Table 4.3; see also Fried & Walgenbach 2020)

For the categorization of our findings regarding standards as interpretative schemes (chapters 5.2, 6.2, and 7.2) and standards as social norms (chapters 5.4, 6.4, and 7.4), we used five different frames to classify meanings, legitimations, and sanctions. The administrative frame refers to reasoning which addresses development roles, internal procedures, and organizational aspects such as remuneration, management decisions, or other administrative aspects of the

Table 4.2 Statistics on gathered data per case

Method		PMA project at CraneSolutions	Siberia project at MedTech	Fidelio project at MedTech	BRT project at MetroEngineers
Participant observations	Amount	3	35	17	16
	Sites	1	1	1	2
	Occasions	Three guided tours on site, one kick-off meeting	Project, milestone, and SQ meetings	Project, milestone, and SQ meetings	Telephone conferences with and without client/supplier, project meetings with and without client, training sessions
	Frequency	Irregular	Twice-weekly	Twice-weekly	Irregular
	Total hours	6	23	15	25
Qualitative interviews	Amount	12	9	5	11
	Participants	8	9	5	9
	Roles	Engineers (software, quality), project manager, homologation manager	Engineers (software, quality), project manager, regulatory manager, risk manager	Engineers (software, quality), project manager, tester	Engineers (software, quality, safety), project manager, team foundation server administrator
	Total hours	16	14	7	16
Online logbook	Rounds	20	23	17	22
	Participants	8	9	5	8[3]
	Entries	56	43	15	40
	Return rate	41%	22%	19%	37%

Continued

[3] During our research, two participants left the organization and one participant joined.

Table 4.2 *Continued*

Method		PMA project at CraneSolutions	Siberia project at MedTech	Fidelio project at MedTech	BRT project at MetroEngineers
Documents (internal)	Amount	1	10		12
	Types	Process model	SOP presentation, different SOP versions, brand brochure		Training material, development and role model, lists of documents and standards, BSc thesis
Documents (external)	Amount	17	34		11
	Types	Annual reports, corporate periodicals, product brochures	Annual and quarter reports, product brochures		Annual reports, sustainability reports, press release
Questionnaire	Participants	Software development manager, accounting staff	Software development manager		Software development manager
	Period	2013–2016	2013–2016		2013–2016

SOP, Standard operating procedure

Table 4.3 Research and analytical questions

Structurationist element of standard enactment	Standards as interpretative scheme	Standards as facilities	Standards as social norms
Research questions	(1) Which sense do standards generate in software developing organizations?	(2) Which power do standards unfold in software developing organizations?	(3) Which legitimations for deviations from standards evolve in software developing organizations?
Analytical questions	(1a) Which meanings do organizational members communicate to reason their engagement in standard enactment? (1b) Which interpretative frames are addressed in view of standards from their point of view? (1c) What sense do further internal and external actors give to standards?	(2a) Which allocative and authoritative resources for standard enactment are reported from software developing organizations? (2b) How do organizational members assess the transformative capacity of allocative and authoritative resources during standard enactment?	(3a) Which forms of deviation from standards are described by organizational members? (3b) Which reasons for deviations from standards are provided by organizational members? (3c) How do organizational members sanction deviations from standards? (3d) How do organizational members attribute responsibility for deviations from standards?
Data sources	Qualitative interviews, field observations	Qualitative interviews, field observations, online logbooks, questionnaire, documents	Qualitative interviews, field observations, online logbooks

organization. We classified meanings, legitimations, and sanctions within a business frame when the organizational members addressed economic and competitive reasons for their actions. In the ethical frame, members used arguments such as the safety of human life, the protection of the environment, or general concepts of wrong or right conduct in their reasoning. In the regulatory frame, we summarized reasoning that referred to legal regulations, assessors, or approval processes. Finally, we grouped meanings, legitimations, and sanctions into the technical frame when technologies and tools such as software or hardware components were the base of the arguments.

In our findings for standards as facilities (chapters 5.3, 6.3, and 7.3), we classified the different resources according to their transformative capacity and their transformative impact for standard enactment (low, medium, or high). For the transformative capacity of resources for standard enactment this means:

- Low transformative capacity: the resource that is believed to supplement standard enactment.
- Medium transformative capacity: the resource that is believed to support standard enactment.
- High transformative capacity: the resource that is believed to be crucial for standard enactment.

Further, we define the transformative impact of resources as their actualized impact for standard enactment. Based on the empirical data, we assessed the transformative impact of each resource in practice:

- Low transformative impact: the resource is considered supplementary for standard enactment.
- Medium transformative impact: the resource is considered to support standard enactment.
- High transformative impact: the resource is considered crucial for standard enactment.

4.5.1 Coding of Data

The coding of data followed a *systematic open coding* (Corbin & Strauss 1990) to conceptualize and categorize the data we gathered from interviews, observations, and logbook entries. We deductively generated codes that represented basic concepts of the field. These codes were continually revised to distinguish them properly and to improve their application when coding further empirical material.

Furthermore, we applied selected codes for a *focused coding approach* (Emerson et al. 2011), with data being sorted along theoretical aspects. We constantly compared important incidents and identified examples on the basis of the analytical questions: (1) organizational meanings of standards (standards as interpretative schemes), (2) descriptions of allocative and authoritative resources for standard enactment (standards as facilities), and (3) deviations from standards, legitimations, and sanctioning of deviations from standards (standards as social norms) (see also Fried & Walgenbach 2020). The coded and selected interview sequences were analysed by using qualitative content analysis thereafter (Mayring 2000).

4.5.2 Data Analysis for Standards as Interpretative Schemes

For the analysis of standards as interpretative schemes, we consider the organizational members as 'interpreters' of standards and as 'knowledgeable agents' (Giddens 1979). Accordingly, we framed the interpretations in the qualitative interviews as organizational accounts of standards as practice. These served as an access to the reality of the organizational members and the organization. The sum of interpretations we collected as codes in our NVivo database represents the interpretative schemes of the organization.

In order to approach the analytical question *Which sense do standards enfold in software developing organizations?* we compiled all interview sequences coded with the codes 'internal standard', 'external standard', and 'slang' in one document (see also Fried & Walgenbach 2020). The code 'slang' was used for organization-specific language. With reference to the analytical question, we coded the thus-collected sequences with 'standard as' as a separate superior code in our NVivo database. The further analytical process was inspired by the approach of condensing the data material to 'cohering metaphors' (Ladner 2014: 146). In line with Giddens (1984), we used this reducing technique to describe the thus-collected 'standard-as' codes as organizational meanings anchored in the interpretative schemes of the organizational members. Statements that were identical in content were collected under a common 'standard as' code. Finally, we selected the codes that provide meanings of standard enactment which motivate the interviewees to participate in the enactment of standards. For example, statements that relate to standards allowing to assess the safety of a product in a reliable manner were collected under the common code 'assurance of human safety'. A summarizing table for each case at the end of the respective chapter provides an overview of all 'standard as' codes as meanings of standards. In the table, we added the applicable signification frame and the different roles that referred to the 'standard as' code in the interviews. Overall, we had a large number of hits for 'standards as' codes for each organization: fourteen hits for CraneSolutions, thirteen hits for MedTech, and fifteen hits for MetroEngineers. In the later comparative analysis of the cases, we then condensed the case-specific meanings of standard enactment for each case. To identify the organizational members' sensemaking (Maitlis 2005) for standard enactment, we complemented our analysis with observational data.

4.5.3 Data Analysis for Standards as Facilities

To investigate standards as facilities during standard enactment, we asked the question *Which power do standards unfold in software developing organizations?* (see also Fried & Walgenbach 2020). We coded the interview transcripts, the observation protocols, and the logbook entries. We selected the codes 'power', 'frustration', 'control', 'hierarchy', 'financial resource', 'personnel as resource', 'knowledge as resource', and 'tools as a resource' from our NVivo-based analysis. We searched for particularly expressive sequences, and selected meaningful parts describing resources, resource limitations, and their need, availability, and effect on standard enactment. We further focused on events in which resources were reproduced during interactions to enact favourable decisions. For the selection of events we analysed the following aspects in the observation protocols: (1) types of events or activities, (2) types of actors, (3) types of behaviour, and (4) modalities of action and used or mentioned artefacts. Additionally, we used information from the questionnaire and the document analysis. From the questionnaire we mainly extracted data on financial resources and employment data over time (2013–2016/17). We analysed documents to supplement information on personnel resources and hierarchies (e.g. organization charts) and gained insights on standards and their enactment by process documentation and written elaborations on different standards and their application (e.g. bachelor thesis, process handbook). A table for each case provides an overview of all authoritative and allocative resources at the end of the respective chapter on standards as facilities. For each resource, we assessed the transformative capacity and impact as described in section 4.5.3.

4.5.4 Data Analysis for Standards as Social Norms

For the analysis of standards as social norms, we examined the research question *Which legitimations for deviations from standards evolve in software developing organizations?* (see also Fried & Walgenbach 2020). We first consulted the interview data in our NVivo database. In a focused coding process, we referred to the codes 'deviance', 'legitimation', 'responsibility', 'danger', and 'frustration'. The relevant sequences were selected and then each assigned to the analytical sub-questions in an extra document. Second, we consulted relevant sequences from the observation protocols coded with 'deviance' and added them to the already existing compilation. In the same way, we analysed the online logbooks; however, they did not reveal any further significant interpretations. The analytical process was directed by the aim of summarizing the empirical material as forms of deviations from standards as thick descriptions. A table for each case provides an overview of all forms of deviations with the corresponding legitimations referred to by the organizational members. A further table summarizes expected sanctions from deviations. For each form of deviation, as well as for each expected sanction, we added the related legitimation or sanctioning frame. Both tables are compiled in the respective chapters on standards as social norms for each case (chapters 5.4, 6.4, and 7.4 in this book). We could thereby reconstruct three forms of deviation from standards at CraneSolutions, four at MedTech, and seven at MetroEngineers.

4.6 Lessons Learned

Investigating organizational deviance from standards in software development was an extensive endeavour which we pursued as a group of researchers over several years in collaboration with three software developing organizations. We worked with a research design selecting five different methods of data gathering and corresponding analysis approaches. During this journey we gained several fruitful experiences on the process of qualitative research from which we will draw some conclusions and lessons learned for future research.

4.6.1 Research Design and Strategy

The complementary combination of multiple qualitative methods within a focused ethnography was especially reasonable for the virtual and often non-linear development work in projects. Depending on the access to the field and the opportunity to conduct field observations, we could complement missing observational data with further interviews, or by motivating the participants to focus on regular logbook entries instead. However, interviews and logbook entries cannot replace the richness of observational data of daily work settings such as project meetings. Observations can capture, for instance, conflicts, which themselves often trigger sensemaking processes.

We chose a minimally invasive research design to cause the least possible disturbances in the daily work settings of the organizational members. This proved to be an important feature to convince the gatekeepers of the empirical collaboration. For instance, for the observations, the project members did not have to account any extra time, since the meetings took place anyway. Although keeping an online logbook was considered as time-consuming, it was also appreciated, since the use of an *online* logbook perfectly fit into the virtual working environment of the software developers.

4.6.2 Sample and Field Access

Access to the field and the depth of empirical investigations were dependent on a trustful relationship with the gatekeepers. The participative co-construction of the research progress, by, for instance, cooperatively selecting the investigated software development projects, as well as the interviewees and participants of the study, was highly beneficial for gaining the commitment of the gatekeepers. However, the relationship was also influenced by the gatekeepers' intentions regarding the empirical investigations. Eventually, for the gatekeepers, our study might have also served as a chance to display the burdens of standard enactment and its consequences to senior management. Even though we investigated three cases, we can only draw conclusions for two industrial sectors since we could not gain access to any organization from the automobile industry, as we had originally planned. We started to contact organizations from the German automobile industry in spring 2015, only a few months before the emission scandal of the German manufacturer Volkswagen was uncovered. None of the companies was interested in collaborating on research on the enactment of standards and organizational deviance at that time.

4.6.3 Data-Gathering Methods

Data gathering was characterized by discontinuities related to the dynamic and unforeseeable nature of project work in the investigated organizations.

For example, since MetroEngineers' BRT project underwent several irregular project stops, it was a challenge to stay integrated in their project work. Meeting changes at short notice sometimes hindered conducting already scheduled observations. Further, data gathering was only possible in a non-parallel manner. For instance, during the acquisition of empirical partners, one of the organizations could eventually not maintain the cooperation, while a new one could be gained later. While we were in the middle of the project work with one company, we had just started to set up the cooperation with the third company. Hence, the knowledge we gained earlier in the first case might have biased the investigations in the later case.

Furthermore, the gathering of data for the phenomenon of standard enactment in software development was challenging. When asked about several incidents during a project meeting at MedTech, the senior software manager explained that 'in fact, the actual work happens during the meetings, on the corridor'. It seems that, even though we chose a variety of data-gathering methods, we could not gain direct access to '*the actual work*' of a software developer and his or her standard enactment. Especially, informal processes such as decision-making on the corridor cannot be captured by interviews or observations of formal meetings. In the following, we discuss some lessons from selected data-gathering methods.

4.6.3.1 Field Observations

We decided to observe regular project meetings where standard relevant topics are usually discussed. In line with Weick, the meetings served as important source 'where most arguments take place in organizations' (Weick 1995: 142). However, the observed meetings differed significantly regarding their settings and dynamic. In MedTech's Fidelio project, the software developers acted in a much more routinized manner, and almost no further sensemaking or even disturbing incidents happened during the meetings. In contrast, during the meetings of the BRT project at MetroEngineers, conflicts appeared regularly between the different project members or the Chinese client; hence we could observe sensemaking of standards as discussions on standard enactment in practice.

Observational data could not be gained in the case of CraneSolutions due to a missing formal meeting culture in the software development unit. We met this challenge by extending the qualitative interviews. CraneSolutions organizational members further used the online logbooks to compensate for the missing observations.

4.6.3.2 Online Logbooks

In our preparations for the research project, we soon understood that regular and frequent observations in a corporate field could be difficult to carry out. In consequence, we complemented our method portfolio with logbooks. We highly recommend to use online logbooks for the empirical investigation of phenomena in virtual work settings (e.g. software development), where frequent access to the field is necessary but sometimes difficult to realise (e.g. high technology organizations), and where investigated phenomena potentially trigger frustration and thus are often not openly addressed. The frustration was communicated more directly in the logbooks. It even seemed that some employees used the logbooks to blow off their frustration about project work and, particularly, about the enactment of standards. In order to stimulate the participants to regularly generate logbook entries, we experienced an increased probability when the logbook method was explained during the interviews at the beginning of each research collaboration. Further, the rate of entries seemed to increase when participants also took part in the meetings we regularly observed. The regular contact with the participants seemed to have created a situation of perceived social pressure to regularly use the online logbook. All in all, the use of logbooks helped us to complement data in turbulent project phases (MetroEngineers) or to compensate for a missing observations (CraneSolutions).

4.6.3.3 Questionnaire

The questionnaire turned out to be rather difficult to apply in research practice. The companies differed in their legal structures, and hence regarding financial reporting. For instance, the company size was relevant for the different aspects the companies gathered in their reports. As well as this, filling out the questionnaire significantly depended on the willingness of and our relationship with the respective gatekeeper. The task itself was rather complex, requiring a lot of time and an understanding of the method's aim by the gatekeeper. Consequently, the resulting questionnaires differed considerably in their structure, which complicated comparison during the analysis. Hence, we focused even more on qualitative data from the other data sources.

References

Alaszewski, A. 2006. *Using Diaries for Social Research*. Thousand Oaks: SAGE.

Alvesson, M. & Deetz, S. 2000. *Doing Critical Management Research*. Thousand Oaks: SAGE.

Bolger, N., Davis, A., & Rafaeli, E. 2003. Diary methods: capturing life as it is lived. *Annual Review of Psychology*, 54, 579–616.

Bowen, G. A. 2009. Document analysis as a qualitative research method. *Qualitative Research Journal*, 9, 27–40.

Brunsson, N. & Jacobsson, B. 2000. *A World of Standards*. Oxford: Oxford University Press.

Bryman, A. 2004. *Social Research Methods*. Oxford: Oxford University Press.

Bryman, A. & Bell, E. 2011. *Business Research Methods*. New York: Oxford University Press.

Corbin, J. & Strauss, A. 1990. Grounded theory research: procedures, canons and evaluative criteria. *Zeitschrift fuer Soziologie*, 19, 418–27.

Denzin, N. 1970. *The Research Act in Sociology: A Theoretical Introduction to Sociological Methods*. London: Butterworth.

Emerson, R. M., Fretz, R. I., & Shaw, L. L. 2011. *Writing Ethnographic Fieldnotes*. Chicago: University of Chicago Press.

Fried, A. & Walgenbach, P. 2020. Theoretical framework to explore organizational deviance from standards. *In:* Fried, A. (ed.) *Understanding Deviance in a World of Standards*. Oxford: Oxford University Press.

Froschauer, U. 2009. Artefaktanalyse. *In:* Kühl, S., Strodtholz, P., & Taffertshofer, A. (eds) *Handbuch Methoden der Organisationsforschung*. Wiesbaden: Springer.

Gey, R. & Fried, A. 2018. Metastructuring for standards. How organizations respond to the multiplicity of standards. *Corporate and Global Standardization Initiatives in Contemporary Society*. Pennsylvania: IGI Global.

Giddens, A. 1979. *Central Problems in Social Theory: Action, Structure and Contradictions in Social Analysis*. London: Macmillan.

Giddens, A. 1984. *The Constitution of Society: Outline of the Theory of Structuration*. Cambridge: Polity Press.

Glaser, B. G. & Strauss, A. L. 1967. *The Discovery of Grounded Theory: Strategies for Qualitative Research*. Chicago: Aldine de Gruyter.

Gobo, G. & Marciniak, L. T. 2016. What is ethnography? *In:* Silverman, D. (ed.) *Qualitative Research*, 4th edn. London: SAGE.

Knoblauch, H. 2005. Focused ethnography. *Forum: Qualitative Social Research*, 6.

Kunz, A. M. 2015. Log-und Tagebücher als Erhebungsmethode in ethnographischen Forschungsdesigns. *In:* Hitzler, R. & Gothe, M. (eds) *Ethnographische Erkundungen*. Wiesbaden: Springer.

Ladner, S. 2014. *Practical Ethnography: A Guide to Doing Ethnography in the Private Sector*. Walnut Creek: Left Coast Press.

Maitlis, S. 2005. The social processes of organizational sensemaking. *Academy of Management Journal*, 48, 21–49.

Mayring, P. 2000. Qualitative content analysis. *Forum Qualitative Sozialforschung/ Forum: Qualitative Social Research*, 1, 1–10.

Meuser, M. & Nagel, U. 2009. The expert interview and changes in knowledge production. *In:* Bogner, A., Littig, B., & Menz, W. (eds) *Interviewing Experts*. London: Palgrave.

Patton, M. Q. 2002. *Qualitative Research & Evaluation Methods*. Thousand Oaks: SAGE.

Piekkari, R., Welsh, C., & Paavilainen, E. 2009. Case study as disciplinary convention: evidence from international business journals. *Organizational Research Methods*, 12, 567–89.

Prior, L. 2016. Using documents in social research. *In:* Silverman, D. (ed.) *Qualitative Research*, 4th edn. London: SAGE.

Roth, P. 2015. Including the diary method in the investigation of practices constituting social innovation networks. *Historical Social Research/Historische Sozialforschung*, 40, 331–50.

Ruparelia, N. B. 2010 Software development lifecycle models. *ACM SIGSOFT Software Engineering Notes*, 35, 8–13.

Schwartz, M. S. & Schwartz, C. G. 1955. Problems in participant observation. *American Journal of Sociology*, 60, 343–53.

Singleton, R. A. & Bruce, C. 2005. *Approaches to Social Research*. New York: Oxford University Press.

Strauss, A. L. & Corbin, J. 1997. *Grounded Theory in Practice*. Thousand Oaks: SAGE.

Van Maanen, J., Manning, P., & Miller, M. 1986. Editor's Introduction. *In:* Van Maanen, J., Manning, P., & Miller, M. (eds) *SAGE University Paper Series on Qualitative Research Methods*. Beverly Hills: SAGE.

Weick, K. E. 1995. *Sensemaking in Organizations*. Thousand Oaks: SAGE.

PART II

EXPLORING ORGANIZATIONAL DEVIANCE FROM STANDARDS IN THE FIELD

In the second part of the book we outline the findings of our empirical investigations on deviance from standards in the three examined organizations—CraneSolutions, MedTech, and MetroEngineers. As illustrated in Figure II.1, we found several different forms of deviations from standards among the empirical cases. Although, these deviations vary in their detailed appearance in each case, we found a number of similar deviations from standard compliance. For instance, in all three cases we traced deviations from standard-related documentation requirements and deviations from required development phases. Further, deviations from standard-required role separation appeared at both, at CraneSolutions as well as at MetroEngineers. Some deviations only appeared in one organization. For instance, at MedTech, deviations from review requirements and interim deviances due to regulatory changes became apparent. At MetroEngineers, we found deviations from testing requirements, from quality management requirements, and from safety integrity levels.

However, as the circles in Figure II.1 show, the deviations differ in their proximity to compliance with standards. For this reason, we condensed these diverging forms into three types of organizational deviance: *attentive deviance*, *over-conformity with standards*, and *non-regulated deviance*. Notably, the figure also shows that the types of organizational deviance from standards are not exclusively represented by each case organization. For instance, although over-conformity with standards generally applies for MedTech, we also found forms of attentive deviance there.

In the following chapters, we illustrate the three types of organizational deviance alongside the three empirical cases. First, the case of CraneSolutions is a striking example of mainly *attentive deviance* (Gey et al. 2020a); second, at MedTech we primarily found the type of *over-conformity* (Gey et al. 2020b);

Understanding Deviance in a World of Standards, Andrea Fried, Oxford University Press (2020).

DOI: 10.1093/oso/9780198833888.001.0001

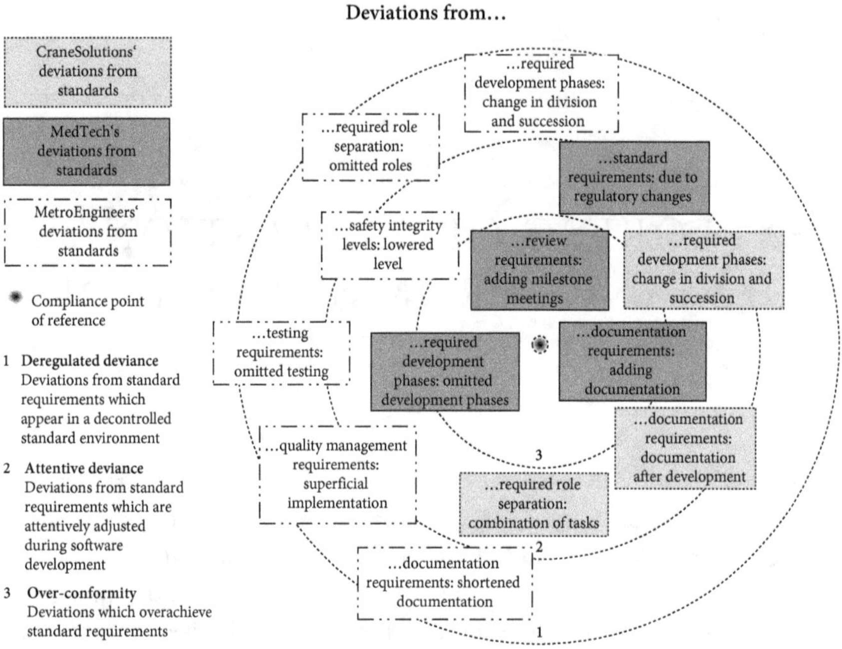

Figure II.1 Empirically deduced types of organizational deviance from standards

and third, *non-regulated deviance* was mostly characteristic of MetroEngineers (Langer et al. 2020b). Based on the structurationist framework, we outline for each case the enactment of standards as interpretative schemes, as facilities, and as social norms (see theoretical framework in Fried & Walgenbach 2020). Further, we explain organizational deviance from standards as a way of how organizations deal with emerging asymmetries and contradictions during the enactment of standards as interpretative schemes, as facilities, and as social norms.

5

Attentive Deviance from Standards at CraneSolutions

Ronny Gey, Sarah Langer, and Andrea Fried

In this chapter we outline organizational deviance from standards in the case of CraneSolutions in the form of *attentive deviance*. We identify three different forms of deviation from standards labelled by the organizational members of CraneSolutions' software development unit: *deviation from documentation requirements* (documentation after development), *deviation from the required development phases* (change in division and succession), and *deviation from required role separation* (combination of tasks). The three deviant practices stand out as characteristic for attentive organizational deviance at CraneSolutions. In order to explain attentive organizational deviance from standards, we illustrate CraneSolutions' characteristic standard enactment by considering standards first as interpretative schemes (signification), and second as facilities (domination); third, the three deviant practices are illustrated in detail from a structurationist perspective of standards as social norms (legitimation). Finally, we discuss reasons for attentive organizational deviance on the basis of contradictions at CraneSolutions.

5.1 Introduction to the Case of CraneSolutions

CraneSolutions is a German, medium-sized manufacturer of heavy machinery for road construction and power plants, with long experience as a manufacturer of high-class cranes. Over the last decades, CraneSolutions acquired several other specialized manufacturers of heavy machinery from related sectors, which made CraneSolutions a world market leader for different, highly specialized products in the niche market for heavy machinery. The production is based on very small quantities—most often only one or two pieces. CraneSolutions customizes all products to the different needs of its clients, which mostly are either state-owned organizations or big companies in the energy or

Ronny Gey, Sarah Langer, and Andrea Fried, *Attentive Deviance from Standards at CraneSolutions* In: *Understanding Deviance in a World of Standards*. Edited by: Andrea Fried, Oxford University Press (2020).
DOI: 10.1093/oso/9780198833888.003.0005

construction sector. We investigated the development of the control system of two cranes for a state-owned, European company, PMA (anonymized) which posed very high demands on the physical requirements of the crane and on standard compliance.

Over the last 3 years, CraneSolutions increased turnover (2013: €127.6m, 2014: €142.5, 2015: €145.1m) and profit (2013: €5.1m, 2014: €6.0m, 2015: €11.1m). However, even though CraneSolutions has been in the position of a market leader for many years, the business reports reveal that the economic situation in the market has become more difficult lately. Since the current order situation has not been satisfactory, CraneSolutions had to cope with compulsory dismissals of employees. The business reports show that the number of employees dramatically fell from 372 in 2013 to about 200 in 2015. Moreover, the level of new orders decreased by about two-thirds in the same period.

Even though the product portfolio of CraneSolutions is quite diverse, the different product sectors share significant economic similarities. First, incoming orders are less dependent on economic trends than in other industries due to the infrastructural criticality of most of CraneSolutions' products. The market, especially in Europe and the US, is characterized by regular replacement investments. When, for instance, a crane is broken, it must be replaced; otherwise, construction processes are critically delayed. Second, the market is much more dependent on political developments, as the business reports of CraneSolutions show. The withdrawal of Great Britain from the EU and the economic sanctions against Russia pose a great risk for future incoming orders at CraneSolutions. Finally, contract negotiations in the industry are rather lengthy, as a software developer explains:

> *And we have the problem that we cannot see far enough in the future regarding projects we will work on.... Around the corner comes a potential client and requires three cranes and then the negotiations start. We speak about two, three years until the contract is signed.* (Software developer 1, interview)

In general, the markets in Asia grew over the last years and CraneSolutions profited intensely from this development. Further, the South American market is supposed to grow significantly in the future. Remote maintenance of the machinery is another important trend that is especially critical for CraneSolutions, since it not only sells its products worldwide but also offers the maintenance service for them.

In the realm of our inquiries on the PMA project, the focus lay on cranes and on the regulation for this specific market. CraneSolutions' cranes are considered as construction and maintenance machines for which relevant standards cover technical requirements for working, running, and travelling these machines, as well as general safety requirements for a plethora of different machines: ditchers, tampers, grinders, spreaders, squeezers, spike pullers, etc. However, as a manufacturer of *cranes*, the company also has to consider EN 13000 which handles the design, construction, and installation of safety devices, information for use, maintenance, and testing of mobile cranes. For the software development of the control systems, CraneSolutions has to consider two other major standards describing compliance measures for the development of safety-related software. As a crane manufacturer, CraneSolutions also needs to follow requirements of the functional safety standard for control systems, the EN ISO 13849. It describes safety requirements and guidance for the design and integration of safety-related parts of control systems, which also includes the design of software.

In the recent past, regulatory demands for cranes increased whenever larger accidents happened, which lead to a very strict market with demanding safety requirements. However, construction and maintenance machines always take on a distinct position among special vehicles regarding regulation and compliance with standards. Formerly, the producers of these machines could rely on a principle that the organizational members at CraneSolutions always referred as *proven in use*. Once a component has been in use for a certain time, it can be regarded as proven in use. It supersedes a formal proof from the producers and significantly reduces approval costs. Moreover, the producers also relied heavily on already certified components for which no further approval process is needed. Yet, a crucial factor for producers of cranes is a well-functioning relationship with their assessors. Due to the niche market, small quantities, and multiple, partly conflicting standards, efforts for standard-compliant development are immense. In negotiation with the assessors, CraneSolutions has to find case-specific solutions to pass the approval process, e.g. product modifications to comply with conflicting standards or additional proofs of safety.

CraneSolutions is an example of the idiosyncrasy of the market of cranes. As a producer of cranes, CraneSolutions has to consider several contradicting standards from different domains of heavy industry. Each of these standards is not fully applicable to CraneSolutions cranes. The *one size fits all* nature of these standards fails in detail. The head of homologation describes this dilemma of CraneSolutions as middle-sized organization producing for a strictly regulated environment:

> *Every piece is custom made, always. We are necessarily a manufactory. It is not like in the automobile industry. That's always criticised by the authorities,*

> *we don't do certain things. We do not make layout plans for the hydraulic system. That's not possible, too much effort. If we draw it we would take as long as to actually build it.* (Head of homologation, interview)

Hence, they established a unit called homologation which coordinates the approval processes for the different products and which also maintains a close relationship with the authorities. Over the years, CraneSolutions established a culture of always trying and finding a customized solution, no matter if it concerns the products or the approval process for these products. A software developer describes it as: '*something typical for CraneSolutions, what you learn is, somehow it will always work*' (software developer 2, interview).

During our inquiries at CraneSolutions, we investigated the software development unit during a development project for an international client, PMA. CraneSolutions developed two cranes and support equipment for a big infrastructural project. The PMA project was organized in flat hierarchies, which characterize organizational structures at CraneSolutions in general. Further, the project manager often changes with a new project, as do role descriptions and positions. The organization seems to be in a constant flux. For the PMA project, they appointed a very experienced employee to guide the project members through the demanding development project. For the crane development, CraneSolutions has to consider several client-specific requirements that render the project particularly challenging. Due to physical limitations of the working environment of the cranes, these have to be custom-designed with a lower height and a more rigid safety system for the crane boom and movements of the different parts within confined working environments.

Further, CraneSolutions applied a new control unit to the cranes, since the formerly used units did not provide the required certifications anymore. In consequence, they had to change the entire software development process to comply with the standard requirements for the new control unit, as the head of homologation describes:

> *There were again new requirements from the German regulatory authority and we could just not do it the old way any longer. CraneSolutions maintain a constant and intense relationship with its assessors from the German regulatory authority. Changing the software development processes is an endeavour that lasts several years longer than the life span of the PMA project itself. Along with the new control unit, they decided to implement a new display for the control system as well. As a consequence, the new control unit also came along*

with a new integrated development environment, the piece of software that the engineers use to develop software code for the control unit.

(Head of homologation, interview)

However, the most challenging aspect of the PMA project is the demanding situation of compliance with standards. Next to the already conflicting demands of standards for cranes and special vehicles, CraneSolutions has to consider requirements provided by PMA itself. Moreover, the cranes will also operate in the network of TransNet (anonymized) which again provides specific standards for the operation of cranes. During the development project, this complex situation led to rather contradictory decisions as the head of homologation describes:

For PMA, we are in the situation that the requirements contradict with the ones of TransNet. For instance the brakes, at PMA you have to brake fast with a short braking distance.... so we had to apply two braking systems.

(Head of homologation, interview)

Another very challenging aspect of the development project is the regulation practice at PMA which is based on a very strict clause-by-clause analysis of the requirements:

The whole process of the authorities is rather obstructive. They practice a clause by clause analysis which is very time-consuming. We have to discuss a lot of issues and to provide evidences for each single small requirement.

(Project manager, logbook)

Though very experienced in crane development, CraneSolutions is not used to the clause-by-clause procedure, an in-depth analysis of each single standard requirement. The very formalistic approach conflicts with the customized nature of its products: customer-specific solutions in small quantities. It further conflicts with the long-practiced approach of developing close personal relationships with assessors, often ending up in a consulting-like relation. CraneSolutions decided to additionally engage a consultancy firm, Crane Consult PLC (anonymized). Crane Consult PLC serves as an intermediate between CraneSolutions, the German regulatory authorities, the regulatory department at PMA, and TransNet itself. Crane Consult PLC was engaged to buffer the conflicting demands from the different standards and authorities and to guide CraneSolutions through the very demanding approval process.

5.2 Standards as Interpretative Schemes in CraneSolutions' Software Development

CraneSolutions' organizational members reported different meanings of standards for their daily work in software development, for the organization, and for the PMA project. We found thirteen different meanings within the software development unit, which provide sense for the employees' engagement in standard enactment. Meanings that refer to administrative and business frames dominate the reasoning of the employees at CraneSolutions. Twelve of the thirteen meanings were similar to the other two cases, MetroEngineers and MedTech. However, one meaning was specific for CraneSolutions: standards as a *tool for knowledge management.* During our inquiries, CraneSolutions was implementing standard-compliant processes. Thus, organizational members at CraneSolutions used standards as facilitators to externalize the process-relevant knowledge of the experienced engineers; standards became a tool for knowledge management. The senior management at CraneSolutions did not engage comprehensively in sensegiving about the signification of standards for the organization and for the PMA project. Negative effects on costs and efficiency dominate their sensegiving for standards towards the members of software development. However, senior management and the owner support the enactment of standards at CraneSolutions by allocating financial and administrative resources. Even though they constantly raise complaints, they accept the necessity of enacting standards due to their meanings as key to the market, as base for certification, and as part of the engineering contracts.

Table 5.1 summarizes the different meanings of standards expressed by members of the PMA project. We complemented the meanings with information about who expressed these meanings and their signification frame. In the following sections we describe the meanings in more detail.

Base for Product Specification

Whenever a machine is built at CraneSolutions, there are standards for the development of this machine to comply with. A requirements manager for the PMA project explains:

> *If there is a standard and somebody* [the customer or the authorities] *says that you have to build a machine based on these standards, then we have to comply with it, absolutely. It is the same daily routine for every mechanical engineering company.* (Requirements manager, interview)

Table 5.1 Standards as interpretative schemes at CraneSolutions

Meaning of standards	Description Standards...	Which project members ascribing meaning	Signification frame
Base for product specification	Define the requirements of a prospective product	Requirements manager, software developer, project manager	Technical
Base for software development processes	Define the design of software development processes	Quality manager, software developer, project manager, head of software development	Administrative
Standardizer of processes	Align processes within the organization and across organizations	Software developer, head of software development	Administrative
Definer of development roles	Enable separate roles for software development projects; define who is allowed to do what	Requirements manager, project manager, quality manager, software developer	Administrative
	Divide power to assure independent quality control	Project manager, software developer	Administrative
Current state of technology	Refer to currently accepted technology but not necessarily the most advanced technology	Quality manager, homologation manager	Technical
Improver of development processes	Help to work more efficiently with defined instructions	Quality manager, project manager	Business
Interface assurance	Reduce costs when finding a suitable supplier	Requirements manager, head of software development, software developer	Business

Continued

Table 5.1 *Continued*

Meaning of standards	Description Standards...	Which project members ascribing meaning	Signification frame
Assurance of human safety	Ensure usability	Requirements manager	Technical
	Ensure quality	Requirements manager, software developer	Business
	Protect society	Project manager, software developer, head of software development	Ethical
Trigger for monitoring	Trigger monitoring and occasions to check the implementation of standards	Project manager, software developer, homologation manager, head of software development	Administrative
Base for certification	Enable transnational product approval	Requirements manager, quality manager, software developer	Regulatory
Key to the market	Prospectively enable market entry if company is certified	Requirements manager, project manager, quality manager, homologation manager, software developer	Business
Part of engineering contract	Bind customers legally; clarify demands from customers	Project manager, software developer	Business
Tool for knowledge management	Document expert knowledge and make it available to stakeholders	Quality manager, software developer, project manager, head of software development	Administrative

For the engineers at CraneSolutions, the standard is the *base for product specification*—an essential requirement which either customers or authorities demand and, as the requirements manager points out, which is a fundamental part of mechanical engineering. When starting to develop a new product at CraneSolutions, right at the beginning, they check the standards: '*We develop a new control unit* [and decide currently] *what we have to consider. We have to comply with these standards*' (project manager, interview).

Base for Software Development Processes

Next to product specification, the standard is also essential for the process of software development at CraneSolutions. For the engineers, it is the *base for software development processes* and bears a meaning as a guiding framework, as the technical project manager emphasizes:

> *The standard is kind of a framework for us. You just need something to guide you. It is good to have a standard which contains certain requirements and rules.... It is definitely considerate to know how something is done in the standard-compliant way and it leads to a satisfactory result.* (*Technical project manager, interview*)

Unanimously, the organizational members reason their engagement in standard enactment with the standards' meaning as a base for software development processes. In practice, different phases form the newly established, well-structured software development process at CraneSolutions. The software quality manager describes:

> *The steps are well structured. We have a requirements phase where we collect all the requirements of the software.... We nail it down in the documents. Then there is the coding phase where we write the software, then there is the test phase. And yeah, then we implement the software at the vehicle, test it again, and ask for approval by the client.* (Software quality manager, interview)

Standardizer of Processes

Another software developer literally explained the meaning of the standard as the *standardizer of processes*:

> *The advantage is that standards mean standardization, that something is on the same level. That is a general condition.... If I do it like this, I don't have to think about it, somebody thought about it already.* (Software developer 2, interview)

To her, standardization means that once the standard is in place, organizational members can rely on its solutions, for instance regarding interfaces and documentation requirements.

Definer of Development Roles

The standards for software development at CraneSolutions not only contain general prescriptions to process or product requirements, but also bear the meaning of a *definer of development roles* to the employees in the organization. The technical project manager of the PMA project reasons for the independence of monitoring behind the strict role allocation:

> *In the standard, they define strictly that the one who develops shall not be the one who tests. It is regulated for each safety level and the specific qualification of the personnel.* (The technical project manager, interview)

Further, he adds that there are different concepts of role allocations for each safety level software development has to comply with. The software quality manager of the PMA project specifies 'definer of development roles' while he lists the different roles involved in the PMA project:

> *Well, the role allocation is fixed. The number of involved employees is fixed and who does what.... if the standard says you need six persons for this safety level then it has to be six persons. We have a quality manager, a system designer, a software designer, a software implementer, a module tester..., we have an integration tester and a validator who tests the functionality onsite at the actual crane.* (Software quality manager, interview)

In the view of the organizational members, the standards are very strict regarding the allocation of the different roles for guaranteeing independent monitoring of development processes.

Current State of Technology

The organizational members at CraneSolutions widely accept that the standard represents the *current state of technology:*

> *When it comes to the current state of software development, the standard covers quite a lot. That's the current state of today's technology.*
> (Requirements manager, interview)

As the requirements manager explains, the standard for software development is comprehensive and covers meaningful technological information for software engineers.

Improver of Development Processes

Before the introduction of standards at CraneSolutions, engineers conducted software development in a rather unstructured way with only little documentation:

> *In the past, we developed software with only little documentation.... And if somebody raised a question, she/he had to walk back and forth between different colleagues involved. And with the standard, we should get a pretty good overview of the process.* (Software quality manager, interview)

However, with the introduction of standard-compliant processes, CraneSolutions develops software in an increasingly structured manner. The organizational members seem to have a '*pretty good overview of the process*', as the software quality manager describes. The organizational members ascribe it to the standards which became an *improver of development processes.* The software quality manager furthers this meaning by explaining the changes regarding bug-fixing and traceability:

> *And by structuring the process I can see where the error is, in which part, in which document.... So, the traceability* [of the development steps] *is really important.... Through this division* [of tasks] *I only have to correct a small part. The rest is clean and clearly structured.* (Software quality manager, interview)

Interface Assurance

During the PMA project, standards provided meaning to the employees of CraneSolutions as a base for procurement. When sourcing a new control unit, a supplier was chosen that could provide a certificate for both the control unit and the firmware that runs on the control unit. The certificate was a must-have criterion, as the head of software development explains:

> *When choosing a new control unit, we have taken care that the software is also certified. Many of the manufacturers of control units will tell you that it is certified. However, if you take a closer look you will discover that only the hardware is certified.* (Head of software development, interview)

For other parts of the crane (e.g. different sensors), organizational members relied on standards to *assure the interfaces* and the provided certificates for components served as base for procurement too.

Assurance of Human Safety

For people in the crane industry, the meaning of standards as *assurance of human safety* is very significant for their daily work. At CraneSolutions, organizational members often connect this meaning with the implementation of 'protective mechanisms' which assure the intended use of parts and products:

> *If you implement it successfully and once you are working with it then it is ideal. You have certain testing mechanisms, protective mechanisms, which result in a solid check-up of your work. You can be sure that everything works as intended.* (Software developer 2, interview)

The technical project manager explains the reasons for the high relevance of standards as assurance for human safety. Disasters trigger new regulation processes on the side of the authorities which increase the rigor of standards each time. Exemplarily, she refers to a catastrophe that happened in Austria in 2000 where 155 people died:

> *If it burns in a tunnel, then you would accept that they* [the authorities] *have much higher standard requirements for the used materials. After each disaster, they check it and they intensify regulation even further. And in detail, it will enhance safety. And these accidents, they are real.*
>
> (Technical project manager, interview)

The acceptance of this meaning of standards is very high among all the employees at CraneSolutions.

Trigger for Monitoring

To become meaningful as assurance for human safety, the standard bears another significance for the employees at CraneSolutions, the standard as a *trigger for monitoring*. The project manager explains the implementation of test routines based on the requirements of standards:

> *There are rules that you must test specific functions at the crane. Accordingly, there is the requirement for test plans and check lists... and that comes from standards which exist for our sort of machines.* (Project manager, interview)

Obviously, due to standard requirements, they implemented test plans and check lists that assist the employees at CraneSolutions to monitor their development processes. With these test routines, CraneSolutions intends to assure a high-quality software development to justify the faith of customers and users.

Base for Certification

At CraneSolutions, standards are the base for the approval process. The requirements manager points out that it is consequently an intended purpose of standards:

> *It is written in black and white in the standard: you must do this and that... and the regulatory authority refers exclusively to these standards. And that's fine, that's what standards are there for.* (Requirements manager, interview)

The requirements manager considers the standard as a *base for certification* when he describes the practice of regulatory authorities exclusively referring to standards during the approval process. Conversely, this means that the certificate signalizes CraneSolutions' compliance with standards. The software quality manager explains that: '*If an external assessor says: "yes, everything's ok, here is your certificate", then they will accept that we comply with the standards*'. To the organizational members at CraneSolutions, standards bear the signification as a base for certification.

Key to the Market

When a product has passed the approval process, CraneSolutions is officially allowed to sell it on the market of the certifying regulatory authority and to operate the machine. Due to this approval, the standard, respectively the issued certificate, functions as a *key to the market*, as the requirements manager argues: '*We are dependent on the "green light", the "thumbs" up of the regulatory authority... otherwise, you won't sell a crane*' (Requirements manager, interview). To the organizational members at CraneSolutions, the meaning of standard as *key to the market* also bears another notion: for competitors not possessing 'the key', the markets are locked. The head of homologation describes the situation in the European market for Chinese companies:

> *If you are in the situation to manage such a complex standard environment and to get the approval, then you know that you can protect your market from external competitors. There are several Chinese manufacturers that compete against us and they are not able to submit a tender for a project like the PMA project.* (Head of homologation, interview)

Apparently, the standards are the key to the market. The standard requirements for the PMA project are exigent in such a way that potential Chinese manufacturers were not able to submit an adequate tender.

Part of the Engineering Contract

Before the beginning of each development project, CraneSolutions and its client sign a contract to specify and fix the requirements that must be fulfilled by both parties. As *part of this engineering contract*, the standard has another relevant meaning to the employees in the organization. The fulfilment of standards is written into the contract:

> *In the contract* [for the PMA project], *they* [the contracting parties] *added an enormous table, they call it technical requirement specification and it lists*

> *every single point a machine must fulfil regarding technology, occupational safety, and environmental directives. And it is specified with several points like fire safety requirements in compliance with EN 45545... at this point, we realised that it is written in a very detailed way in the contract with the client.*
> (Project manager, interview)

The project manager points out that for the different customer requirements several standards are provided. They guide the development and they have to be implemented by CraneSolutions. The project manager summarizes this meaningful aspect of standards: '*If the customer says he wants us to develop according to this standard, then we are bound to it.*' (Project manager, interview)

Tool for Knowledge Management

In comparison to the other two cases, the organizational members of CraneSolutions emphasized additionally the meaning of standards as a *tool for knowledge management*. In the eyes of the engineers, the enactment of standards comes along with the necessity to externalize expert knowledge that ever since resided in the heads of experienced and long-serving employees. The software quality manager describes the situation before the introduction of standard-compliant processes at CraneSolutions' software development:

> *The entire knowledge of the company resides in a few heads. If you need something, you must go and ask this and that person depending on what you actually need. For software, you ask Rick* [head of software development], *for mechanics this person, hydraulics that person, and I think it's not very practical. What do we do if Rick is on sick leave or on vacation and customers would come and ask questions regarding documentation or some parameters? If we do not have a decent documentation, then we are unfortunate.... and that is about to change now.* (Software quality manager, interview)

According to him, customers—but also regulatory authorities—could ask for crucial information about products and processes. When experts at CraneSolutions are not available in these situations, a lack of documentation of the development steps would be disadvantageous in that provided information from CraneSolutions to customers might be unsound. With the current introduction of standards, the software quality manager hopes that this potential information gap will be closed. However, employees at CraneSolutions are aware of the organization-specific situation, as a software developer explains:

> *That's the culture here... a lot is connected to specific persons. Key persons know how it works and there isn't much documentation.... But you must consider that CraneSolutions is a medium-sized company. For big companies with more head count it would work automatically.*
>
> (Software developer 2, interview)

The organizational culture at a medium-sized company like CraneSolutions is shaped by organization-critical expert knowledge that resides in the heads of a few persons. Since the regulatory requirements intensified and the head count in software development grew, the company had to introduce standard-compliant processes and implement new means of documentation. Therefore, the organizational members of CraneSolutions value the meaning of the standards as a tool for knowledge management.

5.3 Standards as Facilities in CraneSolutions' Software Development

CraneSolutions has been implementing standard-compliant processes for the last two years. The company provides appropriate financial resources for the ongoing change process in software development. Facing standard compliance, specific roles (software quality manager, requirements manager) were created which take over standard-related tasks like appropriate documentation or testing from the software developers. However, the software developers still perform a considerable extent of these tasks themselves. Regarding allocative resources, the software developers still rely on software development specific tools (e.g. SVN, CODESYS) for standard enactment. Allocative resources (e.g. SISTEMA) that are specific for the management of standards at CraneSolutions are just about to find their way into software development at CraneSolutions. Table 5.2 summarizes the different resources and their transformative capacity and impact on the enactment of standards at CraneSolutions.

Table 5.2 Standards as facilities at CraneSolutions

Resource	Description	Transformative capacity	Transformative impact
Authoritative resources			
Software quality manager	Implements and manages standard-compliant processes and documents following the V-model; exclusive user of SISTEMA	High	High impact due to central role in the standard enactment process in general
Requirements manager	Manages functional and non-functional requirements; responsible for specifications documents	High	High impact due to central role in the documentation process for specification documents
Project manager	Manages PMA project; crane expert at PMA; sits on standard panel; manages PMA test facilities; distributes standard-related information to colleagues	High	High impact—due to crane expertise and responsibility for several standard-related tasks
Homologation manager	Accompanies the entire approval process; in constant contact with assessors, customers, and standardization bodies	Medium	Medium impact on standard enactment; manages an important interface, yet is detached from actual operations
Software developers	Develops components of software system and compiles standard-compliant documents	Medium	High impact since they are not shielded by organizational arrangements for standard enactment
Standard service	Compiles weekly 'standard ticker' informing about changes in standard environment	Low	Low impact since the product is only an up-to-date newsletter on standards
Process consultant	Designs standard-compliant development processes and several required documents	High	High impact due to expertise and guiding influence in the beginning of process implementation at CraneSolutions
Assessors	Accompanies CraneSolutions throughout the entire approval process; acts as consultant for minor but also major decisions	Low	Due to consultant-like status, assessors have a medium impact even though they are organization-external actors

Continued

Table 5.2 *Continued*

Resource	Description	Transformative capacity	Transformative impact
Authoritative resources			
Crane Consult PLC	Accompanies CraneSolutions throughout the entire approval process for the PMA project	Low	Exercises a low impact since it only forwards strict requirements from the regulation authorities to CraneSolutions and reviews compliance
Allocative resources			
Financial resources	Transformative resource: can be transformed into other resources	High	High impact; financial resources are often debated but still sufficiently provided by senior management
V-model for software development	Defines functional areas, steps, and workflow of a software development process that is aligned in a V-shape	High	Medium impact; not high yet since the requirements are not fully implemented yet
CODESYS	Integrates development environment for standard-compliant development of control software	Medium	Medium impact, since usage of CODESYS assures standard-compliant control software development at CraneSolutions
SVN server	Version-controlled file server for a traceable, comprehensible, and henceforth standard-compliant management of documents and software code	Medium	Medium impact; employees at CraneSolutions use standard-compliant document management with the SVN server
SISTEMA	Software for calculation of performance levels for safety functions	Low	Low impact due to limited scope of application (risk assessment) and users (software quality manager)

5.3.1 Authoritative Resources

5.3.1.1 The Software Quality Manager

As the name implies, the software quality manager plays a very formative role in the enactment of standards and standard-compliant processes at CraneSolutions. Since, above all, the documentation effort has increased over the last years, new roles were created, as the requirements manager reports:

> *Six years ago, when I started here at CraneSolutions, there was one colleague who was doing the documentation for the control units. That wouldn't suffice today.... Due to the wide range of functions a crane has today, we have huge documents, too. Hence, there are colleagues who are working solely on the specifications.... You need two or three people at least.*
>
> (Requirements manager, interview)

The software quality manager is one of these colleagues that deals exclusively with documents like the different development specifications. However, CraneSolutions was looking for somebody to employ for almost 2 years until a former intern took over the position as software quality manager. He explains his tasks:

> *I am responsible for quality assurance of the control software. Until now, I was occupied with the processes and the documentation. You have to have somebody who identifies necessary information from the standards and who advises the others in how to proceed with developing software and who does what. That's important. There are different safety levels and depending on it one is allowed to code and the other one is allowed to test.... And I should maintain an overview. I should look into this and that and if everything has been done correctly.* (Software quality manager, interview)

The software quality manager positions himself at the interface between developers and standards; he passes on important information about standards, advises colleagues regarding standard conform coding and testing procedures, and reviews the work of others. In his work, he tries to take the perspective of an outsider, e.g. an assessor or customer:

> *When I am dealing with standards, I try to put myself in the position of an outsider. I imagine what happens when I come from outside* [the organization] *and I see all the software code. What kind of wishes I had then. And at this*

> *point, I understand the immense importance of documents and comments* [in the software code]. (Software quality manager, interview)

By seeing software development through the lens of third parties, the software quality manager understands the importance of his work for the organization. If, for instance, the documents were not standard compliant, it would be hard for CraneSolutions to convince the assessors and pass the approval process. Hence, the software quality manager emphasizes the importance of his work and the recognition he achieves by other organizational members for ensuring standard-compliant software development at CraneSolutions. Exemplarily, the project manager states:

> *And as the quality guy, Mr Werner* [software quality manager], *who sits right here next door, treads on the colleagues' toes. He has to take care that they work within these newly defined structures and that they write these documents.* (Project manager, interview)

Consequently, the software quality manager has a high transformative impact due to his central role in the enactment of standards at CraneSolutions.

5.3.1.2 The Requirements Manager

Alongside the software quality manager, CraneSolutions created the role of the requirements manager when the demands from standards increased over the last years. His essential task is the documentation of requirements:

> *When I started here, documentation for the development of our control units was a big issue which was also the reason for my engagement here. It means specifications for the control software of our cranes as well as the adequate test specifications. We have been far from doing it as the standard setters or the German regulatory authority require it. So, there was a demand to create additional capacities and I jumped in.* (Requirements manager, interview)

As the requirements manager describes, authorities like the German regulatory authority require all these documents nowadays for the approval process. Compiling these documents is a task they were not doing at CraneSolutions before they introduced the new processes and before they created the role of the requirements manager. During the PMA project, the requirements manager filled out different (sub-) systems and tested specifications, as he describes (e.g. a systems specification for a crane part, the slewing gear): '*Preparation of systems specification slewing gear: requirements for the slewing gear regarding hardware, software, interfaces and visualization were defined*' (requirements manager, logbook).

According to the software quality manager, the roles of the requirements manager and software quality manager are closely interrelated. The requirements manager and the software quality manager frequently sit together discussing standard-related topics and safety functions of the cranes. Due to his intense involvement in standard-compliant documentation, the requirements manager at CraneSolutions has a high transformative impact for the enactment of standards.

5.3.1.3 The Project Manager—Jack of all Trades

The project manager of the PMA project seems like a 'jack of all trades'. Since he has a long experience in the area of crane development, he was chosen as the project manager for the demanding PMA project. Alongside, he has several different tasks at CraneSolutions in relation to the enactment of standard requirements, for instance as head of the unit '*Acceptance and Control*':

> *And, if I think it is relevant for my colleagues, I distribute the information about the changes in certain standards for cranes.... Further, I am the crane expert. So everything concerning cranes is moving over my desk since I am a certified crane expert of the German Accident Prevention and Insurance Association*[1]. *For certain audit purposes you need such a position. And I am also responsible for the testing facilities.* (Project manager, interview)

In addition to the distribution of standards, as mentioned in the previous quote, the project manager is responsible for standards in general at CraneSolutions:

> *Proportionally, I am responsible for this topic* [standards]. *Timewise, it is not a big issue, maybe 10% is even estimated rather high.... I am also in the standard panel* [of a standard for special vehicle] *and I participate in those standard meetings development rounds.... And when those standards are revised, it is a lot of work.... we then also have meetings in-house since it is an important phase for us, when such a standard is revised.*
> (Project manager, interview)

Because of his experience in the crane field, the PMA project manager also sits in the panel for a standard for special vehicles, which is a highly relevant

[1] http://www.dguv.de/en/bg-uk-lv/bgen/index.jsp

standard for CraneSolutions. As PMA project manager, he is at the interface between Crane Consult PLC and the customer PMA:

> *I am quite often on-site at Crane Consult PLC, every 2 or 3 weeks. We have long discussions and they always voice new requests. We have a telephone conference, weekly. And we have another telephone conference together with them and PMA, also weekly.* (Project manager, interview)

The project manager describes his time-consuming meetings and telephone conferences with the customer and Crane Consult PLC. Due to the exceptionally demanding regulatory requirements of the PMA project, this task is often conflict ridden and rather frustrating. Internally, he overlooks the project work, especially regarding the required documentation necessary for the approval process:

> *Either, they tell me how it works and I consider it as sufficient. Or, I contact Mr Leitner* [head of software development] *and tell him that we need to make a document for that purpose so we have something to submit* [to the authorities]. (Project manager, interview)

Due to his experience as a certified crane expert, the PMA project manager is aware of the effects of process change and standard-compliant development on the employees. As he reports, it causes frustration among them:

> *Well, the experienced colleagues often think that you have something against them when you come around asking them to prove that they calculated certain aspects and whether there is an evidence for that. "We never needed that before. What's that? You now come constantly. In the past, nobody was interested in it."* (Project manager, interview)

Part of the project manager's work as head of Acceptance and Control is in the presence and negotiations in national and international meetings of standardization bodies:

> *Applications are made through the DIN Institute to revise a standard and when there are enough claims saying "you need to revise the standard", then it will actually be revised. The revision phase then takes some years and each national standardization body contributes its amendments and eventually it will be discussed in an international meeting.* (Project manager, interview)

Regarding CraneSolutions' potential influence on the discussion and formation of standards within the national and international standardization process, the project manager explains:

> *It depends on how much time you spent in these meetings and on how well you are prepared.... There are also points, however, regarding cranes which we would like to cut out but we do not succeed since it would mean killing the sacred cow.* (Project manager, interview)

Being at the interface between the authorities and the development team, it is the task of the project manager to buffer the outside demands on the software developers. In respect of the criticality of the PMA project and the ongoing implementation of standards, CraneSolutions chose a very experienced project manager with a high transformative impact on standard enactment.

5.3.1.4 The Homologation Managers—Diplomats at CraneSolutions

The homologation team at CraneSolutions is in constant contact with assessors, regulation bodies, or customers, as the requirements manager describes:

> *At CraneSolutions, we have a separate office for the approval process. About two, three colleagues work for it. They are exclusively responsible for product approval. They do not calculate, they do not implement, and they do not sell. They are in continuous contact with the assessors and regulation authorities, with the customer. They are diplomats that reduce the problems. It wouldn't function without them.* (Requirements manager, interview)

The requirements manager compares the three team members of homologation at CraneSolutions with 'diplomats' who ease the different challenges of compliance arising from the often burdensome approval process. The head of homologation explains his tasks for a single project as follows:

> *So, orders or first requests pop in at our sales office.... And when we get down to the details then we have to ask how it works with approval process in these countries. Sometimes you are familiar with it, sometimes not. And then, we approach the regulation authority: "Shortly, we want to make an approval for a vehicle, how does it work?" Then, we get some check lists which we have to process afterwards and see which evidences we have to show. In some countries it is more and in some less.* (Head of homologation, interview)

The work of the 'diplomats' happens behind the scenes as it does for the head of homologation at CraneSolutions. We assume that the homologation manager has a medium transformative impact on the actual enactment of standards at CraneSolutions, since he manages an important interface, yet is detached from actual operations.

5.3.1.5 Software Developers—Troubled by Standards

Software developers at CraneSolutions develop the control system of the crane. The team for the control unit and software development gradually increased in workforce number, as a software developer recounts:

> *We have been two, now we are five. The unit was developed step by step. First, it was Mr Leitner* [head of software development], *then I came to take over the vehicles. Then we realised that we would need another crane developer since Mr Leitner was more and more into project management. And then Mr Klose* [software developer 3] *joined us. Then Mr Werner* [software quality manager] *came to handle all the documentation. When you're a programmer you will sooner or later have the problem that you either code or document, you cannot do both at the same time.* (Software developer 1, interview)

Nowadays, there are five people working in the unit, he explains. Further, he mentions the software quality manager. Together with the requirements manager, he was employed to relieve the developers from quality and documentation tasks. However, software developers at CraneSolutions are still strongly involved in quality assurance related tasks. Exemplarily, software developer 2 describes her typical tasks in the PMA project over a period of 3 weeks in her logbook:

> *Implementation of data logger function for the PMA cranes. Reviews of the systems specification of the PMA cranes. Enhancements of safety and monitoring functions of the PMA cranes. Implementation of the load functions for individual operations at the PMA cranes.* (Software developer 2, logbook)

Moreover, during the approval process for the PMA crane, the software developers fully assist in realising standard compliance, as a software developer describes:

> *For the approval process... we have to deliver certain things in addition. And, we are fully involved in compiling these risk assessments. There is another meeting this Thursday. Hence, we have to hurry with some documents that we*

have to deliver to the customer. These were not so important to the customer in the beginning, but now we need them nonetheless to get the approval.

(Software developer 3, interview)

For the risk assessment in the PMA project, he explains, they were loaded with compiling documents and accompanying meetings in respect of these tasks. Due to an increase in regulation, software development for cranes generally faces an increasing workload. Throughout the unit, the employees have a rather critical view of this development:

A developer has to deal more and more with bureaucracy and it will consume a considerable amount of time in the future. At the university, the engineer constructed, coded, simulated, calculated, he carried out experiments. He wants to tinker, to be creative, to fiddle about. He wants to build or calculate something, he wants to code. What he doesn't want is to fill out documents page by page. (Requirements manager, interview)

The requirements manager describes his understanding of engineering work, whereas documentation is not a significant part. Another software developer describes the difficulties with the different names of the required documents:

The major problem is the functional documentation, all these requirements specifications, and all these wonderful names, the systems requirements specification, software requirements specifications and so on. I have lost track here. (Software developer 3, interview)

Software developers at CraneSolutions still have a high transformative impact on the enactment of standards in their unit. However, they wish it would be less, since they prefer to actually code software instead of documenting it.

5.3.1.6 The Standard Service

In order to be up to date regarding the change and introduction of standards, CraneSolutions employs an internal information service for standards. The service's main task is to compile a document called '*the standard ticker*' which is sent out weekly to inform about the modifications of standards, the withdrawal, or the introduction of new standards.

There are plenty of standards. I don't even know how many standards we actually need to consider. From every field, from industrial safety to electricity

> *standards, from mechanical engineering to environment protection. There are so many standards we have to comply with as much as it is possible. Literally, just as much as is possible: there is always something happening somewhere.*
>
> (Project manager, interview)

From 'the standard ticker' the project manager has to select the relevant information, for instance for the PMA project. Thus, the purchase, interpretation, and implementation of the relevant standard requirements is still up to the project manager and project members who are overwhelmed by information. Therefore, the transformative impact of the standard service for standard enactment is rather low.

5.3.1.7 The Process Consultant—External Expertise for CraneSolutions

When the organizational members in software development at CraneSolutions decided to implement standard-compliant development processes, they first hired an experienced process consultant:

> *We realised that if we still want to sell cranes we have no other choice than to implement it* [standard requirements]. *So, we first hired an experienced consultant. He worked as developer and architect in several standard-compliant software projects for cranes. His task was first of all to raise an awareness for processes and their documentation and how such a compliant software development in a company works. And he designed a process manual, where we describe how we have to compile and manage these documents.*
>
> (Head of software development, interview)

The head of software development explains that the process consultant undertook several critical tasks during process implementation at CraneSolutions (e.g. raising awareness, process manual, systems specification). The software quality manager benefited tremendously from his work, and when the process consultant left CraneSolutions he assumed his tasks:

> *We contracted the external consultant and he helped me a lot in the last 2 years. For instance, he created the first two manuals, process and documentation manual. And since he is gone, I took over this task.*
>
> (Software quality manager, interview)

The external consultant heavily influenced the evolving standard-compliant process landscape in software development at CraneSolutions. He based his work significantly on the V-model for software development and accordingly designed the obligatory specifications in the different development phases, as a software developer explains:

> *We had an external consultant... he guided us in how we can make it.... We work according to the V-model. There are several documents which he compiled together with us. We created the different specifications in order so that we know what belongs to which specification.* (Software developer 3, interview)

During his engagement at CraneSolutions, the external process consultant exerted a high transformative impact for standard enactment in the software development unit.

5.3.1.8 Assessors—Deus ex Machina

The organizational members at CraneSolutions regularly interact with assessors from regulation bodies of the different countries where they sell cranes to. During our investigations, they often seek advice from assessors regarding the approval process:

> *We had an audit by an assessor... we spoke about the content of each document, and we coordinated foresightedly what we should consider content wise in the different tests. And we still had several phone calls about wishes, questions, and requirements: "Please, consider this and that." From the assessor as well as from our side. You are definitely dependent on a good dialogue with the assessor.* (Requirements manager, interview)

The requirements manager points out the 'good dialogue' with the assessors to profit from their recommendations. It seems to be a relation based very much on trust, as if CraneSolutions was seeking fatherly advice. Sometimes, the assessors' counsels even strategically influence the decision-making at CraneSolutions, as the homologation manager describes:

> *And I think CraneSolutions and the assessor came to the conclusion that we could not continue like this. They decided that for the last time, we continue with the old process and, then, we have to start something new.*
> (Homologation manager, interview)

Before they started to implement the new, standard-compliant development process, members of the PMA project were again seeking advice from an assessor. The employees at CraneSolutions ascribe the special role an assessor plays to the circumstance of being a manufacturer of custom-made products in a niche market where standards for cranes and standards for special vehicles partly contradict each other.

Internally, besides the homologation manager and project manager, the software quality manager is at the interface with the assessors, as he explains:

> *I think we will have an assessor here in Germany. He will visit us to take a look at our software development process and raise questions about it. Probably, I will be the person in charge for this part.*
>
> (Software quality manager, nterview)

The assessors are aware of the ever-changing situation in the market for cranes regarding standard requirements and therefore understand the situation of manufacturers like CraneSolutions. The head of software development elaborates on their function for CraneSolutions as buffers of these ever-changing requirements:

> *The German regulatory authority again revised the catalogue of requirements. And our assessor does not think any more about who considers which documents as important. He just looks what the German regulatory authority actually demands and then tells us: "OK, I now need this, and I have to look in those documents". Apparently, it changes all the time for whatever reasons.*
>
> (Head of software development, interview)

The assessors play a very important role in the enactment of standard-compliant processes in software development at CraneSolutions. Often, they are a last resort or act as *deus ex machina*. When CraneSolutions is threatening to fail in meeting the complex and contradicting standard requirements, the assessors would find a solution to save CraneSolutions from the contradictory standard requirements of their software development. Thus, they have a considerable transformative impact on the process of standard enactment. However, given the niche-market products of CraneSolutions, we consider the impact of the assessors as medium on CraneSolutions' standard enactment.

5.3.1.9 Crane Consult PLC

Crane Consult PLC is a globally active consultancy which provides technical guidance, assurance, and special engineering services to its clients facing operational and regulatory challenges. The project manager, who interacts regularly with Crane Consult PLC, describes the company's organizational structure:

> *[T]hey have two independent groups. The submission group collects and structures all the documents which follow the standard requirements. Then they assess whether there is enough evidence to fulfil the standard. Thereafter, they pass it to the other group. That's the actual approval group which reviews again whether they can accept the available documentation. And at the end, they assess whether CraneSolutions fulfils all requirements and they issue a certificate. And if there are points that are not accepted, then we have to apply for concessions from PMA.... That is each time a huge effort.*
>
> (Project manager, interview)

The approval process for the PMA project in England is a huge effort, the project manager explains. Foresightedly, CraneSolutions engaged Crane Consult PLC to assist with this task. As the project manager regularly reports, Crane Consult PLC takes over several documentation tasks in the approval process. For instance, he wrote in his logbook:

> *The licensing office in England (Crane Consult PLC) has to collect and check all the documents needed for approval inter alia also those for software safety and the control system. To date, we considered only traditional topics from the crane business.... There were no software related questions yet.*
>
> (Project manager, logbook)

In the words of the project manager, Crane Consult PLC generally reviews every single document CraneSolutions needs to hand in for approval. Furthermore, it is engaged in standard related research:

> *They* [the consultants] *were also involved in research on standards and comparisons among them. For instance, they figured out which requirements from the standard for special vehicles match the specific requirements of the customer.... We would not be able to do that.* (Project manager, interview)

The project manager mentions the standard for special vehicles and how Crane Consult PLC worked on matching the standard with the specific customer requirements of PMA. However, Crane Consult PLC's engagement with CraneSolutions is limited to the PMA project only and it therefore holds a low transformative impact on standard enactment in software development at CraneSolutions.

5.3.2 Allocative Resources

5.3.2.1 Financial Resources

CraneSolutions has a long history as a producer of high-class cranes. During the last years, turnover (2013: €130m, 2014: €145m, 2015/16: €148m) and profit (2013: €5m, 2014: €6m, 2015/16: €12m) constantly increased. With their cranes, they produce for a small but profitable niche market, and the allocation of money for necessary investment maintaining the high quality of their cranes was never questioned. However, in the last 3 years the total order quantity and the investments decreased due to a general decline in the market. The economic development also affected the situation for the employees and, since 2015, the workforce was reduced by about 40 per cent within 2 years.

Alongside this development, CraneSolutions decided to implement standard-compliant processes for their software development unit which uses up resources on a large scale, as the head of software development describes:

> *Well, the owner is still not happy about how many hours we took and still need. We are still not finished yet. But yeah, he has to go through with it. From time to time, he complains, but it is of no use and it has to go forward... and then, suddenly,* [the research budget] *was way bigger than planned.... You cannot estimate how many hours it will take if you haven't done it once before.*
> (Head of software development, interview)

He estimates around 10,000 working hours for the whole journey of implementing the standard-compliant software development processes. Apparently, the owner of CraneSolutions frequently complains about the huge budget. However, as the head of software development mentions, the owner has no other choice than to continue with these organizational changes. A software developer explains the reasons for it:

> *When there were no standards, we struggled with the owner about more personnel: "Well, wait, they* [additional employees] *cost money, why do we need them again?" That's hard.... If there is a standard saying "you have to*

> *have it!", what should the owner do? He has two options. He can have them* [additional employees] *or not, whereas in the second case he won't sell the crane.*
> (Software developer 1, interview)

Since regulations for the market of cranes require compliance with standard requirements, CraneSolutions invests massively in adequate organizational structures, according to these statements. In practice, according to the project manager, writing in his logbook, developing in a standard-conform way is very demanding and inflates the costs for the PMA project at CraneSolutions:

> *Regarding compliance with standards, there is such a level of detail which tremendously inflates the expenditures for an approval. That's good for the assessors and bad for us and the customer. However, PMA pays everything without further questions.* (Project manager, logbook)

As project manager, he considers it fortunate that the client, PMA, covers all costs regarding the assessment without further inquiry. Even though CraneSolutions allocates enough financial resources for the implementation of standard-compliant processes, it is not a straightforward task to *actually* implement processes. Financial obstacles for standard compliance are mentioned by the project manager:

> *We are happy if we find any supplier at all that produces the two or three cabins we need per year. If we tell them that they have to consider this standard they will refuse. The cabins mostly are individual products and very expensive anyway.... As manufacturer of special machinery, it is such a little quantity.*
> (Project manager, interview)

Since CraneSolutions produces only small quantities, they also source small quantities of parts. For their suppliers, producing in a standard-compliant manner for a minor customer is, however, a costly endeavour. In turn, suppliers pass these costs for standard-compliant development of parts on to CraneSolutions, which makes sourcing a costly endeavour.

The senior management provides sufficient financial resources for the enactment of standards in software development and, hence, the financial resources provide a high transformative impact. As a manufacturer of single custom-made products for a small niche market, CraneSolutions and its customers obviously accept the costs for the changes in the development process they undergo.

5.3.2.2 V-Model for Software Development

When the employees at CraneSolutions started to implement standard-compliant processes in software development, they used the V-model as a reference for their development processes according to the standard for special vehicles. The requirements manager explains the relevance of the V-model for the approval of the regulatory body:

> *To obtain the approval for a crane we need the approval from the regulatory authority. And this is based on a standard where they recommend using the V-model for the development of software for crane applications.... There is a big documentation effort in the V-model which we did not follow before we implemented the standard. It is a lot of work, we had to develop capacities and generate new positions that will create the documents. It is not rocket science, but it is a lot of work.* (Requirements manager, interview)

Since CraneSolutions started to implement the recommendations of the V-model, it created several new positions (e.g. software quality manager, requirements manager) in the company that handle the documentation tasks. Despite all efforts, the organizational members at CraneSolutions also acknowledge the advantages of the new processes:

> *It is very reasonable to develop according to the V-model. We can intercept defects quite early. For instance, if we detect something during the requirements phase we can stop and re-do the specific requirement. It is definitely better than detecting the error during the test phase because I would have to start again, develop and test. This consumes time, a lot of time.*
>
> (Software quality manager, interview)

The software quality manager points out that the early detection of errors saves a lot of time, something they obviously did not accomplish before the introduction of the V-model, on the one hand. On the other hand, throughout our inquiries, the software developers complain about burdensome requirements of the V-model for the organization. A software developer reasons:

> *If you have fifty employees who design something, then you have to implement such measures. Such models like the V-model they apply to bigger organizations and then the question comes up: what are smaller organizations doing with it? You would need a V-model 'light' or something similar and that's the problem here.* (Software developer 2, interview)

The V-model is the central reference model for software development at CraneSolutions. Thus, it has in our reading a high transformative impact for the enactment of standards at CraneSolutions. However, the recommendations are not fully implemented yet due to the comparatively bulky standard requirements for medium-sized organizations like CraneSolutions.

5.3.2.3 CODESYS

CODESYS[2] is an integrated development environment for the development of controller applications in line with the IEC 61131-3 standard for programmable controllers. In the automation business, often the development environment is bundled with the hardware, the actual control unit. CraneSolutions sources the control units and the development environment from the same supplier. The head of software development describes the advantages of CODESYS and the sourcing approach at CraneSolutions as follows:

> *For our single-piece production it's much easier. If you have a series product you only have the effort* [of assessment] *once. Then you can also have your development environment assessed and certified. But if we do it for every single crane then we would have a big problem.... When we were looking for a new control unit on the market, we thus required a device which includes a certified development environment. That would save us a lot of work. We would just hand over the certificate to the assessor and tell him: look, it is certified, someone* [another assessor] *looked into it already. You only have to assess the parts that we built ourselves.*
>
> (Head of software development, interview)

He elaborates that the usage of a certified development environment, like CODESYS, saves a lot of effort regarding the assessment of the control software. As a producer of single-piece products, he adds, CraneSolutions would not be able to handle the costs for a single assessment process for each crane it delivers. Moreover, while using CODESYS, the software developers at CraneSolutions can produce also software code that automatically complies with the requirements of the IEC 61131-3. Overall, CODESYS is of considerable importance for a standard-compliant development at CraneSolutions and disposes a medium transformative impact.

[2] https://www.codesys.com/

5.3.2.4 SVN

Apache™ Subversion®[3] is an open-source version control system, often abbreviated by the employees as SVN or SVN server. The employees at CraneSolutions file project documents and the software code on the SVN. In doing so, they comply with standard requirements for documentation:

> *Every new software code as well as all the documents for the V-model we put it on the SVN server. And the SVN does the correct versioning in the way the assessor likes it. So it is comprehensible and traceable.*
>
> (Software developer 3, interview)

The software developer emphasizes the factors comprehensibility and traceability for a standard-compliant development which they accomplish at CraneSolutions while using the SVN. The SVN was introduced due to an initiative of a further software developer, who explains the advantages of the SVN in more detail:

> *[E]verybody can access the information of the project for any given time in the project.... Thus, I always insisted to have this SVN. It concerns not only documentation [but also] the control software, it is always both.... I can comprehend at what time which version was the actual one and which changes were made. Hence, for an older project I can refer to the actual documents at that time, what was required and where did we go from there.... That's all much easier to handle.* (Software developer 1, interview)

With SVN, the software developers realise traceability of any document or any piece of software code throughout the lifetime of a development project. If an assessor or a customer inquires about a specific status of a document at a certain time, the employees at CraneSolutions can easily access this information through the SVN. This makes the SVN a powerful tool for the enactment of standards at CraneSolutions, yet with a medium transformative impact since it is not a *designated* standard-compliant tool for document management.

5.3.2.5 SISTEMA

SISTEMA (Safety Integrity Software Tool for the Evaluation of Machine Applications) (Huelke 2008) is a software tool for the application of the safety standard EN ISO 13849. It was developed by the DGUV, the Institute for

[3] https://subversion.apache.org/

Occupational Safety and Health of the German Social Accident Insurance[4], and given away for free use to manufacturers of machines and control units. In several logbook entries, the software quality manager describes his work with the software where he calculates the performance levels of different safety functions. Exemplarily, he points out the use of SISTEMA in one of his entries:

> *We calculate performance level values (PL values according to EN 13849) of the safety functions by using the SISTEMA software. Afterwards, we compare these actual values with the estimated values from the risk assessment. This is to test whether we developed sufficient safety functions regarding risks and hazards.* (Software quality manager, logbook)

The software quality manager describes his calculations of performance levels with SISTEMA to compare it with the planned values during risk assessment. During an interview, the software quality manager also refers to the usage of SISTEMA:

> *For the evaluation of safety functions, we work with the relevant standards and also a special software, SISTEMA. It's easier to calculate the values. You just enter all the different input values and the software shows the final result. We then estimate if we are still able to reach a satisfactory safety level. If not, we have to change something or buy other components.*
>
> (Software quality manager, interview)

The usage of SISTEMA significantly eases the software quality manager's task to ensure a safety-oriented and standard-compliant software development. However, the scope of the software is limited to risk assessment only, and therefore we estimate a low transformative impact.

5.4 Standards as Social Norms in CraneSolutions' Software Development

5.4.1 Legitimation of Organizational Deviance from Standards

Strict compliance to standards is an insoluble challenge for CraneSolutions. Its development process is per se deviant because it is a producer of cranes, and as

[4] http://www.dguv.de

such it cannot fully comply either with standards for cranes or with standards for special vehicles. The experienced project manager explains the situation in detail:

> *For the crane part we rely on the EN 13000. However, we cannot rely on it completely since the standard* [for mobile cranes] *doesn't fully cover special vehicles. Then we refer to this standard in those points relevant for special vehicles. And again, we cannot fully comply with this standard as well. Hence, we have two C-standards that fit somehow but not fully. Consequently, we cannot assure conformity to European regulation based on standards only.*
>
> (Project manager, interview)

The project manager of CraneSolutions is aware of the deviant approach for the company's cranes based on a strict standard-only assessment of software development. Members of the PMA project regularly legitimize deviations in their software development due to inadequate standards (regulatory frame). The project manager continues his explanations:

> *Of course, we do not fulfil certain points, certain standards. It is a bit difficult and you have to explain why. Normally, the standard is made for special vehicles. A crane clearly is such a machine; however, there are 100,000 different ones. A standard cannot fit in all points to every machine. There are certain points we cannot fulfil.... We are a crane and it works differently. Thus, we solve certain things differently. So, there is a lot of justification needed.*
>
> (Project manager, interview)

The project manager mentions quite different types of machines that fall under the same standard for special vehicles. Thus, the standard is designed quite generic and CraneSolutions must justify uniqueness of its products to the assessor during the approval process. The requirements manager describes the cooperation with the assessor:

> *It doesn't mean that we know what we have to write in all the specifications for all the different functions. That's still an iterative process. And we are in constant dialogue with the assessor. It is a fruitful cooperation, he helps with crucial points. But it is not written in detail, what we have to fill in. We have to fiddle around in what level of detail we have to describe the contents.*
>
> (Requirements manager, interview)

As the requirements manager mentions, the cooperation with the assessor is an iterative process. The organizational members at CraneSolutions often cannot fully assess in advance whether they act in compliance with standards, since it all depends on the negotiation process with the assessor. The uncertain situation regarding standard-compliant development processes clearly stresses the employees at CraneSolutions. The project manager compares it with '*walking on eggshells. You will only prove it for sure in the moment when you are on trial*' (Project manager, interview).

We found another reason for the unclear situation of compliance at CraneSolutions in the actual process change that the software development unit undergoes. The software quality manager summarizes:

> *That is the first project where we develop with the new process. Thus, there are still former practices present. These happen again and again.*
>
> (Software quality manager, interview)

As he names it, practices from the former software development processes are still being used and the employees do not yet possess the entire knowledge to comply with the standard requirements, or to assess the state of compliance for their own processes.

Moreover, the homologation team at CraneSolutions resides on the interface between the software developers and the regulation authorities. Questions whether they develop products in compliance with or in deviance from standards at CraneSolutions are processed by this unit. Since they act as 'diplomats' (see section 5.3), these tasks are rather hidden to the software developers, which consequently affects their ability to assess the status of compliance for their development activities.

For the PMA project, we found two further aspects that rendered it more difficult for the software developers to report on compliance or deviance in software development. Since the regulatory situation is rather complex in the PMA project, CraneSolutions engaged Crane Consult PLC which acts as consultant for the approval process (see section 5.3). It also acts as mediator between the software developers and regulatory authorities and further blurs the ability of the software developers to assess standard compliance. At the end of our inquiries, the PMA project had been delayed massively due to political developments in the UK. The head of software development explains:

> *From our perspective, the machines are ready.... The client doesn't accept the machines at the moment because they do not need them. The money for the infrastructure project was cancelled and, thus, they now have plenty of time to look into regulation topics.... It could lead to plenty of additional work with*

these approval documents for us.... Here and there, we might stumble into a compromise or a pragmatic solution.

(Head of software development, interview)

The head of software development states that the budget for the PMA project was on hold on the client side. He is worried about the consequences and the strict approval process that could follow. Hence, the assessments of the regulatory authorities are still missing in the PMA project. The organizational members at CraneSolutions remain in an uncertain situation about the state of compliance for their cranes.

Considering the special circumstances at CraneSolutions, we reconstructed three deviations from standards, which are summarized in Table 5.3.

5.4.1.1 Deviation from Documentation Requirements—Documentation after Software Development

The requirements manager of CraneSolutions describes the deviation from standardized documentation requirements as a common practice in software development. Developers often document not until the actual development is finished, even if they are aware of the necessity to document in parallel:

I would call it ideal to compile the documents while the software is being developed. That's how it should be. In a small organization like ours, it is often just not feasible. Documents are not part of our day-to-day business. They can be compiled during development, which they are already when there have been free resources among the colleagues. If that's not the case, if day-to-day business is too demanding, if there are urgent customer projects then we would always focus on that. And we would only document afterwards.

(Requirements manager, interview)

The requirements manager legitimizes this deviation by the day-to-day business which he considers as more urgent than writing documents (business frame). Further, he mentions that the actual size of CraneSolutions matters as well. In his eyes, the organization is too small and cannot allocate sufficient resources to handle a standard-compliant documentation process which he calls '*ideal*' (administrative frame). He adds that the software developers at CraneSolutions would comply with this documentation requirement if sufficient resources were available.

Table 5.3 Legitimation of deviations from standards at CraneSolutions

Forms of deviation	Legitimation of deviation	Legitimation of which project members	Legitimation frame
Deviation from documentation requirements	Processes are not fully embodied by employees	Software developer	Administrative
	Required development process is an ideal prototype	Requirements manager	Administrative
	Day-to-day business is more important	Requirements manager	Business
	Deviance saves cost	Requirements manager	Business
	Deviance saves efforts	Requirements manager	Business
	Deviance saves time	Head of software development, software developer	Business
	Deviance increases flexibility	Head of software development	Administrative
Deviation from required development phases	Linearity of V-model is impractical according to process consultant	Head of software development	Technical
	Deviance saves time	Head of software development	Business
Deviation from required role separation	Role concept is difficult to implement and handle due to small team	Head of software development, software developer, project manager	Administrative
	Deviance saves costs	Software developer	Business
	Deviance saves time	Software developer	Business
	Deviance saves effort	Head of software development	Business

A software developer expresses another legitimation for deviation from documentation requirements:

> *These processes are defined, though not yet fully embodied. Actually, for the control system, we had to finish the program first, so that the crane could go to the test field and, thus, we didn't do the paperwork. However, it should be the other way around. But that's reality.* (Software developer 3, interview)

The software developer legitimizes the approach to document after the actual software development by time pressure (business frame) and being able to test the software directly on the test field. He argues that the processes are not yet fully embodied (administrative frame). Since the new development processes were introduced only recently, many of the software developers still keep to the old practices.

The head of software development furthers another justification for the deviant approach to first develop and to document afterwards. Even though the external process consultant is considered as an expert for standard-compliant processes, he also compiled documents retrospectively when he was working for CraneSolutions:

> *The function was quite extensive and had to be reviewed by the assessor. And then he* [process consultant] *compiled the documents afterwards which should have been there before. They* [the process consultants] *describe the function of the crane and what the software has to do. And all these documents had to be given to the assessor then.*
>
> (Head of software development, interview)

5.4.1.2 Deviation from Required Development Phases—Change in Division and Succession

The head of software development justifies deviation from the required development phases with evidence from the process consultant:

> *That's what the process consultant said: it is not possible to linearly pass the V-model in a way that you only continue when the previous step was finished. You will not finish it in this way. You are allowed to do it somehow in parallel. However, you cannot start with a step whilst the input documents are not ready.... Though, for the crane which is down there* [on the testing field], *it happened like this due to a lack of time. And we knew that from the very beginning.* (Head of software development, interview)

Citing the process consultant, the head of software development explains that a linear processing of the different phases of the V-model is not possible in practice (technical frame) and that phases can be handled in parallel as long as the input documents are in place. The software developers are aware of this deviation within the PMA project. The head of software development legitimizes deviation from the required division and succession of development phases by a lack of time (business frame) and the expertise approval of the process consultant.

The software quality manager describes another example from the PMA project for deviation from the required development phases:

> *I don't know when we start with the software requirements specification. There are still no drafts, even though the software is done.... And next week, we already test the crane, we do system tests. I really don't know what I should do regarding documentation and process compliance.*
>
> (Software quality manager, interview)

As the software quality manager explains, several documents are still missing, while the software development for the crane is already finished. However, these documents are to be included in the system test phase which soon starts. Hence, the software quality manager shows concerns about how to start his task without several crucial input documents.

5.4.1.3 Deviation from Required Role Separation—Combination of Tasks

We found a third form of deviation, with the head of software development reporting about deviation from the required role separation:

> *Sometimes, someone who was not allowed to do both tasks actually did both tasks in the end.... In the end, you just have to take care that the right person signs. When you only have a small team, it is really hard to comply with it* [role separation] *strictly. We try it* [role separation] *as much as possible. However, sometimes you have to be pragmatic, you have to find a solution.*
>
> (Head of software development, interview)

As the head of software development describes, software developers sometimes execute tasks that should have been accomplished by another employee, due to the role separation required by EN 50126. However, he points out that this form of deviation officially disappears when the documentation of these tasks is signed by the person who should have accomplished the task. The head of software development legitimizes this deviation form by the small size of his development team (administrative frame) and the positive consequence of saving costs, time, and effort by deviating from the standard requirements (business frame). He adds further:

> *In the beginning, they* [the authorities] *have been very motivated about the RAMS* [Reliability, Availability, Maintenance, and Safety—defined in EN 50126] *process. We consider some aspects as a matter of course. However, some aspects are just not feasible for us, not feasible economically, impossible. It's different if you have a series production. But for a single product? No way.*
>
> (Head of software development, interview)

In the eyes of the head of software development, it is impossible to implement certain standard requirements, since the economic effort would be too high (business frame). He justifies the deviant approach of CraneSolutions' software development by the singularity of the company's products, since the cranes are single products in small series.

5.4.2 Expected Sanctions from Deviance

The situation for expected sanctions from deviance at CraneSolutions reflects the specific regulatory circumstances of the organization—due to generic standards, both from the craning side and from the special vehicles side. CraneSolutions' cranes cannot comply fully with any of these standards. Hence, CraneSolutions anticipates and accepts organizational deviance in software development and relies on negotiations with the assessors about specific regulatory solutions for its cranes. Consequently, the software developers are not involved in these discussions and are hardly aware of deviations and of specific sanctions from deviant behaviour. Further, since the implementation of standard-compliant processes is still ongoing, the knowledge on new processes is not robust enough among all the employees. Thus it seems difficult to evaluate deviation from development processes and resulting sanctions.

Table 5.4 summarizes the expected sanctions from deviance at CraneSolutions. Among the different expected sanctions, business sanctions dominate at CraneSolutions. In particular, its organizational members frequently voiced the opinion that deviations from standards save costs, time, and effort (business frame).

Table 5.4 Expected sanctions in the case of standard deviations at CraneSolutions

Sanctioning frame	Expected sanctions on project members in the case of deviations
Business frame	Loss of markets Approval by client Saving on development costs Saving efforts on standard implementation and compliance monitoring
Administrative frame	Delays in the development process Flexibility in the development process
Regulatory frame	Disapproval from the assessor As long as unnoticed by the assessor
Ethical frame	Not mentioned
Technical frame	Not mentioned

Deviation from the required development phases by changing division and succession can be sanctioned negatively and lead to delays in the development process (administrative frame). The software quality manager points out that due to missing input documents he cannot accomplish his tasks in the final testing phase:

> *All these intermediate phases between system design and system test are missing actually while I should start with the final phase. How is that possible?*
>
> (Software quality manager, interview)

However, the same delays in the development process can lead to a gain in flexibility (administrative frame). The head of software development explains the deviation from the required parallel execution of documentation and development:

> *Sometimes you have to code something quickly to be able to continue works down there* [e.g. on the test field or in the hardware manufacturing]. *In that case, documentation is only second.... You have to be flexible depending on how and when certain things are needed.*
>
> (Head of software development, interview)

While developing first and documenting afterwards, the head of software development explains that the software developers can hand over the crane control software to other hardware development or testing tasks in a timely manner (business frame).

A common feared regulatory sanction is the disapproval from the assessor (regulatory frame). The software quality manager sums up:

> *The assessor has to give his OK. We develop software and in the end the assessor says: yes, you have done all right.... Compliance with these standards is acknowledged only if an assessor says: yes, everything is alright, here is your certificate.* (Software quality manager, interview)

The approval by the client (business frame) was mentioned as another sanctioning aspect when deviating from the standard procedures. The project manager describes the scenario:

> *For this specific crane we used the new hardware.... They* [the client] *insisted to comply with EN 13849. This was possible only by using the new hardware and they acknowledged that they wouldn't demand documentation for a while.* (Project manager, interview)

Following the project manager, the client insisted on using a new control unit which necessitates another approval process for the control unit of the crane. To complete the crane in a timely manner, the client waived documentation at short notice. CraneSolutions followed the client's request and, hence, received the client's approval (business frame) as a constructive sanction.

For CraneSolutions, compliance with standards equals having the opportunity to manufacture and sell its products on the respective market (regulatory frame). This way, it avoids economic sanctions (business frame). The requirements manager explains:

> *Even though the means are often highly questionable, as long as we are still able to implement all the requirements, we do implement them. Otherwise, you won't sell a crane.* (Requirements manager, interview)

However, the most prevalent sanctions for deviance from standards mentioned at CraneSolutions are constructive business sanctions such as saving costs, efforts, and time (business frame). It was referred to as being '*pragmatic*', as '*finding a solution*', as focusing on the '*day-to-day business*', or as avoiding '*economically not feasible*' requirements. Exemplarily, the requirements manager explains:

> *In a small organization like ours, it is often just not feasible. Documents are not part of our day-to-day business.* (Requirements manager, interview)

Further, the project manager mentions how deviations would not lead to any sanctions at all in the first place:

> *It is what it is, and we cannot comply with every single standard requirement. And it doesn't matter as long as nobody notices.* (Project manager, interview)

The project manager is aware that organizational deviance can only be detected when someone, e.g. the assessor, detects it (regulatory frame). Hence, up to that point, deviations go uncovered.

5.5 Attentive Deviance from Standards at CraneSolutions: Negotiating the Asymmetries

In the following, we summarize the appearance of attentive organizational deviance with standards and present contradictions during the software developing project PMA at CraneSolutions. We provide explanations why CraneSolutions deviates from standards by attentively adjusting standard requirements with assessors and clients. All in all, we found three forms of deviation from standards: compiling the required documentation only after software development; the change in division and succession of the required role separation; and the combination of tasks as deviation from the required role separation.

Regarding related contradictions at CraneSolutions, as described in Fried and Walgenbach (2020), asymmetries can occur, first, when standards are not appropriately represented as interpretative schemes, facilities, or social norms in organizational practices. Second, contradictions can emerge *between* standards as interpretative schemes, as facilities, or as social norms. Generally, since CraneSolutions works in a niche market with conflicting standards, standard compliance is a special challenge, making negotiations and adjustments necessary. Attentive deviance appears here as challenging the standard in order to find a special solution with external approval, a specialized approach which the project manager describes as '*walking on eggshells*' (project manager, interview). CraneSolutions' approach to standard enactment is outlined in Figure 5.1.

In order to explain attentive organizational deviance at CraneSolutions, we illustrate the enactment of standards as (1) interpretative schemes, (2) facilities, and (3) social norms. We discovered only one asymmetry and no secondary

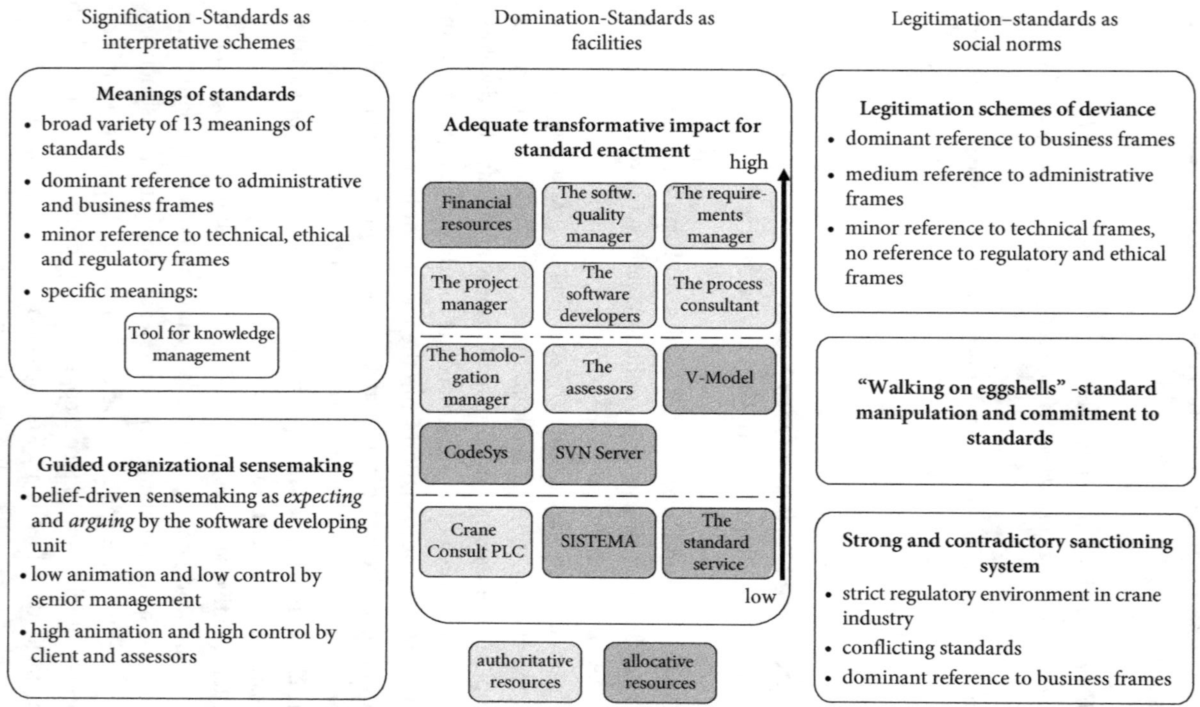

Figure 5.1 Standard enactment in CraneSolutions' software development

contradictions between the structurationist aspects (interpretative scheme, facility, social norm) of standards.

5.5.1 Standards as Interpretative Schemes: Guided Organizational Sensemaking

Regarding standards as interpretative schemes at CraneSolutions' software developing unit, we traced thirteen different meanings of standards, whereas most of them are similar to the meanings of MetroEngineers and MedTech. Among them, administrative and business frames were dominant and only minor references were made to technical, regulatory, or ethical frames when describing the signification of standards for CraneSolutions.

Although engagement in sensegiving for standard enactment is rather restrained and little controlled by senior management at CraneSolutions, we found evidence of *guided organizational sensemaking* (Maitlis 2005). The employees of the software developing unit at CraneSolutions are comparably active in providing sense for the enactment of standards, for instance due to the enabling chance of standards as a *tool for knowledge management.* Standards give an opportunity to systematically document expert knowledge at CraneSolutions. Even more though, external actors such as the assessors, consultants, and client play an essential role in CraneSolutions' sensemaking for standards. Since they extensively animate and control the sensemaking process by discussing standards in regular consultations, meetings, and monitoring, organizational sensemaking at CraneSolutions takes on a *guided* form. CraneSolutions implemented a homologation unit as a systematic, organized approach coordinating the approval processes and maintaining a close relationship with the assessors. Hence, assessors, consultants, and clients serve here as active 'sense-givers' (Maitlis 2005) in regular discussions on standard enactment, while the members of the PMA project also engage in sensemaking by constructing their own accounts of standard enactment.

These accounts become apparent in one case-specific meaning for standards at CraneSolutions: as a *tool for knowledge management.* It implies sensemaking for standards as *arguing*, since the new standard enactment process is used as an argument to strategically accumulate and make available the process knowledge of experienced employees for software development and to monitor the compliance of the development process. However, we also find sensemaking as *expecting* at CraneSolutions when employees refer to the former approach of product approval, the approach of *proven in use*:

CraneSolutions expects the approval of compliance with standards as it has ever since gained approval for certain product components once they had been in successful use for a certain time.

5.5.2 Standards as Facilities: Appropriate Transformative Impact of Most Resources for Standard Enactment

At CraneSolutions, we can generally see an appropriate availability of allocative and authoritative resources for standard enactment, with many resources deploying a high or medium transformative impact. However, we find some asymmetries among the transformative capacity and impact of some authoritative and allocative resources. Since resources at CraneSolutions appear as tightly tailored to their specialized, innovative niche products, this customized capacity does not always fit certain standard requirements. For instance, the small size of the software developing teams does not meet the standard requirements of the V-model, for instance to enable standardized, separated development roles during software development. Thus, typical tasks for standard enactment are shared among the roles of the requirements manager, project manager, and software quality manager. As well as this, the software developers at CraneSolutions still perform a large part of standard enactment. Furthermore, the extensive involvement of external authoritative resources, especially consultants and assessors, stands out at CraneSolutions. In comparison to the other cases, CraneSolutions' efforts on compliant standard enactment are constantly and intensively supported by external consultants and assessors to solve the demanding approval process. Moreover, CraneSolutions invests in authoritative resources for the standard renegotiations with standardizing bodies. For instance, the project manager represents CraneSolutions' interests in these time-consuming processes.

5.5.3 Standards as Social Norms: Selective Manipulation of and Commitment to Standards—A Strong but Conflicting Sanctioning System

At CraneSolutions, standards are enacted as social norms even though the enactment process faces a characteristic challenge: since CraneSolutions' products apply to conflicting standards of special vehicles and cranes, compliance with both standards is hard to accomplish. Hence, the ongoing adjustment of standard requirements is necessary. As a consequence, CraneSolutions is necessarily *committing* to standard requirements standards as well as *manipulating* them.

The account of 'walking on eggshells' (project manager, interview) implies that negotiations and adjustments of standard compliance with assessors and clients are a necessary trial and error process of standard enactment. Moreover, CraneSolutions' characteristic approach of standard enactment as 'walking on eggshells' seems *committed* and *manipulative* at the same time: employees at CraneSolutions actively challenge the standard in cooperation with assessors and clients in order to find specialized but safe solutions in the day-to-day operations.

Concerning CraneSolutions' patterns of legitimizing deviance from standards, we found a dominant reference to business frames such as savings on effort, time, and costs. Software developers of the PMA project referred less to administrative frames and technical frames and not at all to regulatory or ethical legitimations.

Regarding the sanctioning system, business sanctions were most dominant, with the loss of markets as the imperative external sanctions to be avoided by attentive organizational deviance from standards. CraneSolutions generally faces a strict regulatory environment in the crane industry with demanding safety requirements. At the same time, however, the standard implementation at CraneSolutions is still ongoing and thus an appropriate internal sanctioning system for deviance from standards is not yet in place.

In summary, conflicting standard requirements make attentive organizational deviance a necessary and pragmatic solution for CraneSolutions. At the same time, the conflicting standard requirements offer CraneSolutions the opportunity to scrutinize some of the standard requirements in a *reflexive* way: to comply with standards is as vital as to ensure the company's economic objectives, and thus to be able to sell its unique crane solutions on the market. Deviations from standards are not hidden but attentively adjusted with the affected stakeholders to ensure reliable, innovative products for its niche markets.

Even though the findings on organizational deviance at CraneSolutions represent ambitious efforts for compliant standard enactment, they show partly temporary deviant practices, which would potentially risk certification but are attentively adjusted during or after the development process. CraneSolutions' efforts for a standard-compliant development are immense because it works in an environment with demanding standard requirements. Moreover, conflicting standard requirements lead to the challenge of finding product-specific solutions to pass the approval process. We found a sophisticated practice of standard enactment at CraneSolutions which we refer to as *attentive organizational deviance* from standards. As knowledgeable agents of standard enactment, the employees of the software development teams answer the conflicting standard requirements and the demanding approval process for certification with negotiating and adjusting the standard requirements with assessors and clients. Moreover, attentive organizational deviance from standards is both necessary and possible due to CraneSolutions' specific position as an influential member in a niche market, allowing for special solutions. Further, attentive organizational deviance is based on time-consuming negotiations and external expertise by consultants and eventually the approval by assessors.

References

Fried, A. & Walgenbach, P. 2020. Theoretical framework to explore organizational deviance from standards. *In:* Fried, A. (ed.) *Understanding Deviance in a World of Standards.* Oxford: Oxford University Press.

Gey, R., Langer, S. & Fried, A. 2020a. Attentive deviance from standards at CraneSolutions. *In:* Fried, A. (ed.) *Understanding Deviance in World of Standards.* Oxford: Oxford University Press.

Gey, R., Langer, S. & Fried, A. 2020b. Over-conformity with standards at MedTech. *In:* Fried, A. (ed.) *Understanding Deviance in a World of Standards.* Oxford: Oxford University Press.

Huelke, M. 2008. *SISTEMA: A Tool for the Easy Application of the Control Standard EN ISO 13849-1.* Sankt Augustin: Institute for Occupational Safety and Health of the German Social Accident Insurance.

Langer, S., Gey, R., Karadzhova-Beyer, D. & Fried, A. 2020b. Deregulated deviance from standards at MetroEngineers. *In:* Fried, A. (ed.) *Understanding Deviance in a World of Standards.* Oxford: Oxford University Press.

Maitlis, S. 2005. The social processes of organizational sensemaking. *Academy of Management Journal,* 48, 21–49.

6

Over-Conformity with Standards at MedTech

Ronny Gey, Sarah Langer, and Andrea Fried

In this chapter we illustrate over-conformity with standards as we encountered it in the case of MedTech. We generally reconstruct a tight enactment of standards in this company. However, we also identify four different forms of deviations, which appear as deviations from standard requirements, from required development phases, as well as from review and documentation requirements. Most striking with MedTech, however, are deviations that overachieve standard requirements in the SOP, such as additional meetings and documentation. With the purpose of explaining over-conformity with standards, we outline MedTech's distinctive enactment of standards in this chapter. We show that missing contradictions in the enactment of standards lead to over-conform development processes.

6.1 Introduction to the Case of MedTech

MedTech is the ophthalmology business division of a large, multinational medical technology business group, based in Germany. The medical technology business group itself is a subsidiary of a large traditional German holding originally founded in the nineteenth century. Historically, the group developed from merging with another medical technology company and is publicly traded on the stock exchange today. Since then, the medical technology business group has taken over further international companies active in the same field to build a multinational group. The group owns production sites in Europe, the US, and Japan. As a manufacturer, the medical technology business group has two strategic business divisions: one in the field of surgical microscopes and the other in ophthalmology. We had the chance to investigate the software development for the projects Fidelio and Siberia of the ophthalmology division at the business group's headquarters in Germany.

Ronny Gey, Sarah Langer, and Andrea Fried, *Over-Conformity with Standards at MedTech* In: *Understanding Deviance in a World of Standards*. Edited by: Andrea Fried, Oxford University Press (2020). © Oxford University Press.
DOI: 10.1093/oso/9780198833888.003.0006

As stated in the business report, the aim of MedTech's business group is to be a market and technology leader in microsurgery and ophthalmology with substantial growth. Over recent years, turnover of the business group increased constantly by about 7 per cent and reached an annual turnover of €1.088bn in 2015/2016. Between 2012 and 2015, it had a constant profit of about 13 per cent of turnover. Further, it spent consistently about 11 per cent of turnover on in-house research & development. In 2015, about 2,900 employees worked in the overall business group.

In recent years, the industry for medical devices has been strongly influenced by several trends (Johner 2017; VDI 2017). The ongoing demographic change in important markets like Europe, the US, China, and Japan has continuously increased the demand for medical devices. German medical technology companies enlarged their turnover to a record maximum of €29.2bn in 2016 (Johner 2017; VDI 2017: 4). MedTech is competing with international corporations in a highly prosperous market for medical technology. Further, digitalization has significantly changed the medical device industry. Software handles more and more functionality in medical devices and service functions are automated. 'Big Data', the 'Internet of Things', and mobile applications form the basis for these developments. In consequence, the demand for software in medical devices at MedTech increased tremendously over recent years:

> *For instance* [in the Siberia project], *we only have one electrical engineer and one construction engineer…, two systems engineers and the project manager, and the residual majority, that is software in the moment, that is madness.*
>
> (Systems engineer, interview)

Above all, the regulations for medical safety will increase in the future. As a global player, MedTech operates in markets with differing regulatory systems. Efforts for product approvals will increase as MedTech extends its presence into emerging markets with developing and frequently changing regulatory systems like China and Brazil. However, the US and the European markets still dominate MedTech's turnover and efforts for regulation in these markets is of highest priority. Hence, MedTech strictly follows the prescriptions of both the European and the US system. The European Medical Device Directive (93/42/EWG) was announced in 1993, and transformed into German legislation as the Medical Device Act (EN 13485, EN 14971, EN 62304, EN 60601). EN 13485 ('Medical devices—quality management systems—requirements for regulatory purposes') describes the requirements for comprehensive quality management systems for medical devices. The standard EN 14971 applies to risk management for medical devices. The standard EN 62304 defines the application of medical device software and software lifecycle processes. Hence, it is the most important standard for software development at MedTech. Finally, EN 60601 considers safety and performance of medical electrical equipment. Further, the guidelines of the US Food and Drug Administration (FDA) are critical to software development at MedTech. Several official FDA 'guidance documents' (among others, 'General Principles of Software Validation'; 'FDA Reviewers, and Compliance on Off-The-Shelf Software Use in Medical Devices'; 'Mobile Medical Applications') need to be considered for software development at MedTech.

In response to the requirements of the different standards for software development, MedTech developed a sophisticated approach to handle these often conflicting demands from multiple standards. We labelled this approach previously as metastructuring of standards (Gey & Fried 2018). Over the years, MedTech developed specialized roles (e.g. software quality managers), specialized tools (team foundation server (TFS), IBM Rational, integrated management system (IMS)), and an internal standard document, the SOP for software development, which integrates the different, sometimes conflicting requirements. Since the enactment of standards lies in the hands of specialists, the software developers are not directly confronted with standard requirements as such, but with the directives in the SOP.

Apart from meeting the standard requirements, the approval process for the different (supra-national) regulatory systems is crucial for software development at MedTech. It is very demanding and significantly ties up resources in the organization. For MedTech, compliance with standards is the key requirement for passing the approval process. Henceforth, due to the criticality of this function, MedTech centrally coordinates its efforts regarding standards, regulation, and the approval process within a regulatory affairs unit.

In the realm of our investigations, we studied two different ophthalmology development projects at MedTech and the software developers' challenges of developing standard-compliant software. In the first project, called Siberia, MedTech developed a device replacement for retinal laser therapy within the field of conventional eye treatment. Several hardware parts of the laser device have been discontinued by the suppliers and could not be sourced anymore. With the new hardware, MedTech aims for several enhancements of the device (less invasive, enhanced procedure, lower energy levels). The Siberia project was planned with a duration of more than 3 years from April 2014 to July 2017. In the beginning, the software development team consisted of two developers and the software project manager. However, it increased significantly in the course of the project and temporarily hosted seven developers since the product requirements were changed permanently and new features were added frequently.

For the second project, called Fidelio, MedTech scheduled a new software release for an already existing diagnosis device in the field of optical eye biometry in September 2015. The device measures several variables of the eye, including axial length, cornea radii, cornea diameter, and anterior chamber depth, which are required for the precise calculation of artificial lenses. The release includes new calculation formulae, a better treatment workflow, and increased software usability. Again, in the course of the project, new product requirements were constantly brought in by the product management team.

Besides a strict regime regarding standards and safety regulations for MedTech, both projects highlight two other typical aspects of software development at MedTech. First, the projects are characterized by a high number of external staff, especially among the software developers and testers: '*when I started here, it was even more. We had about 50 per cent externs*' (software developer 3, interview). This past development seriously threatened a continuous application of software development. Nowadays, the rate has decreased to 30 per cent—a rate that most of the employees still consider as too high and which is therefore often debated among the employees. Second, at MedTech the relationship between software development and product management is partly conflictual. The relationship is shaped by ever-changing requirements and increasingly shorter product release cycles, which challenge the software developers in accomplishing a straightforward and continuous software development.

6.2 Standards as Interpretative Schemes in MedTech's Software Development

The organizational members in MedTech's software development team reported different meanings of standards for their daily work, for the organization, and for the different projects they work on. From analysis of the interviews, we identified thirteen different meanings, which provide sense to the employees for their engagement in standard enactment. Distinctly most prominent among the signification frames are administrative frames followed by technical frames. In comparison to the two other cases in this book, business frames seem to be not that dominant for the signification of standard enactment. The meanings of standards greatly resemble the ones at MetroEngineers and CraneSolutions. However, three meanings are specific for MedTech: standardizer of terminology, rules of the game, and non-relevant for software developers.

First, in contrast to the other cases, *terminology* is highly standardized over the different development projects. Employees used the same terms for roles, documents, milestones, and other concepts relevant to the development process. Second, *standards as rules of the game* are an integral part of MedTech; their importance for product development and market entrance is unquestionable. Standards as taken-for-granted by the software developers are the rules of the game and, as such, senior management accepts the enactment of standards as necessity. Moreover, they support standard enactment by allocating financial and administrative resources for standard-compliant software development. By doing so, they provide sense for members of the Fidelio and the Siberia project to find a shared understanding of compliant software development. Thus, senior management is very engaged in sensegiving for standard enactment, whereas the software developers have no need to provide any sense. This is further illustrated by the third meaning *non-relevant for software developers.* Since standard requirements are centrally and regularly translated into the binding SOP by the software quality assurance department, standards as such are not present for software developers.

Table 6.1 summarizes the different meanings of standards expressed by members of the software development teams at MedTech, and describes each meaning of standards in more detail.

Base for Product Specification

Standards serve as a *base for product specification* for the software developers at MedTech. The systems engineer of the Siberia project describes this meaning using an example from his work with laser applications:

> *Whenever you are unsure about certain things or when you have a question, you have to look it up every now and then; you have to look into the standard occasionally. That's how it is.... The general standard for laser applications prescribes many things a laser has to have.... And to be honest, let's not deceive ourselves, I think there is no developer who knows everything. That's not possible. It lives and it changes all the time.* (Systems engineer, interview)

Table 6.1 Standards as interpretative schemes at MedTech

Meaning of standards	Description Standards...	Which project members ascribing meaning	Signification frame
Base for product specification	Define the requirements of a prospective product	Software developer, software quality manager, software project manager, software architect, systems engineer	Technical
Base for software development processes	Define the design of software development processes	Head of risk management, software project manager, software quality manager, software developer	Administrative
Standardizer of processes	Align processes within the organization and across organizations	Software developer, head of risk management	Administrative
Definer of development roles	Separate roles for software development projects; and define who is allowed to do what	Software quality manager, software project manager	Administrative
	Divide power to assure independent quality control	Software project manager	Administrative
Standardizer of terminology	Align communication within the organization and across it	Software quality manager	Administrative
Interface assurance	Ensure documentation for development of technical interfaces	Software project manager	Technical
Current state of technology	Provide reference for currently accepted technology, but not necessarily the most advanced technology	Software developer	Technical
Improver of development processes	Work more efficiently with defined instructions	Software quality manager	Business
Assurance of human safety	Protect society	Software developer, software quality manager	Ethical
	Ensure usability	Software developer	Technical
	Create consumer trust	Software developer, software quality manager	Business
	Ensure quality	Software developer, software quality manager	Business
Base for certification	Enable transnational product approval	Software project manager, software developer, head of risk management	Technical
Key to the market	Open prospectively the markets for the company if certified	Software developer, head of quality management, head of risk management	Business
Rules of the game	Function as rules of the game of medical technology	Software quality manager	Administrative
Non-relevant for software developer	Are not directly affected by developers	Software developer, software project manager	Administrative

As a base for their product development, the software developers in few cases still directly turn to the standard when they are looking for advice in terms of technical requirements for product development. Since it seems impossible to know everything about his work subject, the systems engineer refers to the standards as a knowledge base. Further, he points out constant changes in applicable technologies that need to be addressed in standard updates.

Base for Software Development Process

When organizational members design, implement, and enhance the processes for software development at MedTech, they primarily refer to standard requirements. For instance, for the development of medical devices it is the Medical Device Act:

> *The demand for having SOPs? That is derived from the German Medical Device Act or from the ISO 13485 or 9001 respectively. That is the ISO for quality management which clearly states that you have to define resources. Therefore, you have to have a process. In addition, it says that you have to define a development and manufacturing process.*
>
> (Head of risk management, interview)

The head of risk management points to the mandatory processes for development and manufacturing processes, for example. The SOP for software development functions as the organizational implementation of this standard requirement. Throughout the development work at MedTech, the project members of the Siberia as well as the Fidelio project guide and help each other by pointing to the requirements of the SOP. The first implementation of an SOP for software development traces back to 2006:

> *SOP software development? Since 2006 or 2007, at that time we wrote the first version. Before, we had a SOP for product development in general which dates back to 2002.... At that time, there was not much content. It prescribed that there had to be a design phase, an implementation phase, an approval phase. Today that is much more specified, who and what, and it's quite complicated.*
>
> (Software project manager 2, interview)

The guiding prescriptions of the SOPs are accepted by the organizational members as the *base for software development processes.*

Standardizer of Processes

Standards align the processes of all development projects across MedTech. The organizational members recognise the standards as *standardizers of processes.* A software developer describes this aspect with an example from the requirements management:

> *If you read our requirements, they all sound similar and that makes it easier as if someone writes a novel and another one only a few words. If it is standardized it is easier to read, you are faster, and it has advantages.*
>
> (Software developer 3, interview)

The interviewee points out that all software developers formulate product requirements in the same way, so that they are applicable independent from the developer. The result of standardized processes is then standardized work deliverables.

Standardizer of Terminology

Efficient communication is an important aspect for collaboration in organizations. For the employees at MedTech, standards standardize not only processes across the organization but also the terminology (*standardizer of terminology*) used in the documentation of development processes. The senior software manager explains:

> *So, the software processes were harmonized across the different sites at MedTech. That means no matter which site is talking about a milestone 2.1, everybody knows what that means. That helps a lot.*
>
> (Senior software manager, interview)

He underlines the importance of the consistent use of definitions and concepts, like a mutual understanding of certain milestones. The software quality manager exemplifies this by the use of similar abbreviations at MedTech:

> *And there are all these abbreviations. They are kind of guided by the SOPs. There is an SOP for software development and there is one for the development of devices in general. And all these terms, PRS* [product requirement

specification] *for instance, relate to the entire device and as such also to the hardware.... And all those abbreviations in the formulas or in the software are derived from the SOP.* (Software quality manager 2, interview)

Since many abbreviations are used according to the SOP, terms, definitions, and concepts in the communication across MedTech are standardized.

Definer of Development Roles

The standard defines not only each phase of the development process but also the different roles that are involved in the development of software (*definer of development roles*):

> *The software quality* [department] *is derived from the standards. They require an independent panel which assesses the software quality.... We introduced a software quality department here around 2008. Before, the software developers tested their own code. And there is this inherent risk. If you control yourself, you are not fully independent.... So, different roles were created. Responsibility was distributed over several management levels in such a way that there are no conflicts anymore. And this is all due to the standard.... The units for regulatory and clinical affairs are quite big. This comes from the standard and the developments in the different countries. Medical approvals become more and more restrictive and difficult. You have to establish huge units for that.*
> (Software project manager 2, interview)

The software project manager mentions several roles that were created at MedTech in line with the standard's requirements: software quality, regulatory affairs, and clinical affairs. They represent a role and task separation at MedTech which is triggered by standards. Today, these three tasks at MedTech are accomplished by 'huge units', as the software project manager explains.

Interface Assurance

As *interface assurance*, the standards encompass two different meanings based on the understanding of interfaces. First, the software developers at MedTech emphasize the importance of standards for the definition of technical interfaces:

> *Standards require that you provide documents identifying the technical interfaces. That's a relatively high effort.*
>
> (Software project manager 1, interview)

Standards require a precise documentation of the technical interfaces of a software product which makes it possible to comprehend the functionality of the technical interface. However, second, interfaces can also exist in customer–supplier relationships, as the senior software manager explains:

> *If we qualify a new supplier or if we make a software audit, then of course I look up the standards. They* [the suppliers] *have to show me their documentation. Then I can see whether they are in line with the standards.... And if I see that they are completely different to us, then I go back to the standards to figure out whether they are still compliant or not.*
>
> (Senior software manager, interview)

At MedTech, they assess their interfaces with the suppliers by verifying the supplier's documentation process. Consequently, when suppliers document compliant with standards, they demonstrate a shared understanding of the development process with MedTech.

Current State of Technology

A software quality manager at MedTech describes standards as the *current state of technology*:

> *A standard reflects always the current state of the art. If you want to do something new then you might have a problem. For highly sophisticated applications, you might not find a suitable standard* [laughs]. *So, for instance, if you work in ultrashort pulse applications or at the university in general—there you might not find a standard.* (Software quality manager 2, interview)

The software quality manager emphasizes the suitability of standards which, among others, depends on the novelty of certain technologies. He explains that new technologies, like ultrashort pulse applications, will trigger the development of suitable standards since there is a lack of standards. The standard as the current state of technology reflects the accepted state of a technology but not necessarily the newest.

Improver of Development Process

A software developer describes the consequences of standards for developments at MedTech. To him, standards appear as an *improver of development processes*:

> *We have standards for coding, since everybody has his own coding style—otherwise it would look completely different. This is something you have to standardize. It has to look similar to make it comprehensible for third parties in a faster way.... I will finish faster if I understand the code of the others more quickly. There are pros and cons. Of course, it is a lot of effort. At first, you invest in a 'topic' to react faster in certain situations later.*
>
> (Software developer 3, interview)

The software developer points out that they use the same coding style across software development at MedTech. Moreover, this is also applicable to test descriptions and software code, milestone documentation, and most of the documentation effort in the organization. However, he keeps things in perspective by emphasizing the efforts of the developers in terms of training and getting used to new development routines. In the end, the invested efforts may turn into an advantage: they save a lot of time and the developers are able to read and understand faster the software codes of their colleagues.

Assurance of Human Safety

We consider the industry for medical technologies as risk averse and, thus, very safety oriented. Standards are an important aspect of safety. A software developer views standards as a way to *assure human safety*:

> *The standards shall ensure that the product is safe: first, for the user, for patients, and also for the company since we cannot deliver a defective product. It is a very hard frame we have for medical devices. However, it doesn't hinder us that much, since we have to consider several safety requirements for the product anyway.* (Software developer 1, interview)

In her eyes, the medical staff and the patients are the people to be protected. Moreover, she considers human safety as significant for MedTech to avoid products harming human safety. Assurance of human safety is a shared meaning among the employees. She also explains that MedTech has internalized this habit for a long time and develops in line with safety requirements.

Learning Opportunity

The meaning of standards as *learning opportunity* has two different aspects for employees at MedTech. First, several trainings are offered for employees regarding SOP-compliant software development:

> *The last time, two standards were updated. So, we have to prepare trainings for these standards and our internal process, our SOP. We have to prepare mandatory trainings for our SOP every second year or even every year. And laser application, we have to do it every year. Even when the standards didn't change, you have to repeat these trainings.*
>
> (Software quality manager 1, interview)

The software quality manager explains that every time the SOP changes, they adjust training modules which the developers have to attend and to later apply in their daily work. Further, some of these modules have to be repeated constantly. Second, the employees of software quality, regulatory affairs, and clinical affairs who directly deal with standards participate constantly in standard-related training.

Base for Certification

The system engineer of the Siberia project illustrates the meaning of standards as a *base for certification*:

> *At the beginning of each project, you have to choose the applicable standards in cooperation with the regulatory* [affairs] *unit. There is a list including all worldwide relevant standards you need for worldwide approvals.*
>
> (System engineer, interview)

The relevant standards at MedTech are the base for a worldwide certification of the product. For this reason, MedTech always identifies them at the beginning of each development project.

Key to the Market

Once products of MedTech have passed the approval process, they are allowed to enter the market of the certifying country. Thus, another aspect of standards becomes evident—they are a *key to the market*, as a software developer explains:

> *The authorities stipulate the standards. And these standards are determined by the markets where you want to sell the devices. You have to pass certain approvals. Otherwise you are not allowed to enter the market.*
>
> (Software developer 1, interview)

The intended markets determine which standards MedTech needs to comply with. The standards are considered as key: when MedTech complies with them, it is allowed to access the market with its products.

Rules of the Game

Very representative for MedTech in general is the meaning of standards as the *rules of the game*. The software quality manager explains this signification very appropriately:

> *We have the standard and it is like in a game. You have to know the rules of the game before you start.* (Software quality manager 1, interview)

The production of medical devices is the game that MedTech plays and the standards represent not less than the rules of this game. In this description, the software quality manager emphasizes the rigour of standards: they have to be accepted, understood, and followed by MedTech; otherwise, the disposal of medical devices would not work.

Non-Relevant for Software Developers

Another symptomatic aspect of standards as interpretative schemes at MedTech is represented in the meaning as *non-relevant for software developers*. A software developer describes the minor relevance of the standards as such for his work:

> *The developers do not have to deal as much with the standards, if you are solely a software developer. The whole system is broken down into a system specification, and then there are module and component specifications. And it is specified in a very detailed way what we have to do and by doing so we already comply with the standards. Hence, it is not necessary to think about whether you comply with the standards or not. Usually, if you implement the requirements then everything is fine.* (Software developer 1, interview)

The design of the mentioned module and component specifications originate from MedTech's SOPs. As long as the software developers follow the requirements of the SOP, they simultaneously comply with standard requirements. The standards as such are not relevant for software developers, since the software quality assurance department regularly translates the standard requirements into SOP.

6.3 Standards as Facilities in MedTech's Software Development

Throughout our inquiries, the employees at MedTech had access to a plethora of different allocative and authoritative resources for the enactment of standards. The handling of standards and the translation into internal directives is well institutionalized in the organization. Hence resources for standard enactment are also firmly institutionalized at MedTech. Different standard-related functional areas are served by several roles (e.g. the software quality manager, regulatory affairs manager, risk manager, software testers) which emerged in response to the requirements of market regulation by standards (e.g. Medical Device Act, FDA guidelines). MedTech provides sufficient financial resources for standard enactment and the resulting accomplishment of standard-related tasks. Consequently, the software developers are shielded from standard requirements by the internal standard document, the SOP, and the central unit handling standards, the software quality unit. The software quality unit is responsible for monitoring the enactment of standards in software development at MedTech. The SOP is the most powerful allocative resource at MedTech and results from intense efforts for structuring their standard enactment. Table 6.2 summarizes the different resources and their transformative impact.

Table 6.2 Standards as facilities at MedTech

Resource	Description	Transformative capacity	Transformative impact
Authoritative resources			
The powerful software quality managers	Implement and manage standard compliant processes; design and maintain SOP, document templates and deliverable list.	High	High impact due to their central role in the process of standard enactment.
The shielded software developers	Develop software for medical devices and follow standard compliant prescriptions of the SOP.	Low	Low impact; they are shielded from standard requirements through organizational arrangements (e.g. software quality manager, SOP).
The software project managers—mediators between the units	Manage software parts of the projects (e.g. Fidelio, Siberia).	Medium	Medium impact; they moderate software development needs and standard requirements between different stakeholders in a project.
The senior software manager—mediator between the units	Manages software development at MedTech; supervises the software development projects (e.g. Fidelio, Siberia).	Medium	Medium impact; moderates between software development and the other stakeholders in the organization (e.g. software quality).
The software testers	Test the software code and the final product; accomplish documentation and reviews.	Low	Exercise medium impact due to documentation and review tasks they are taking over from the software quality managers.
The regulatory affairs manager—the interface to the world of standards	Manages regulatory requirements for each product and passes information to the development projects.	Medium	Medium impact; work is highly standard relevant, however, they participate only in the beginning and in the end of projects.
The risk manager	Perform risk management based on standard requirements for the development projects.	Low	Low impact due to limited responsibility regarding standards (standard enactment only for risk management; standards only one risk amongst others to monitor)
The product manager—advocate of the market	Manages the medical device during the entire product life cycle.	Low	Low impact due to a lack of knowledge about standards and standard enactment in the organization.

Continued

Table 6.2 *Continued*

Resource	Description	Transformative capacity	Transformative impact
Allocative resources			
Financial resources—often discussed, seldom denied	Transformative resource: can be transformed into other resources.	High	High impact; even though it is often discussed, financial resources are sufficiently provided by the higher management.
The powerful SOP	Internal standard document for software development at MedTech. Defines processes, milestones, roles, and documents.	High	High impact; central resource for standard enactment; central product of the metastructuring process around standards at MedTech.
Document templates	Defines the design and content of required and recommended documents for a standard compliant development.	High	High impact due to their importance for the entire standard compliant documentation process.
The software deliverables list—a tiny list only, of high importance though	Defines the required and standard compliant documents per milestone.	High	High impact; highly debated in the beginning of each project and strictly followed once it is finally defined
Milestones—slicing the development process	Milestones for the completion of development phases.	Medium	Medium impact; milestones are often aligned to the formal approval process.
Integrated management system—the chamber of compliance	Document management system for standard compliant documents for the approval process.	Medium	Medium impact; often used during audits from the authorities
Team foundation server	Requirements management system, used for design documents, source code management, bug tracking, and versioning.	Medium	Medium impact; could be higher if only one tool for requirements management was used.
IBM rational	Requirements management system, used for requirements and tests.	Medium	Medium impact; could be higher if only one tool for requirements management was used.

6.3.1 Authoritative Resources

6.3.1.1 The Powerful Software Quality Manager

The software quality manager plays a central role in the enactment of standards and the SOP as the central standard document at MedTech. One of the software quality managers explains his tasks:

> *We work for 20 per cent on general quality topics, performing audits or carrying out trainings for software developers. Further 20 per cent, I work in smaller projects…and the remaining 60 per cent are for the Fidelio project whereupon each week is different.* (Software quality manager 2, interview)

Besides the work as software quality managers for the software development projects, the software quality managers conduct audits and carry out employee training periodically or when significant changes of the SOP are made. Consequently, the software quality managers claim responsibility for all standard-related tasks at MedTech:

> *We, from the quality side, we are responsible that things are in line with the standards. With the EN 62304, we have a specific standard to comply with. And once the device is ready, we have to make the approval.… The documents have to be structured and formatted in a certain way; otherwise they* [the regulatory authorities] *throw it back to us.*
>
> (Head of software quality, interview)

The head of software quality derives the significance of the software quality work from the necessity of correctly implemented standard requirements—in this case, the structure and format of documents. Otherwise, MedTech would not be able to pass the approval process. At MedTech, the software developers perceive the software quality managers as the ones to ask about standard-related questions: '*If I need detailed information, I would always ask software quality: "What should I fill in there, what do I have to do?"*' (software developer 1, interview).

The standards require software quality roles in development processes nowadays. A software project manager explains why:

> *For instance software quality, it comes from the standards. They require an independent authority that assesses the quality of software. Therefore, these*

> *roles came up. With software quality, we started about 2008. Before, we only had software development and they managed both programming and testing. But, if you monitor yourself, there is always the risk of not being independent.*
> (Software project manager 2, interview)

The software quality unit at MedTech is the authority in the organization that assesses software quality independently from the software developers. At MedTech, the first software quality roles were implemented in 2008. Over time, the software quality unit grew to a veritable unit:

> *[W]e formed a department together with regulatory affairs which was one person only at that time. We were fewer people. I was the third software quality manager when I started .... Now, we are seven software quality managers.*
> (Software quality manager 2, interview)

Nowadays there are seven employees working as software quality managers. Regulatory affairs later became a sub-unit on its own. Software quality managers are highly safety-oriented. They are considered as risk-averse, which can be estimated by their approach to bug fixing of software code: 'a fix is a high risk itself. It might mess up the code more than it helps. And at this point, I am always on the safe side' (software quality manager 2, interview).

During the project meetings for the Siberia as well as the Fidelio project, the software quality managers constantly scrutinized the quality of software (see Box 6.1). They obviously have the highest transformative capacity among all roles at MedTech.

6.3.1.2 The Shielded Software Developers

Software development at MedTech has increased over recent years. Nowadays, it makes up a large share of the development activities in general. Some of the product releases are even software releases only. Software developers thus represent the biggest group at MedTech. During recent years, regulation has increased and software developers have noticed these changes in their daily practices:

> *The first thing I've noticed was that I have to write a huge amount of tests now...we have to apply about double the effort now.... That's the first thing coming from regulations. We have to make sure that the code is safe and does the right thing. And we make a lot of effort to write test plans.*
> (Software developer 3, interview)

Box 6.1 Observation protocol: design review meeting, Siberia, 24 September 2015

In the project Siberia, the team holds a design review meeting. The software project manager, Michael, presents both the hardware- and software-related development steps of the last months. While Michael presents a specific diagram of a state-machine, the head of software quality, Tom, comments sharply: 'I don't want to see this logic in [this part of the device]'. A hot discussion evolves where Michael tries to defend the diagram and the states he used. However, Tom and the senior software architect of another project are not satisfied: 'Guys, sorry, this is no safety concept. We have to keep [this device] clean, it has to be safe.' Michael, puzzled and frustrated, adds: 'You have to explain that again. Do we really need a separate state for the software?' At this point, Bruce, the senior software manager, jumps in and somehow ends the discussion: 'if Tom asks for it, then the assessors will ask as well'. At the end of the presentation, time is running out and Bruce asks snippily, while looking to the present software quality managers: 'and now, the verdict of the jury, please'. After the meeting, Bruce explains the rigour of the software quality regarding the documentation of the development efforts: 'We call it bus or lottery principle. If someone gets hit by a bus the next day or if a person wins in the lottery, then she is gone and the knowledge as well'.

The software developer mentions the tremendously increased test efforts as the most significant change over the years. Moreover, they introduced new practices like code review and organization-wide standardized ways of commenting on the software code. Management considers the software developers as the technical core of the organization and therefore shields them from excessive administrative or standard requirements. The software project manager handles these tasks, as one of the software developers explains:

> *We would like to do it this way, but the standard would not allow us to do it in this way since it is too dangerous or so. Therefore, they* [software project managers] *have a conflict there. Moreover, Kate* [software project manager 2]... *tries to intercept these things so that it would not concern us* [the software developers]. (Software developer 3, interview)

Next to software project managers, the senior management at MedTech implemented further roles to separate the software developers from the increased amount of different tasks: testers and software quality managers. SOPs are a further mechanism to reduce complexity for the developers. Consequently, software developers as well as other developers at MedTech are not affected by standards directly but align their development work to the SOPs:

> *I am not so much into it* [the standards]. *Rather, our SOP guides me.... Nevertheless, there are new topics and there is no standard for it yet.... And, at this point, the developer has to deal with the standard, what does it mean? However, that is rather an exception.*
>
> (Software project manager 1, interview)

The software project manager argues that developers only deal with standards in exceptional cases, for instance, when there is no established standard for a specific topic yet. Finally, the head of software quality emphasizes an important fact:

> *Software development is not only responsible for the code to do what it should do. It is also about the things around it. They have to think about the appropriate tools, strategies for automating certain things, to build up test equipment. That is quite specific, we from the software quality, we do not have a say in this. That lies firmly in the hands of the developers.*
>
> (Head of software quality, interview)

Even though the organization encapsulates the software developers by implementing separate roles and the SOP for software development, software developers are still responsible for their direct development environment (e.g. development tools, test equipment, and process automation) and its compliance with standards.

6.3.1.3 The Software Project Manager and Senior Software Manager—Mediators between the Units

For the software part of each project, a software project manager is appointed. According to the head of software quality, it became necessary since the administrative tasks of the software developers grew constantly:

> *It makes sense to install a specific software project manager for the software developers. The developers are real developers and they have to compile more*

and more documentation. It increased constantly over the last years. Not every developer is keen on planning and this sort of jokes. It has been found practicable to have someone who communicates to the overall project leader, who makes the planning, the architecture, the design.

(Head of software quality, interview)

The software project manager links the software developers and the rest of the development project: the overall software project manager, the product manager, the software quality, regulatory affairs, and risk managers. One software developer explicates the interest of a software project manager in standard enactment:

For sure, the software project manager because he wants to reach his milestones. And it is part of the milestones to pass all the tests. And the tests are passed when we implemented the standards and the whole program, when the test report is ready and signed. (Software developer 1, interview)

The higher-level supervisor of the software project manager is the senior software manager who coordinates the different software development projects. The senior software manager often discusses standard-related issues with other managers and with the members of the software quality unit:

If it were about software, people would come to me first. And, I am then discussing these issues with the software quality managers. . . . And we have a second senior software manager here at the site. We often sit together and discuss these issues. . . . It can be about regulations, about purchases. For instance, how do we implement automatic testing for a specific system or product?

(Senior software manager, interview)

Further, the senior software manager ensures the practicability of the software development task in light of the demands from standard requirements and administrative tasks. The senior software manager sits at the interface between software development and higher management. She/he often explains peculiarities of the software development process and the underlying interplay with standards to members from the higher management, as one software quality manager highlights:

That is a peculiarity of software development. You don't see what runs under the hood. Non-experts are not able to assess software. There are often voices

> *why we are so slow. Sometimes we need six months for a bug fix since it's not so easy. It is hard to make our point. But it is the task of Bruce* [senior software manager]. *He knows these peculiarities. Nevertheless, already his boss does not.*
> (Software quality manager 2, interview)

6.3.1.4 The Software Testers

In the past, software developers tested their software code themselves. Recent standard requirements, however, required that MedTech has to increase its testing efforts. MedTech implemented a new role, the software tester. The field description in Box 6.2 portrays the motivation for this role.

The software developers at MedTech do not appreciate testing as a work task and react reluctantly when confronted with testing needs. Nowadays, ten software testers work at the software development unit of MedTech. They perceive their work as based on requirements coming from standards for medical devices:

> *The tests base on the requirements. The requirements base on the design and all this is based on regulations regarding specific topics. Therefore, it all runs through to the tests....* (Tester, interview)

By virtue of the proximity of their task to the software quality managers, the testers also accomplish software quality-relevant tasks. The same tester explains: '*even now* [as a tester], *it already affects me. I work on the documentation, I do reviews for documents*' (interview). Due to their quality-related testing tasks, the

Box 6.2 Observation protocol: software quality meeting, Siberia, 12 January 2016

Software quality meetings for the Siberia project take place fortnightly. During one of these meetings, a discussion started about how to integrate the new tester in the project. The head of software quality wants to recruit a software developer for testing purposes. One of the two software quality managers adds: 'everyone has to suffer a bit'. The software project manager reacts a bit irritated while he tries to defend the software developers and their core task, the development: 'too much testing demotivates the developers. You should not do that all the time'.

management at MedTech expanded the testers' responsibilities towards documentation and reviews. Hence, the transformative impact of the testers for standard enactment can be valued as medium.

6.3.1.5 The Regulatory Affairs Manager—The Interface with the World of Standards

A software project manager deduces the forming of a regulatory affairs unit from the increased need for specialists for standards and regulation:

> *These units* [regulatory affairs]...*and their size nowadays is due to the standards. Achieving medical approval is getting more restrictive and much more complicated. You have to develop whole departments. All these rules, the standards, it is so complicated; it has to be done by specialists.*
>
> (Software project manager 2, interview)

In each development project, a regulatory affairs manager oversees the regulatory requirements for the product to be developed. A regulatory affairs manager himself describes his tasks:

> *We take care of the approvals in the different countries and the standards we have to comply with to enter the market there. We inform the project team about the requirements of these standards.... Our task is actually not to implement the standards.... Later on, we make the approval for the different countries. Especially in the US, this is challenging. You have to write many reports and collate documents. At this point, we are much more involved in the process.*
>
> (Regulatory affairs manager, nterview)

As the regulatory affairs manager explains, the team of regulatory affairs is not involved in the actual standard implementation. They act in the beginning of each project, when they inform about regulatory requirements for each country where MedTech wants to sell its products. Moreover, they are active at the end of a project when it actually comes to the approval of the product against each national authority. Thus, he distinguishes his domain from the tasks of the software quality as follows:

> *Quality management takes care about the quality of the documents. They should be formally correct and usable. They should be in English, etc. In the end, we only pick what we have to deliver* [for approval].
>
> (Regulatory affairs manager, interview)

The software quality team is responsible for the correct standard implementation. Standards are software quality business, whereas law and regulation are the domain of regulatory affairs: '*we consider legal changes via regulatory affairs. However, changes in standards, that is the task of software quality*' (head of software quality, interview). Thus, the transformative capacity of the regulatory affairs manager is lower than the software quality managers' but still on a medium level.

6.3.1.6 The Risk Manager

Risk management and the tasks of the risk managers at MedTech are based on the requirements of the standard DIN EN 14971 as part of the Medical Devices Act. They are responsible for the enactment of DIN EN 14971 and therefore must take considerable actions to implement a standard-compliant risk management. They act jointly with the quality management team (among others, software quality) in a centralized unit:

> *Quality management has four teams. We work for the hardware development and we do both risk management and quality management for hardware. For software, we do only risk management.*
>
> (Head of risk management, interview)

However, in the daily business of MedTech, the risk management unit is not engaged in the enactment of standards to the same extent as the software quality managers or even the members of the regulatory affairs unit. Consequently, the risk managers' transformative impact for standard enactment is rather limited.

6.3.1.7 The Product Manager—Advocate of the Market

At MedTech, product managers are responsible for guiding the success of a product in a certain market. The product managers do not engage in standard enactment. However, the success of the product depends on the homologation in certain markets, and hence on standard-compliant development. A software developer places responsibility on the product managers, since '*they want to sell their products. This means, they can only enter the markets if they respect the existing standards*' (software developer 1, interview).

However, among the team members of the development projects at MedTech, there is the opinion that the product managers do not possess the necessary knowledge on standards and the sensibility regarding their enactment

Box 6.3 Observation protocol: milestone meeting, Fidelio, 6 October 2016

After the team of the Fidelio project have accomplished important features of the new product, they hold an informal milestone meeting where they present this development step to the product managers and members of the higher management. Martha and Kate alternately present the finished features with a PowerPoint presentation and a live demonstration of the new software version. The product managers question the new features in a rather cool manner and make suggestions on how to change certain aspects of the product: 'Why can't we just call the button and the menu like [name]?' The senior software manager, Bruce, explains ironically: 'these names are standardized as well. People usually know it, some [the product managers e.g.] don't'. Further in the presentation, a discussion arises concerning the versioning of the software, where the product managers do not understand the idea of explicit versioning of each part of the software and the software itself. Again, Bruce jumps in with a grin: 'versioning is a regulatory requirement since it is a medical device'. The overall project manager adds: 'ignoring it is close to breaking the law'.

in the routines of the software developers (see Box 6.3). It seems that product managers have a low transformative capacity for standard enactment.

6.3.2 Allocative Resources

6.3.2.1 Financial Resources—Often Discussed, Seldom Denied

MedTech has produced medical devices for several decades. It is a well-established producer of high-quality medical technology. Over recent years, turnover increased constantly by about 7 per cent and reached about 1 billion Euros in 2015. Between 2012 and 2015, the company was very successful, with a constant profit of about 13 per cent of turnover. Further, it consistently spent about 11 per cent of turnover on in-house research & development.

Throughout the software development projects, employees address financial resources when either the need of personnel becomes obvious (see Box 6.4) or when they discuss the situation of temporary staff at MedTech.

Box 6.4 Observation protocol: software quality meeting, Siberia, 3 April 2017

During many of the observed project meetings at MedTech, discussions arise about the deployment of developers or testers and the fact that there is either only a low project budget available or not enough personnel. Exemplarily, in the Siberia project software quality meeting, the software project manager, Michael, reports: 'on the subject…we have money [ironically]. We cannot finance Steve [a tester] anymore after June'. Higher management cut the budget and the tester has to work for a project which now has higher priority. However, Steve is needed again in September.

The enactment of standards and regulatory requirements at MedTech is time-consuming and costly. A software quality manager explains:

> *Standards are so complicated, that's a lot of effort. Many people work for it for a lot of time. That is a lot of money. An audit in the USA? We have to check everything before the assessor gets here. A lot of money and a lot of time.*
> (Software quality manager 1, interview)

The software quality manager especially emphasizes the costly approval process for selling MedTech's products in the US market. Due to different national regulations, different standards have to be met, which consumes financial resources. Employees at MedTech accept this situation since they see no alternative to these costly tasks:

> *It's a huge effort but we should accept that, we have to do it. And we have to plan for it and communicate it. It doesn't help to save time in the beginning which we would need anyway at the end.* (Head of software quality, interview)

The head of software quality particularly stresses the efforts at the beginning of each development project, which entails planning and communication of standard- and SOP-related requirements. Finally, employees perceive the cost-intensive production of medical devices at MedTech as self-evident:

> *But hey, we are* [MedTech]. *We cannot come with cheap parts. We are dedicated to the brand MedTech. However, a good device costs money, it's expensive.*
> (Software developer 2, interview)

At MedTech, for the enactment of standards of the medical device industry and the enactment of the SOP, employees consume a considerable amount of financial resources.

6.3.2.2 The Powerful Standard Operating Procedure

The SOP for software development is the internal standard document for the software developers at MedTech. Developing a customized SOP is suggested by the US FDA for each medical technology company. The head of risk management explains:

> *SOP means standard operating procedure.... Since we release our products to the US market, we decided to align our concepts to the US regulation system... and it says that the producer has to have SOPs for certain topics.... That should be the same for the other producers of medical devices.... It makes no sense otherwise.* (The head of risk management, interview)

SOPs are widely used in the medical device industry. The FDA requires SOPs for specific functional areas like software development for medical devices. The SOP for software development at MedTech guides the software developers through the complex task of standard-compliant software development. The SOP prescribes steps in the development process, project phases and milestones, and documentation requirements such as document templates. MedTech derives the requirements of the SOP from the different requirements of all the standards it has to comply with globally. In consequence, when the standards change, MedTech adjusts the SOP and the software development processes as well (see Box 6.5).

At MedTech, the software developers and other members of the development projects strictly follow the prescriptions of the SOP for software development. The employees recognize the importance of the SOP for the realization of standard compliance. A software developer explains that if something is written in the SOP, it was derived from a standard:

> *We carry out code reviews... a developer performs a visual check of the code of another developer.... that is supposed to come from a certain standard. It prescribes that there has to be something like this.... I don't remember which standard it is. But it has to come from the standards, there has to be a safety aspect.* (Software developer 3, interview)

MedTech produces medical devices for different global markets. It consequently has to consider a plethora of standards for software development.

Box 6.5 Observation protocol: software quality meeting, Siberia, 24 September 2015

During a biweekly software quality meeting, the team members discuss recent changes in the SOP and how they affect the actual project documentation. Carsten, the projects software quality manager, explains: 'So, we have a new SOP. The templates changed as well. And we have to adapt the project's documentation accordingly. There is a new header and new footer area.' Further, the SOP now includes a cybersecurity part and a new scale for error assessment. Carsten asks to consider these templates from now on as they had been discussed in the recent SOP training. According to the software project manager, Michael, the SOP looks almost the same as 10 years ago. He adds smilingly: 'Shall I retrieve an old document?' The team members are not very amused about the additional efforts for the project. However, they take it in good humour, as they seem to be very used to it.

Regarding the software developers, enacting SOPs bears a tremendously important advantage. A software project manager describes:

> *It is an advantage that I don't have to deal with that. There are standards in different countries which are changed frequently. I would have to read them all. There are specialists for that. And they create a guideline* [SOP]*: if you follow these instructions, you comply with all rules in the world. That saves a lot of work. I might not understand everything... but I don't have to deal with these issues.* (Software project manager 2, interview)

While working with SOP instead of different standards, the software developers are encapsulated from the complex and ever-changing demands of the standard requirements. Even though the SOP reduces complexity for the software developers at MedTech, the SOP itself is an equally demanding task due to its number of requirements for the software development process. Thus, many mandatory trainings for the SOP are offered frequently:

> *Each quarter we have a training for the SOP. Mostly when changes to the standards come in. Well, not only changes but also optimizations.*
>
> (Software developer 3, interview)

The SOP is a powerful resource with a high transformative capacity. It is the most important document that guides the software development process at MedTech. Most organizational members refer to this document during software development on a regular basis.

6.3.2.3 Document Templates—'Follow me Strictly'

The employees at MedTech compile a significant number of documents. To a large extent, these documents are the same for all projects, which allows project members to adapt them efficiently to other projects. Hence, MedTech chose consistent document templates:

> *That is really transparent, we have a template for each type of document. It defines the document structure and we are not allowed to change it.... And by following it, we are sure that we conform fully.... It would be insane if the developers had to deal with it, right?* (Software architect, interview)

The software architect mentions another advantage of consistent templates. If they follow the templates, the software developers at MedTech likewise comply with the regulatory requirements. Effectively, software development complies with the most important standards for MedTech. The head of software quality explains: '*If you use the templates you can be sure about complying to the DIN EN 62304 and the FDA guidelines*' (interview). With these harmonized document templates, MedTech guarantees that quality assurance is standardized across MedTech. However, the process of changing these documents is cumbersome. Software developers have to come to terms with templates that sometimes appear counterintuitive or even erroneous (see Box 6.6). In summary, the document templates have a high transformative capacity.

6.3.2.4 Software Deliverables List—A Tiny List only, of High Importance though

In the practice of software development at MedTech, the software deliverables list is very present. Its use is mandatory and specified in the SOP. For specific milestones, the employees at MedTech have to compile a defined number of documents:

> *It is a list of documents which we have to compile for a certain milestone.... We compile a certain amount of documents for each component of the software.... There is a requirements document, a design document, a test plan,*

Box 6.6 Observation protocol: software quality meeting, Siberia, 6 February 2017

During a routine software quality meeting, Michael and Tom discover an error in a SOP-defined Word template. Tom, the head of software quality, explains that the testing itself needs to be traceable: 'I want to understand, who tested what'. Michael, the software project manager, answers that according to the template this is only necessary for the errors discovered. Bruce, the senior software manager, comes to Michael's defence: 'I would interpret the table [of the template] here in the same way as Michael did'. Apparently, Michael strictly followed the document template. However, the document template is erroneous, as they found out in this particular software quality meeting.

> *a test report. You need it for each component.... And there are higher level documents which developers do not touch. That's only for software quality or testers.... That's about forty documents in total that we have to write for our Fidelio project.* (Software developer 3, interview)

The software developer of the Fidelio project only processes certain documents. Testers and especially the software quality managers handle the other documents on the software deliverables list. A software quality manager describes the main purpose of the software deliverables list:

> *For each release, you compile such a list so that you know which documents belong to this release.... And you can easily find these documents through their number and version. You would find it quickly in the integrated management system where all these documents are stored. There are more than 1000 documents now.* (Software quality manager 2, interview)

The deliverables list is a guideline for the software quality managers of what documents they have to deliver for a certain release. For their work in a project, it is one of the most important documents. It retains the status of a development project and the product under development. For standard enactment, the software deliverables list is a powerful resource. The members of the development project define the software deliverables list in the beginning of each project:

> [The deliverables list] *is defined at the beginning of each project.... You can add or leave out parts, that's allowed, as long as the quality manager signs it. Nevertheless, if the list is accepted then you have to deliver all these documents.*
> (System engineer, interview)

As the system engineer explains, once the software quality manager accepts the software deliverables list, it is mandatory to compile all the defined documents at the end of the specific development phase for the milestone.

6.3.2.5 Milestones—Slicing the Development Process

In the SOP for software development at MedTech, milestones for different development phases are defined:

> *There are different phases for us. Then, we have all these milestones: M1, M2.1, M2.2, M3, M4. That is all planned in advance. M2.1 is feature complete, so the developers should have implemented everything at this point.*
> (Software quality manager, interview)

The software quality manager exemplarily points to milestone M2.1 which is particularly important for the software developers at MedTech. M2.1 is a milestone linked to the formal approval process, as a software developer explains in a logbook entry:

> *We reached milestone M2.1. That's an official milestone of our development process. It will be submitted to the authorities and, hence, it is documented accordingly. With this milestone, we would like to have a product that contains all defined features.* (Software developer 3, logbook)

The milestones for software development at MedTech reflect the temporal requirements for product approval in the different countries. They are an important measure of the progress of a development project.

6.3.2.6 The Integrated Management System—The Chamber of Compliance

The integrated management system is a document management system in which are stored all documents that matter for proving standard compliance and meeting regulatory requirements:

We have kind of a document management system called integrated management system. That's a huge Excel table. There are all official and signed documents for a specific project.... and there is a search function to get information more quickly. And you can sort it regarding locations and topics. In addition, you have to take care that it is the latest version. (Software developer 1, interview)

The software quality managers as well as the senior software manager consult the integrated management system for document-related questions in their daily routine. During audits of the different national authorities, the use of the integrated management system facilitates the challenge to pass these audits. When documents change and new versions are released, these are immediately reflected in the integrated management system. The senior software manager explains the use of the integrated management system with an example of changed SOPs (see Box 6.7). Overall, the integrated management system holds a medium transformative capacity.

6.3.2.7 Team Foundation Server and IBM Rational

MedTech uses two different software solutions for managing requirements, tests, and tracking of software development efforts. The software developers use the team foundation server for design documents, source code management, bug tracking, and as a versioning system for their software code. They deploy IBM Rational for managing requirements and the test plans:

We use IBM Rational for the requirements and the test plans. For the design documents, we use the team foundation server. Further, we use the team

Box 6.7 Observation protocol: discussion with senior software manager, Siberia, 19 October 2016

After the regular meetings, the senior software manager, Bruce, often explains to us the particularities of software development at MedTech. In one of these conversations, we discuss the different SOP versions and their evolution over time. Bruce shows us the integrated management system, where all documents are stored in a library-like manner. He explains that if you would like to check certain changes over time, you only have to look in the integrated management system. During audits, employees at MedTech regularly consult the integrated management system to get the correct document version for specific requests of the assessors.

foundation server for source code management, bug tracking, and the versioning system. We do not have an interface between the team foundation server and IBM Rational.... we wanted to but it appeared not to be practical. The requirements are changing all the time... until shortly before we finish implementing it.

(Software architect, interview)

All the team members of both projects, Fidelio and Siberia, use both software solutions in their daily development routine. Whereas the use of such software tools is not a standard requirement itself, they both facilitate the standard requirements regarding documentation, traceability, and verification. Hence, both tools are powerful allocative resources for standard enactment at MedTech with a medium transformative capacity. The head of risk management explains the advantages of IBM rational:

That is traceability. We have to ensure traceability. And IBM Rational is a wonderful program for that. I can link different modules.... I have a certain point in the risk plan; that we shall not exceed certain temperatures. And then, I can link it to the specification that defines these material properties.

(Head of risk management, interview)

6.4 Standards as Social Norm in MedTech's Software Development

6.4.1 Legitimation of Organizational Deviance from Standards

On the one hand, the employees in the investigated development projects at MedTech share the view that compliance with standards is part of their success and long-term survival in the medical technology market. On the other hand, compared to the two other cases in this book, MedTech appears to the employees as an exceptional case in view of the strict compliance with standards. If deviation is discussed among the employees at MedTech, then it is rather framed as overachieving than underperforming standard requirements. A software quality employee stated in comparison to his previous work experiences:

Standards are more strictly followed here in this company since we have a whole group dealing with standards. In the medical technology sector the audits, the controls, and laws, for instance the EU law, are stricter.

(Software quality employee 1, interview)

The strict standard compliance at MedTech materializes in the regulatory affairs unit which is a separate unit dealing with standards and certification strategies full time. As a legitimation for the strict standard compliance, the software quality manager points to the distinctiveness of the medical technology sector with its strict standards and legal regulations. Further employees, like the tester, mention the regulatory affairs unit as a sign of strict compliance with standards as well:

> *They* [regulatory affairs unit] *are relatively strict here in the company but that is simply their job. It is pointed out directly to the risks and that is their role.... In other companies where I have worked, they did not have a department like that. In this case however, it surely is okay if a problem is examined as precisely.... It could be the case that if a problem is reported from a customer..., then we have to ban the product or block the delivery.* (Tester, interview)

As a legitimation for the strict compliance of standards, the tester refers to the product safety and the potential avoidance of product problems, which would eventually lead to economic losses and additional efforts due to a product ban. Hence, she assesses the strict standard compliance at MedTech as helpful and necessary. A similar notion can be reconstructed from the following:

> *They definitely take care of the standards being implemented in our SOP. That is simply what they are obliged to. I think that is a must.... I know that there are companies with an ISO 13485 certification where the development process looks differently. Surely, you can also manage it with less rigid process instructions. However, the question always is: do you still understand what you have once done? Moreover, the interesting thing is indeed: the standard is one thing, the certification another one. The third aspect is that you have to get approval for every possible market and you have to adapt your SOP accordingly, so it is only one document at the end and you can get certification worldwide.*
> (Head of software quality, interview)

The head of software quality legitimizes the strict compliance with standards with the sheer necessity in the medical technology sector. However, he gives some additional legitimations for MedTech's strict approach: the chance of receiving a certification and the worldwide validity of the SOP for certifications. Altogether, the head of software quality assesses the strict compliance with standards as a precondition for selling products worldwide.

The senior software manager also refers to certification when he describes MedTech's compliance with standards:

> *Regarding the certification, if you consider the regulators, who then say: we are the ones who audit the standard and when they interpret the standard in a form completely contrary to ours, then we have a problem. Mostly, you do not start discussing with the regulatory authorities and say: you are not right, your interpretation of the standard is wrong. The game goes the opposite way. That is the danger, which makes it all more demanding. You want to counteract this concern. That is the topic of risk affinity: we certainly do not want to develop for 4 years and then realise afterwards: Oh, we have interpreted the standard in the wrong way, a little too lax, stupid game, two more years of clinical studies. Instead, we rather say: ok, the standard says that, in the strictest interpretation, that would mean to do it like that; ok let us implement it like that. This will cost us altogether 1 year extra, but we eventually are still faster than if we would take the risk and then we would need another 2 years of reworking. That is a real area of tension.* (Senior software manager, interview)

The senior software manager refers to MedTech's standard interpretation as the strictest possible. He connects the decision for strict compliance with MedTech's cautious risk management approach. In the range of possible interpretations of standards, MedTech does not take any risks regarding the receipt of a product certification. According to the senior software manager, however, it means investing additional efforts in the short run but saving time and costs in the long run.

Some employees also view MedTech's strict compliance with standards critically, as the last example shows:

> *Well, there always is the question: How much do you invest to satisfy the authorities? You can surely also get a little obsessed about it. And I have that feeling here in the company. They try so hard to manage everything in these audits so smoothly, without ever challenging: let us do less and let us then see how they react. I think that is not quite legitimate.*
>
> (Software developer 2, interview)

The forms of deviation from standards shown in Table 6.3 will support the software developer's critique of enacting standards too 'smoothly' in several different ways regarding standard enactment.

Table 6.3 Legitimation of deviations from standards at MedTech

Forms of deviation	Legitimation of deviation	Legitimation of which project members	Legitimation frame
Deviation from standard requirements	Regulatory changes of standard requirements necessitate re-adaptation of documentation	Head of risk management, software quality manager	Regulatory
Deviation from required development phases	Practicability of the SOP for the actual development process	Senior software manager	Administrative
	Internal standard procedures should not obstruct the software development work	Senior software manager	Administrative
	Official permission due to a less safety critical release of a product	Software project manager	Regulatory
Deviation from review requirements	Interest and role of the lead of software quality: responsible representative towards external assessors	Senior software manager	Administrative
	Additional opportunity to clarify audit-relevant questions already at the beginning of the development work	Senior software manager	Regulatory
	Adjust time expectations of involved external partners	Software project manager, software developer	Business
	Adjust product requirements of the product management	Software project manager	Business/ administrative
	Adjust delivery deadlines of the general management	Software project manager	Business
	Deviance saves costs in the long run	Software project manager	Business
	Deviance saves time in the long run	Software project manager	Business
Deviation from documentation requirements	MedTech's fear to do anything wrong and thus to eventually loose product certification	Software project manager	Regulatory
	MedTech's general cautious approach to risk assessment	Software project manager	Business
	Practicability of the SOP for the actual development process	Software developer	Administrative

6.4.1.1 Deviation from Standard Requirements—Interim Due to Regulatory Changes

In his description, the head of risk management explains how the change of a standard creates a form of interim deviation from standard requirements, which is due to regulatory changes:

> *Our product has expired on the first of March in Brazil and a new law was introduced, and it was clear we have to deal with it.... We have to use the 62304* [the standard IEC 62304], *but we originally wanted to reuse partial functions from the predecessor model but that has not been developed in compliance with 62304.... If in doubt, that means redesign, project delay, to decide when we can manage this in terms of resources, how many resources do we need for rewriting. These are the hard consequences, every time a standard is changing. On a regulatory basis, we have to be compliant with them anyway but it is fatal if the standards change in the meantime. Then you have additional expenses for things you had not thought of.* (Head of risk management, interview)

Due to changed regulations, MedTech has to adapt the processes, documentation, and eventually the design of the product in order to become compliant again. Consequently, MedTech's processes and documentation are temporarily deviant from the new standards or updated standard requirements. Legitimation for this deviation derives from the external process of changing standards and the practical necessity of a certain amount of time to re-adapt to the new regulation (regulatory frame). However, the head of risk management especially stresses the additional efforts and expenses that need to be mobilized to overcome this temporary deviation and to comply with standards again. A quality assurance employee who is responsible for standard compliance at the project level further underlines the aspect of time:

> *Now we have had all the fuss with Brazil where they had changed a law overnight, so that we have a gap now because we could not manage to adapt the documentation as quickly as needed to receive the certification again. Legal changes enter via the regulatory affairs division and standard changes should come in via the quality* [assurance] *division. And then, certainly, we have to check to which degree the processes still fit.*
>
> (Software quality manager 2, interview)

It becomes evident that both the head of risk management and the quality assurance employee experience this deviation from standards as stressful and effortful, with negative consequences such as reworking, project delays, or even loss of certification.

6.4.1.2 Deviation from Required Development Phases—Omitted Development Phases

The senior software manager of MedTech explains a deviation from the required development phases defined in the SOP of software development:

> *Especially the software development process gives us the opportunity to adapt the process—we call it tailoring. For a specific process, if smaller or bigger, we can leave out or add parts, simply change things in the development process, in order to reduce or intensify the procedure when we would normally not do that.... However, that depends on the people, the people who can play with it and who have the knowledge and the appropriate experience to say: ok, that is the process, that is the frame I can move within. I would like to deviate from that, I will write it down, I will give clear reasons for it, and then I will go this separate path, which is possible and will be approved.... That is why I would rather link it to the people than the process as such.*
>
> (Senior software manager, interview)

The software development SOP specifies all relevant phases of the software development process but also leaves room for adapting the rules of the SOP to the actual development process. The senior software manager explains the possibility of adding or leaving out parts or phases of the development process. According to the senior software manager, any deviation from the SOP, however, requires good reasoning and approval by the certification bodies. Legitimation for this deviation is drawn from the practicability of the SOP for the actual development process (technical frame). Interestingly, the senior software manager attributes responsibility for this form of deviation to the employees at MedTech. He stresses the point that deviation as a separate path from the SOP is only for the courageous and experienced employees at MedTech. This is supported by an explanation of the software project manager, who indicates the minimal scope of deviations at MedTech:

> *We are allowed to deviate from the process, but that is only for very very little trivialities.... A real deviance happens only when you say, ok, let us have an M4* [Milestone 4] *immediately instead of an M3* [Milestone 3] *before, since you do not have to take a user-acceptance-test. Because you do not actually change anything regarding the measurement procedure of the product but*

Box 6.8 Observation protocol: milestone meeting, Siberia, 26 June 2016

At the beginning of a milestone meeting, the software project manager ironically introduces his presentation: 'This is software milestone M4, which actually is milestone 3 but now called M4.1'. Later in the meeting, the service manager points to the heading of the review document which says 'M4' instead of 'M4.1'. While the software project manager changes the heading in the review template for the milestone meeting, the senior software manager ironically asks: 'Do you think this template change is allowed?' Some other participants are laughing. The senior software manager explains that they decided to set up this milestone 4.1 as a hybrid milestone, hence deviating from the milestone sequence as required in MedTech's SOPs: it is both a milestone M3 and has already accomplished parts of milestone M4.

you only add a printer, for instance. Otherwise though, the rules are mostly followed. (Software project manager 1, interview)

The software project manager labels 'a real deviance' at MedTech as an intentional deviation from the sequence of process milestones as required in the SOP. However, as legitimation he cites the official permission of leaving out standard required tests due to a less safety-critical release of a product (regulatory frame). Thus, the legitimation itself is within standard-compliant notions of a software development process. Box 6.8 shows the application of a 'hybrid' milestone as deviation from the required development phases at MedTech.

The ironical tenor of both the software project manager and the senior software manager shows how bizarre some of the requirements from the internal SOPs appear to the employees at MedTech. Responsibility for the bizarre situation thus is indirectly ascribed to the SOP as an organizational authority.

6.4.1.3 Deviation from Review Requirements—Adding Informal Milestone Meetings

Box 6.9 illustrates how the employees at MedTech decided to implement a voluntarily milestone as deviant from the internal SOP. We reconstructed this deviation from review requirements since the additional milestone is not a

Box 6.9 Observation protocol: milestone meeting, Siberia, 24 September 2015

During our investigations, we discovered that some of the milestone meetings we attended where informal milestones in addition to the milestone sequence as required in the SOP. After such an informal design review, the software manager explained to us that the design review used to be part of the internal SOP but now is an optional meeting. However, the head of the quality assurance department re-implemented the design review as an additional milestone meeting, since it gives the possibility to clarify questions, which are also frequently being asked by external audits. The structure of the design review is guided by the documentation structure, which makes the design review even more complex than before. However, the senior software manager adds that the need of the design review is decided in view of the development project's size. During the design review meeting the head of software quality assurance takes a central role and keeps on asking about and reminding of standard relevant issues like safety and testing. The senior software manager defends him: 'If Tom [head of software quality assurance] is asking this, external bodies will ask this as well'.

mandatory standard requirement and even more complex than the previous mandatory milestone. As legitimation for the implementation of the additional, informal milestone, the senior software manager refers to the interest and role of the head of software quality (administrative frame). As MedTech's representative towards external assessors, he legitimizes this deviation by the additional opportunity to clarify audit-relevant questions at the beginning of the development work (regulatory frame). Responsibility for this deviation thus is directed towards the head of software quality as an interface with the assessors. His central role becomes evident in the design review meeting when defending another employee's legitimation with regard to standard certification.

The head of software quality himself assesses the milestones as an important and thorough feature of development work, which should be strictly complied with:

We have a lot of milestones and I find it very important. I am rather a proponent of living them restrictively. That also means to delay them sometimes and to

> *say 'With this milestone we document the current state of the project'. Some see it differently and are rather optimistic.... But it is no use if you have a milestone and it is not worth the paper you have signed. That must be corresponding.*
>
> (Head of software quality, interview)

However, a second example from another development project at MedTech shows further legitimations for the implementation of additional informal milestone meetings. The software project manager of project Fidelio describes in his online logbook the informal feature milestone as a contributing event with several advantages:

> *Feature milestone with the product management: once a requirement (customer view) is implemented by the software development, it is introduced to the product management. The aims of these milestones are: to make the progress visible for external partners, to align implementation and expectations, to have the possibility to change, i.e. the requirements (cost-neutral).Close before the finalization it is too late for changes or it leads to delayed delivery.*
>
> (Software project manager 2, logbook)

The online logbook entry shows that the additional, informal milestones, for instance with the product management, have advantages for meeting external expectations, such as the time expectations of involved external partners, product expectations of the product management, or delivery deadlines of the general management (business frame). Again, the deviant approach of over-complying seems to save costs and time in the end (business frame).

6.4.1.4 Deviation from Documentation Requirements—Adding Documentation

Box 6.10 illustrates how some employees see MedTech's compliance with standards as exaggerated. The software project manager complains about MedTech's documentation efforts being even more than the assessors expect.

This practice can be reconstructed as deviation from regular documentation requirements by adding additional documentation. As a legitimation, the software project manager refers to a general fear at MedTech to do anything wrong, which eventually would mean losing the certification for their products (regulatory frame). Responsibility for the increased documentation is directed outside the project work at the level of general management or subordinated quality management. Both the software project manager and the

Box 6.10 Observation protocol: regular planning meeting, Fidelio, 6 June 2016; milestone meeting, Fidelio, 16 February 2017

After a regular planning meeting of project Fidelio, the software project manager explains several aspects regarding the increase of documentation over time. He points out that the documentation has expanded enormously from fifteen to forty documents nowadays. As a reason for the increase, he mentions that MedTech is documenting too much since there is the fear of doing anything wrong; hence, it is documented more than the assessors expect.

In a later milestone meeting the topic of documentation comes up for discussion again. While pointing to a pile of documents about 40–50 cm high, the software project manager explains that this is the software documentation only, which means half of the entire documentation of the development project. It encompasses already about 1000 pages, printed on both sides. Moreover, at milestone M4 there will be another 1000 pages on top. The software project manager and the software quality assurance employee are making jokes about the eventual totalled weight of the documentation being about 25 kg. After the meeting the software quality assurance employee stresses that during the last 4 years a lot more documents were added. This, however, gives no indication of the increase in complexity and effort, since some former documents with 100 pages now have 280. The software quality assurance employee underlines that the increased documentation heavily influenced their work during the last years.

software quality manager see this form of overachieving deviation from standards as an increasing hindrance to their daily development work.

The advice of an external software consultant underlines the perceived overachieving compliance with standards at MedTech (Box 6.11). The senior software manager refers to MedTech's cautious approach to risk assessment as legitimation for the extensive documentation (administrative frame). He wishes for a less anxious argumentation of risks at MedTech. During the initial meeting with the senior software manager at the beginning of our investigations, he described this practice at MedTech as 'working in a comfort zone' and wished to challenge standards more often since certification bodies have never complained so far.

Box 6.11 Observation protocol: software quality meeting, Siberia, 3 October 2016

During a software quality assurance meeting for the project Siberia, the software project manager tells the story of a consultation at MedTech with an external software standard expert. The consultant claims that he could narrow MedTech's risk analysis document down from 300 to 3 pages. The senior software manager adds that it is often advised to MedTech that they assess risks too anxiously: 'We see risks, where, in doubt, there aren't any. We should argue risks differently.'

6.4.2 Expected Sanctions from Deviance

Regarding the expected sanctions at MedTech, it is obvious that the regulatory pressure from legislation is very high in the field of medical technology, since the safety of human life is affected:

> *Well, these are the regulatory requirements which are different in each country. Some say: The things, which are not tested in our country, will not enter our market. The USA is doing that on product basis. They have clearly verbalized in legislation which products are harmless and which require conducting a study. And that is to be accepted by us.*
>
> (Head of quality management, interview)

Organizational deviance from standards is directly connected to legislative penalties in the respective countries (regulatory frame). Economic sanctions thus can be expected from deviations when MedTech is not able to sell the products (business frame). The system architect puts it clearly:

> *The product management, they want to sell their products. They can only enter the markets if they comply with necessary standards.*
>
> (System architect, interview)

However, as well as this, detrimental consequences for the safety of human life are mentioned as an expected sanction from deviance (ethical frame). One of the testers states with regard to the strict regulations:

> *That is how it is like in the field of medical technology, where I absolutely appreciate that you pay close attention to what is happening and that the authorities control it. . . . I find it important because if I am myself lying under a robot or in front of a device, I want it to work reliably. . . .* (Tester, interview)

Further sanctions are related to the software project manager's and the software quality manager's roles. When asked about his interest in standards, the system architect points out:

> *The quality manager, because they are the ones made responsible. The software project manager certainly, since he or she wants to eventually meet his or her milestones and part of the milestones is the question if the tests are passed. They are passed if all the standards and the whole program is enacted.* (System architect, interview)

Not only the disapproval of the software quality manager (administrative frame), but also the software project manager's deviation from milestone deadlines (administrative frame) are administrative sanctions expected from deviance from standards. Milestone deadlines are part of the incentive system at MedTech by writing them into the agreement of objectives for the senior software project managers. Thus, deviations from the milestone deadlines have negative consequences for the bonus payment. Regarding technically related sanctions for deviance, we can only reconstruct the expected higher practicability of software development at MedTech (technical frame) and the resulting efficiency for the actual development work.

Regarding overachieving deviations from standards such as adding milestones and documents, we can also depict several expected sanctions (see Table 6.4). In the light of business sanctions, we can see the additional investments of time and effort in the short run (business frame), for instance the immense efforts for documentation. In view of the expected regulatory sanctions, deviation as adding milestones or documentation is expected to increase the probability of a successful certification (regulatory frame). Further, this deviant approach as overachieving earns approval by software quality management, and product and general management not only for meeting standard requirements but also for adjusting to their time and product expectations (administrative frame). Hence, it is expected that deviation as adding milestones and documentation saves costs and time in the long run. Eventually, this practice is also rewarded with a positive attribute of

Table 6.4 Expected sanctions in the case of standard deviations at MedTech

Sanctioning frame	Expected sanctions on project members in the case of deviations
Administrative frame	Disapproval by software quality manager
	Loss of bonus payments for the project manager
	Approval by software quality manager for meeting standard requirements
	Approval by product management for adjusting to their time and product expectations
	Approval by general management for adjusting to their time and product expectations
	Reaffirming MedTech's risk avoidance culture
Business frame	Loss of markets
	Additional investments in the short run
	Saving on development costs in the long run
Regulatory frame	Legislative penalties
	Increased probability of certification in time
Technical frame	Increased efficiency in development work
Ethical frame	Damage to human life

consistency, since it fits MedTech's general cautious approach to risk assessment (administrative frame), as shown in the introduction (section 6.1).

6.5 Over-conformity with Standards at MedTech: Missing Contradictions

In this section, we summarize the appearance of over-conformity, present contradictions and provide essential explanations why MedTech deviates from standards by overachieving standard review and documentation requirements—even if for some standard requirements, such as processes and documentation, MedTech deviates only temporarily and mainly due to changes in the national standard requirements. As we described in Fried and Walgenbach (2020), contradictions can occur as asymmetries between structure and interaction—first, when standards are not appropriately represented as interpretative schemes, facilities, or social norms in organizational practices; second, contradictions emerge *between* standards as interpretative schemes, as facilities, or as social norms. Since MedTech generally follows a narrow interpretation of standards, its approach to standard enactment is excessively compliant. MedTech's over-conformity with standards is outlined in Figure 6.1.

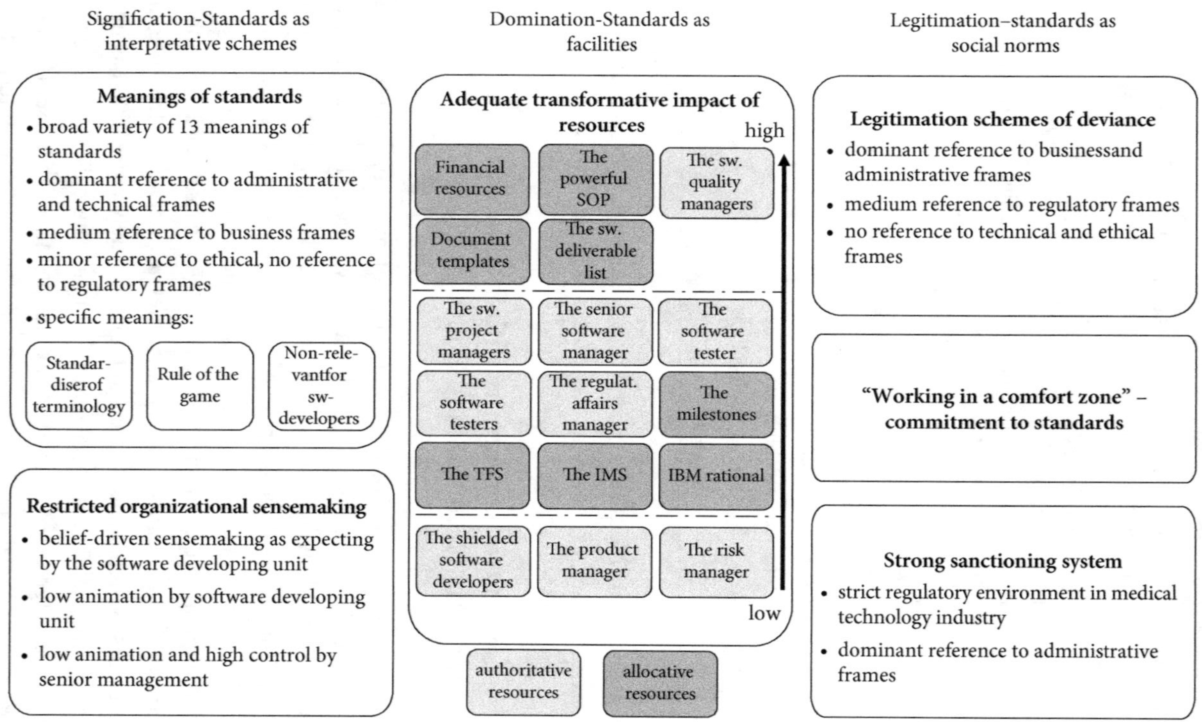

Figure 6.1 Standard enactment in MedTech's software development

In order to explain over-conformity with standards as a form of organizational deviance at MedTech, we will illustrate standards as they take effect as interpretative schemes, as facilities, and as social norms. We could not discover any secondary contradictions or any asymmetries.

6.5.1 Standards as Interpretative Schemes: Restricted Organizational Sensemaking as Expecting

Considering standards as interpretative schemes at MedTech, we traced a broad variety of thirteen different meanings of standards mainly referring to administrative and technical frames. Interestingly, administrative frames stand out here as a strong source for the sensemaking of standards compared to the cases of MetroEngineers and CraneSolutions in this book (chapters 5 and 7). This indicates MedTech's narrow interpretation of what compliance with standards requires. Several meanings referring to administrative aspects such as roles (definer of development roles), processes (standardizer of processes), and process rules for software development (base for software development processes) show the administrative importance of standards for MedTech.

Furthermore, we identified a restricted organizational sensemaking for standards at MedTech. Restricted sensemaking represents a highly controlled but rarely animated process producing similar, narrow accounts of signification (Maitlis 2005). The three case-specific meanings give evidence of this: first, since standards are taken-for-granted, they are fully accepted as rules of the game among the project members. Second, with the meaning of the standard as the standardizer of terminology we found a mutually shared understanding of standards forming the communication organizational members refer to in daily practice. Hence, they standardize documents and process steps company-wide in a similar way. Third, senior management does not animate sensemaking for standards among those who are most affected by them, but rather highly controls how standards are to be interpreted by means of the SOPs. Represented in the meaning non-relevant for software developers, software developers, in contrast, hardly have any room for their own sensemaking regarding standards. The software developers find themselves in what MedTech's senior software manager called the 'comfort zone'. Translated and predefined by the central software assurance quality unit, they seem to accept the predetermined interpretive schemes, with no alternative attempts for interpreting standards.

According to Weick's idea of belief-driven sensemaking (Weick 1995), at MedTech we consequently identified a strong belief in the way MedTech enacts standards combined with the expectation that this is the solution of how software development should be organized in the future. As the senior software manager's metaphor of MedTech as finding itself in a 'comfort zone' expresses, standards are hardly scrutinized in software development. In other words, they are taken-for-granted.

6.5.2 Standards as Facilities: Appropriate Transformative Impact of Resources for Standard Enactment

Regarding standards as facilities, senior management at MedTech provides overall sensible authoritative resources (i.e. software quality manager, senior software manager, regulatory affairs manager) and allocative resources (i.e. financial resources, SOPs, document templates, software deliverable list) to facilitate standard enactment in an appropriate manner. As well as this, the relation regarding the transformative impact of authoritative and allocative resources seems quite balanced at MedTech. Financial resources are invested sufficiently to ensure standard-compliant software development, for instance, when daily monitoring the implementation of standards by the software quality manager or when ensuring the awareness of international changes of standard requirements by the regulatory affairs unit. Resource allocation at MedTech is often discussed and thus not free of conflict; overall, however, we assume an appropriate transformative impact of resources, since they stabilize and support standard enactment.

6.5.3 Standards as Social Norms: Commitment to Standards and a Strong Sanctioning System

Regarding the legitimation frames compared to the other documented cases in the book, at MedTech we see an emphasis on business and administrative legitimations for over-conforming enactment of standards. Organizational members further referred to regulatory legitimations. What we found at MedTech is what Weick (1995) describes as commitment to social norms. Commitment aims at binding actions to efficiency while, however, reducing flexibility, learning, and adaption at the same time. At MedTech, organizational members work within a 'comfort zone', hardly deviating from standards in the sense of underperforming standard requirements. According to Weick, commitment is, besides manipulation, one of the possible action-driven processes of sensemaking. At MedTech, we detected manipulations that were, however, only temporary when national or international regulatory authorities changed standard requirements, for instance, in the case of a law change for medical devices in Brazil.

The dominant reference to administrative frames is also the basis for sanctioning deviance. We identified that MedTech experiences strong regulatory pressure relating to strict legislation in the medical technology sector. At the same time, we perceived a high probability of detection (Tenbrunsel & Messick 1999) of deviations from standards at MedTech. Furthermore, at MedTech potential external sanctions from assessors are complemented by internal sanctions. We found an institutionalized system of monitoring and approving standard enactment. For instance, employees of the software-developing unit refer to sanctions such as the approval of software quality management, or product or general management for meeting their standard-related requirements. A further example is the loss of bonus payments when not complying to SOP, for instance, when certain milestones of the development process are not met. Internal and external sanctioning opportunities thus form a comparably strong sanctioning system.

In summary, the software developing unit at MedTech is embedded in a rich environment of meanings for standard compliance; diverse, powerful resources to appropriately enact standards; and a strong sanctioning system. We can hardly discover any severe contradictions regarding standard enactment at MedTech. If we can retrace deviant practices at MedTech, they appear as interim forms, or minor forms, or as overachieving standard requirement in order to uphold certification or to save time and costs in the long run. In fact, the distinctiveness of the medical technology sector with strict standards and legal regulations demands strict compliance with standards; however, MedTech's over-conformity with standards is characterized by even overperforming these standards, e.g. by informally adding meetings or documents. Implicitly, besides the regulatory logic there is a business logic inscribed in this over-conforming approach to standard enactment: holding additional meetings not only gives the opportunity to constantly keep an eye on audit-relevant questions during the development work but also enables MedTech to meet time and product expectations as well as delivery deadlines. However, in the light of standard enactment at MedTech, it seems as if wishes for challenging the 'comfort zone' appear as unintended consequences of the over-conformity with standards at MedTech.

Eventually, this could lead to a future secondary contradiction: the strict organizational sanctioning system at MedTech could sooner or later conflict with the wish to fulfil economic objectives which are driven by fundamental innovations, potentially challenging existing standard requirements (Benner & Tushman 2003).

References

Benner, M. J. & Tushman, M. L. 2003. Exploitation, exploration, and process management: the productivity dilemma revisited. *Academy of Management Review*, 28, 238–56.

Fried, A. & Walgenbach, P. 2020. Theoretical framework to explore organizational deviance from standards. *In:* Fried, A. (ed.) *Understanding Deviance in a World of standards.* Oxford: Oxford University Press.

Gey, R. & Fried, A. 2018. Metastructuring for standards: how organizations respond to the multiplicity of standards. *In:* Jakobs, K. (ed.) *Corporate and Global Standardization Initiatives in Contemporary Society.* Hershey, PA: IGI Global.

Johner, C. 2017. Trends in der Medizintechnik. Johner Institut. https://www.johner-institut.de/blog/karriere/medizintechnik-trends/.

Maitlis, S. 2005. The social processes of organizational sensemaking. *Academy of Management Journal*, 48, 21–49.

Tenbrunsel, A. E. & Messick, D. M. 1999. Sanctioning systems, decision frames, and cooperation. *Administrative Science Quarterly*, 44, 684–707.

Vdi 2017. Medizintechnik—Trends und Perspektiven. In: Kraft, M. (ed.) *VDI—Thesen und Handlungsfelder*. Dusseldorf: VDI Verein Deutscher Ingenieure.

Weick, K. E. 1995. *Sensemaking in Organizations*. Thousand Oaks: SAGE.

7
Non-Regulated Deviance from Standards at MetroEngineers

Sarah Langer, Ronny Gey, Diana Karadzhova-Beyer, and Andrea Fried

In this chapter we illustrate *non-regulated deviance from standards* as we could trace it in the case of MetroEngineers. We found six different practices labelled by the organizational members of MetroEngineers' software development unit as deviant from standards. There are rather generic practices such as *deviation from the required role separation by omitting roles*, *deviation from the required development phases by their change in division and succession*, and *deviation from documentation requirements by shortening documentation.* There are also more case-specific deviant practices such as *deviation from quality management requirements*, *from testing requirements*, and *from safety integrity levels.* All in all, this variety of deviant practices at MetroEngineers is a characteristic of non-regulated deviance. With the purpose of explaining non-regulated deviance from standards, we outline MetroEngineers' distinctive standard enactment by examining standards from a structurationist perspective. We describe the six deviant practices mentioned above in more detail. In conclusion, we discuss explanations for non-regulated deviance based on asymmetries and contradictions in standard enactment at MetroEngineers.

7.1 Introduction to the Case of MetroEngineers

MetroEngineers is an engineering services division, part of a large, globally active engineering company situated in Germany. The engineering activities of MetroEngineers are divided into two business units: *Development* with engineering in the automotive and rail sector and *Manufacturing Engineering* with production-IT, planning, and fixtures. The investigated unit *Development*

Sarah Langer, Ronny Gey, Diana Karadzhova-Beyer, and Andrea Fried, *Non-Regulated Deviance from Standards at MetroEngineers* In: *Understanding Deviance in a World of Standards.* Edited by: Andrea Fried, Oxford University Press (2020).
DOI: 10.1093/oso/9780198833888.003.0007

at MetroEngineers is active in the railway vehicle construction sector, focusing on the development of components or entire rail vehicles such as high-speed trains, subways, and trams. Depending on the industrial clients' expectations, the development projects range from initial vehicle design to new development of railway vehicles, or only mechanical and software parts, to production maturity, or their upgrade. All development projects are delivered as engineering services, not as manufactured products.

According to annual business reports, MetroEngineers significantly increased turnover in 2013/14 (2012/13: €24.1m, 2013/14: €34.5m) mainly due to some large projects in the Chinese market. However, the initial profit turned into a massive loss in 2013/14 due to a decline in orders from markets in Brazil, Russia, and India, and necessary investments in the development work for the rail and automotive division, e.g. an increase in personnel expenses. The loss in profit continued to increase in 2014/15 (€5.82m), with turnover falling tremendously to €27.3m. The number of employees at MetroEngineers rose from 290 in 2012/13 to 382 in 2014/15. At the same time, the loss was further compounded by enlarged receivables from unpaid customer invoices. In 2016, MetroEngineers was put up for sale by the parent company due to its overall lack of profitability. The engineering services division was finally sold to a private equity firm in autumn 2016.

The markets in Europe and the US, but primarily in Asia are important business areas for MetroEngineers. This is due to a general trend in the rail industry, with worldwide urbanization and growing megacities as motors of economic development. Especially the Chinese railway market has evolved to be the biggest and most dynamic market, where investments are being made in high-speed trains and metros. Approximately 20 per cent of worldwide investment in the rail sector is in China (Li & Leenen 2012: 143). In its business report, MetroEngineers points to the Asian market as a promising target, with expected increasing demand for new rail vehicles, especially in urban areas. With the European railway market, however, MetroEngineers expects a rather stagnant development.

Corresponding to these challenges, we investigated the engagement of the software developing unit in the new product development project BRT (anonymized) for a Chinese client between October 2015 and June 2017. The development project's task was to develop a complete prototype of a suburban railway vehicle. The project was organized in multiple units, integrating electrical, mechanical, and software systems, as well as quality and safety management at MetroEngineers. It was characterized by a time-intensive interaction with the client. Hardware-related software development processes for a safety-critical environment were part of the development project. MetroEngineers' software developers were responsible for the development of the train control and monitoring system, a system that controls and monitors train equipment and functional processes. In former projects, MetroEngineers used train control and monitoring systems provided by one specific provider, in effect gaining significant experience from these systems.

As a means of coordination, the development process was divided into a concept phase of 4 months with weekly project meetings of all engineers engaged in the project. It was followed by a construction phase of 10 months with an estimated completion of development by the end of 2016. However, due to delays, the end of the development project was extended to June 2017. At this time, the situation at MetroEngineers regarding the BRT project was very uncertain, since the company was due to be sold. At the project level, the employees cast serious doubt on whether the prototype would be assembled at all by the Chinese client. Further, they were unsure which claims might still come from the client.

The BRT project represents MetroEngineers' new development challenge: development of a complete rail vehicle. It has been a relatively new business area for MetroEngineers, beginning approximately in 2013. When we started our investigations, the new quality manager in MetroEngineers' software development unit was still developing a standard-compliant process for the rail vehicle software development. The European standards DIN EN 50126, 50128, and 50129 are the basis of this development process. They were developed by CENELEC (the European Committee for Electrotechnical Standardization) and translated by the German Institute for Standardization (DIN). In DIN EN 50126, RAMS is defined as reliability, availability, maintainability, and safety. Further, a process was set up for managing RAMS based on the system lifecycle. The standard defines a systematic process for specifying requirements for RAMS. DIN EN 50128 describes compliance measures for the development of safety-related software for railway control and protection. It prescribes requirements for organizational structure and the relationship between organizations and the division of responsibility. Further, criteria for the qualification and expertise of personnel are provided. DIN EN 50129 is applicable to the functional safety of railway signalling systems. The three standards can be applied likewise to heavy rail systems, light rail, and urban mass transportation. However, compliance with these standards is a very challenging task. Even the big European rail vehicle producers, which participated in designing the standards, are struggling nowadays to comply with the standards for rail vehicle development (Fuchs 2011; Oelsner 2017).

Interestingly, compliance with European railway vehicle standards is expected within the BRT project by contract with the Chinese client. This is a new situation for the software development unit at MetroEngineers, since, for the first time, the development of a complete railway vehicle is their responsibility. In the past, the software developers were developing '*as usual*', which means not necessarily compliant with European standards due to MetroEngineers' former status as a component deliverer only:

> *When I had started here, everything worked along the quick and dirty method. There has not been a lot of documentation.... The company originated from providing single systems for other big rail vehicle producers, and back then it was enough. They instructed from above: you have to do this and that, they did it like that, and done!* (Quality manager, interview)

At that time, MetroEngineers had provided software development services only as components for big rail vehicle producers. Hence, standard-compliant software development processes were not a special requirement for the software developing unit.

As stated by the quality manager, even though part of the contract, compliance with European standards is obviously not mandatory for entering the market in China. The quality manager explains: '*That is why they would like to have them* [standards] *always as part of the contract, to have the possibility to later sell the train on the European market*' (quality manager 1, interview). However, the situation of regulation in the Chinese market is not transparent to MetroEngineers. The quality manager explains that: '*[s] ince the First World War they did not build trams anymore* [in China]. *And there is nobody with know-how, who knows how it works*' (quality manager 1, interview). In China, they only began in the last 10 years to develop and produce trains, metros, and trams on a broad scale. Before, they were dependent on imports and joint ventures with experienced producers from Europe, North America, and Japan. Therefore, regulation is also a new topic in China; a potential future Chinese standard is possible at any time. In addition, the Chinese client is not transparent on the regulatory environment (Heras-Saizarbitoria & Boiral 2012). Thus, it confuses the organizational members at MetroEngineers:

> *That* [approval process] *is the task of our client who is the final producer of the train. Which steps are needed and if they are necessary in the first place, it is*

not transparent to us and it is not communicated how this should work. They tell us "let us take care about these issues" and they seem to be not worried at all about any restrictions. (Project manager, interview)

Apart from these standards concerning software development, employees at MetroEngineers have to select from a wide range of available functional standards touching every part of rail vehicle development, from mechanics to electricity, and safety in general.The development project seems to be facing serious challenges to being compliant with European standards.

7.2 Standards as Interpretative Schemes in MetroEngineers' Software Development

Members of the software developing unit at MetroEngineers referred to a broad variety of meanings concerning standards in general but also in view of the BRT project. In the interviews, we discerned fifteen different meanings within the software development unit which provide sense for their engagement in the standardization of the software development process. Among these meanings, administrative, business, and technical frames dominate the reasoning of the employees at MetroEngineers.

Two meanings were specific for MetroEngineers compared to CraneSolutions and MedTech. First, as *proof of workload*, the standard-compliant process documentation also provides evidence of the workload that is to be compensated by the client. Second, since the standard is an indisputable norm, it is the base for its meaning as *argument*. However, standards and their signification for MetroEngineers' BRT project are discussed throughout the development process among the team members. Moreover, on several occasions, members of the software developing unit tried to convince members of the electrical and mechanical units to implement the functional safety standards common in the European market. The reaction of the electrical and mechanical units, however, was dismissive. Furthermore, the senior management of MetroEngineers did not pay any attention and was even reluctant to support the enactment of standards; hence no sense for standards was provided. The senior management did not engage in formal or informal sensegiving regarding the signification of standards for the BRT project. There was little attempt to support the initiative of the software developing unit in finding a shared understanding for their daily efforts to comply with European standards.

Table 7.1 shows an overview of the interpretative schemes of standard enactment by the software developing unit at MetroEngineers. We complemented

Table 7.1 Standards as interpretative schemes at MetroEngineers

Meaning of standards	Description Standards...	Which project members ascribing meaning	Signification frame
Base for product specification	Define the requirements of a prospective product	Quality manager, project manager, safety manager, software developer, mechanical engineer, TFS admin	Technical
Base for software development processes	Define the design of software development processes	Software developer, quality manager, project manager, safety manager	Administrative
Standardizer of processes	Align processes within the organization and across organizations	Quality manager, project manager, safety manager, software developer	Administrative
Definer of development roles	Separate roles for software development projects; define who is allowed to do what	Project manager, quality manager, software developer, safety manager	Administrative
Interface assurance	Ensure the suitability of suppliers for components and services	Quality manager, software developer, project manager, mechanical engineer	Technical
	Reduce costs of finding a suitable supplier	Project manager, mechanical engineer	Business
Current state of technology	Act as a reference for currently accepted technology but not necessarily the most advanced technology	Project manager, safety manager, electrical engineer	Technical
Improver of development processes	Help to avoid mistakes in product development	Quality manager, software developer	Technical
	Save financial resources	Quality manager	Business
Assurance of human safety	Protect society	Quality manager, project manager, safety manager, software developer, mechanical engineer	Ethical
	Ensure product usability	Quality manager	Technical
	Create consumer trust	Project manager	Business
	Ensure quality	Project manager, safety manager, software developer	Business
Trigger for monitoring	Trigger monitoring and occasions to check the implementation of standards	Quality manager, software developer, project manager	Administrative

Learning opportunity	Trigger learning regarding, for example, development practice, role separation, and resource allocation	Project manager, quality manager	Administrative
Part of engineering contracts	Bind customers legally; clarify demands from customers	Quality manager, project manager, safety manager, software developer, mechanical engineer, TFS admin	Business
Proof of workload	Trace development efforts due to documentation requirements; provide evidence for accomplished workload for the customer	Software developer	Administrative
Base for certification	Provide evidence for functioning product	Software developer, project manager	Technical
Key to the European market	Prospectively enable market entry if company is certified	Software developer, project manager, quality manager, mechanical engineer	Business
Argument	Trigger routines that are taken for granted	Safety manager, quality manager, software developer, project manager, mechanical engineer	Administrative

these meanings with information on who expressed them and their signification frame. We describe the meanings in more detail in the following text.

Base for Product Specification

According to MetroEngineers, standards reduce the scope of possible actions. Standards have a significant influence on the development process. They are directly integrated into the functional requirements of the product; thus, standards serve as a *base for product specification*:

> *The functional requirements from these standards are integrated and they form the basis for the development of the concept and the actual implementation of the concept.* (Project manager, interview)

Base for Software Development Processes

Besides the requirements that are derived from contract or from the technology itself, standards are a significant source of product and process requirements in the eyes of the organizational members. Depending on the type of standard, they create meaning not only for the product but also for the process of development activities at MetroEngineers (*base for software development processes*). Referring to the latter, employees at MetroEngineers regard standards as a cause for process implementation:

> *And then, according to the standard, there is the testing. And, at the time we had nothing, neither process nor tools. And then, we started to design a process, to enhance our tools, to define specifications for it, tool validation and so on.*
> (Software developer 1, interview)

Enacting standards for the development processes means to enhance the existing processes or to implement entirely new ones for software testing. Hence, MetroEngineers implemented steps for software tests and tool validation. Standards essentially define the processes:

> *In the end, it is like a guide of how I should proceed, of what I should pay attention to, which things don't work at all.*
> (Quality manager 1, interview)

Standardizer of Processes

Standard enactment means aligning most of the software development processes to standards. This brings standards into a guide-like position for the software development activities not only at MetroEngineers but also in the whole railway vehicle sector (*standardizer of processes*):

> *In the railway vehicle sector, the standards are defined in such a detail. They represent concrete work instructions. They really dictate our everyday work for us.* (Quality manager 2, interview)

Definer of Development Roles

However, the decision for standard compliance not only affects the design of processes but also motivates role and task-separation in software development. For the employees of MetroEngineers, the standard *defines development roles*:

> *In the standard for software development you find a concrete role concept. There is a massive division of power: who is allowed to do something and who is not.* (Quality manager 2, interview)

With the definition of new roles, MetroEngineers creates new positons and hierarchical levels. It means that organizational charts and power relations between existing and newly created roles change as well:

> *Besides project management, we have a quality manager now. Second factor is the requirements management. Since the standards are translated into requirements, I can check where the standards have been applied.*
>
> (Project manager, interview)

Besides appointments of the quality and requirements managers, employees reported the creation of new positions for verification and testing.

Interface Assurance

We extracted a further relevant meaning of standards defining the environment of software development of MetroEngineers: the standard as *interface assurance*. Standards provide the possibility of finding suitable component or service suppliers according to their compliance with the necessary interfaces for technical systems. This leads to an efficient flow of the development process and eventually for the development work: '*[i]f there were no standards, you would certainly have a considerable interface effort with each supplier*' (quality manager, interview).

Current State of Technology

Only a generally accepted state of technology can serve as interface assurance. The safety manager states:

> *So, nobody argues, it is the standard, it is the state of the art. And, I do not have to argue with the construction engineer to design it differently.... I can tell him: "here, it is written in the standard, take a look".*
>
> (Safety manager, interview)

As such, the standard as *current state of technology* also bears some disadvantageous meanings for MetroEngineers: '*[i]t is disadvantageous now that standards mirror somehow a state of the art at a certain time*' (project manager, interview). It takes some time until new technologies form the basis for the development of a new standard.

Improver of Development Processes

Moreover, employees at MetroEngineers view standards as enablers for software development resulting in fewer mistakes. Hence, the standard is framed as an *improver of processes*. Even though the implementation of standards is associated with obstacles, they are nevertheless judged rather positively: '*[i]t's not that it is simply a drag shoe* [a railway jargon metaphor for hindrance or chock] *to us, it's actually the fact that the standard supports us to avoid such mistakes*' (quality manager 2, interview). Further during the interview, the same quality manager added another important aspect highlighting the standard as an improver of processes:

> *It is a certain effort, but it is double and triple worthy. I am saving on these iteration steps, again and again, back and forth. I avoid messing this up. And that saves pure money.* (Quality manager 2, interview)

Assurance of Human Safety

Another significant aspect of defining the environment of software development is the standard as *assurance of human safety*:

> *It is also important to have guidelines in place that protect the general public. So that development has to follow a certain framework in such a way that the products are safe and usable in the end. It should conform to what in our country or in the EU is considered as standard.*
>
> (Quality manager 1, interview)

To our interviewees, enacting a standard means to enact a safety-relevant framework which enables the production of safe products.

Trigger for Monitoring

The customers and potential users can trust these products. To justify the trust of customers and the potential users, the standard further encourages the intense monitoring of processes:

> *[E]verybody takes care that the standards are used and implemented. And the project management together with the quality management should check that everything is compliant and that it* [the product] *does what it should do.*
>
> (Quality manager 1, interview)

As the quality manager mentions, the standard implementation as well as usage need to be monitored; employees from project and quality management should take responsibility for monitoring the standard enactment. Thus, standards are a *trigger for monitoring* here.

Learning Opportunity

Moreover, for some employees, enacting standards means to enjoy a *learning opportunity* regarding their development practice, especially concerning project settings, role separation, and resource allocation:

> *So, there are certain settings, what kind of trades do I need, how the trades must be separated from each other, which roles can or need to be run independently of each other.... So, from the normative side we learned a lot about how to allocate ourselves.* (Project manager, interview)

These meanings of the enactment of standards show that standards not only carry the rigor of rules, but also appear to the employees of MetroEngineers as flexible enough to adjust them to their local needs from a software development perspective.

Part of Engineering Contracts

Even if not legally required, standards are *part of the engineering contract* between MetroEngineers and the Chinese client. The customer contract is a legal resource which includes standard compliance as a binding objective:

> *Currently, it is literally written* [in the contract], *the standard GB 732* [a Chinese standard] *is to be fulfilled—this would mean, for me, everything that is written in there.* (Quality manager 2, interview)

If the standards were not fixed in the contract, the interpretative schemes of, for example, 'basis for product development' or 'definer of roles' would not be dominant in the conceptions of the employees.

Proof of Workload

Once the employees comply with standard requirements, for instance regarding documentation, standards gain importance as a *proof of workload* and hence as a basis to account for the incurred costs:

> *So, in the end, it is a documentation of your work, what have I done?... Actually, you can even prove with it: I have already done this and that and I would like to have money for it now.* (Software developer 2, interview)

The process documentation can thus provide evidence for the workload in software development. The process documents serve as proof when demanding client payments for the development service. A complete documentation enables traceability of development efforts and can be used to detect non-compliant development. The standard-compliant documentation proves the development work to the customer and surprisingly appears as an additional benefit.

Base for Certification

Organizational members also mentioned a rather formal meaning of standard enactment: standards as a *base for certification*. One primary goal of enacting standards—the certification—can be achieved because standards provide the basis for it:

> *As said, things that concern the protocol, where data are exchanged, that is what we have to fix this year. With that, there is a basis, on which you can run certification. That means, the producer can say: "okay, we know the protocol, look, we have a certificate, and it works".* (Software developer 2, interview)

The interviewees reported that being certified is a commonly accepted goal of the organization and its members. Certification was hardly questioned throughout our inquiries.

Key to the European Market

Complying with the standard and becoming certified obviously signifies the *key to the European market* for MetroEngineers:

> [Our client] *intends to construct the railway vehicle in such a way that it can be licensed also on the European market. And then, in order to get a license for the European market: 50126, 28, 29,* [DIN EN 50126, 50128, 50129] *there is no alternative.* (Software developer 2, interview)

For the employees at MetroEngineers, complying with the functional safety standards for railway development (EN 50126, 50128, 50129) synonymously stands for the *key to the European market*. The manufacturers need to prove compliance with standards to the European authorities in the railway sector to license their railway vehicles.

Argument

Finally, the standard as an *argument* highlights the very heart of the meaning of standards: a standard becomes *the* standard based on an agreement on commonly acknowledged rules. If these rules are generally accepted, they do not need to be questioned again:

> *The standard gives you precise instructions for action. And, these are not subject for discussions since it is the standard. Right? Nobody argues about it, that is clear, that is the standard, that is the state of the art and I do not have to argue with the constructor to tell him you have to do it differently.... Then I don't have to discuss with him, I can simply say: "Look, it is written in the standard".* (Safety manager, interview)

7.3 Standards as Facilities in MetroEngineers' Software Development

In general, the availability of authoritative and allocative resources at MetroEngineers was critical throughout our investigations from the very start of the BRT project until the end of our inquiry. Most importantly, adequate financial resources for standard enactment are not provided either from the client or from the higher management. Most of the authoritative resources were established only recently, shortly before (safety and quality managers), or even during our inquiry (requirements manager, TFS administrator). However, in practice, these positions massively lack power to implement standard-compliant processes. In compensation, MetroEngineers relies on interns as low-cost resources or technical solutions such as the TFS. Allocative resources often materialize based on standard requirements, e.g. the role concept, document templates, or the V-model. However, most of the authoritative and allocative resources significantly lack transformative capacity. Table 7.2 summarizes the different resources and their transformative impact. Subsequently, we elaborate on the different resources at MetroEngineers in more detail.

Table 7.2 Standards as facilities at MetroEngineers

Resource	Description	Transformative capacity	Transformative impact for standard enactment
Authoritative resources			
The heroic project manager	Manages BRT project and train control and monitoring system sub project	High	Medium impact due to the lack of financial resources and resistance from the electrical and mechanical engineers
The quality manager—motivated and frustrated likewise	Implements and manages standard-compliant processes, designs role model, V-model, and document templates for standard-compliant development	High	Medium impact due to the lack of financial resources and resistance from the electrical and mechanical engineers
The frustrated safety manager	Manages and controls safety-relevant development in line with requirements of functional safety standards	High	Medium impact due to the lack of financial resources and resistance from the electrical and mechanical engineers
The diligent software developers	Develop the TCMS in line with different requirements	Medium	Medium impact; however, they wish it would be higher since certain standard requirements are not implemented due to the lack of financial resources
The tenacious engineers	Design the electrical and mechanical systems in line with different requirements (customer, product, standard, safety, etc.)	Medium	Low impact on effective standard enactment since they show resistance to certain standard requirements, especially regarding processes and testing
The emerging requirements manager	Manages functional and non-functional requirements	High	Low impact since it was only recently implemented; however, more impact is expected in the future

Continued

Table 7.2 *Continued*

Resource	Description	Transformative capacity	Transformative impact for standard enactment
The TFS administrator—the master of technology	Manages TFS and designs standard-compliant processes	High	Medium impact, which would be higher if all employees would use the TFS
The powerful interns	Develop products and processes in the realm of their department; undertake R&D work	Low	Low impact, since they are the compensation for the lack of financial resources
Allocative resources			
Financial resources—which resources?	Transformative resource: can be transformed into other resources	High	Low impact since there is no budget from higher management for standard enactment. Low and unreliable budget from the client
The role concept of DIN EN 50128	Defines roles and positions for the software development process	High	Medium impact due to the lack of financial resources and resistance from the electrical and mechanical engineers
Document templates following DIN EN 50128	Defines the design and content of required and recommended documents for standard-compliant development	High	Medium impact due to the lack of financial resources and resistance from the electrical and mechanical engineers
The V-model for software development	Defines functional areas, steps, and workflow of a software development process that is aligned in a V-shape	High	Medium impact due to the lack of financial resources and resistance from the electrical and mechanical engineers
The TFS—a never-ending story	Mighty management tool for (standard) requirements and V-model-oriented software development	High	Medium impact since the implementation is not yet finished; concerns from certain users regarding usability

TCMS, Train Control and Management System.

7.3.1 Authoritative Resources

7.3.1.1 The Heroic Project Manager

The project manager of the BRT development project also heads the software developing unit's part of the project. The project manager established the train control and monitoring system development unit and also more generally the software development at MetroEngineers:

> *It was my task to establish the department which could provide this service* [TCMS development] *to the rail vehicle projects. And, since April 2013, I am building up the department, the last two and a half years. Until now, we increased from one to twenty-five employees. We built up all the necessary expertise, the tools, the processes. And we now develop the control system for rail vehicles.* (Project manager, interview)

The head of the train control and monitoring system development became project manager for the whole BRT development project of the train vehicle. He is very committed to the enactment of standards at MetroEngineers. Exemplarily, he explains establishing a '*lessons learned*' meeting for the software developing unit at MetroEngineers:

> *That's my personal attitude. That is not official. It* [a 'lessons learned' meeting] *is neither forbidden nor mandatory to do it regularly. We regularly hold it for our department. Tomorrow there is a 'lessons learned'* [meeting] *for the internal tool development. In my opinion, it is useful. However, it is not the usual approach in this company. This is due to the approach to think from project to project. There are always different project members and, often, they are not gaining any experience from the former projects.*
> (Head of the train control and monitoring system development, interview)

To date, the software developing unit is the only one dealing profoundly with the enactment of standards and with the establishment of compliant processes and tools. In this endeavour, the project manager does not benefit from the support of the senior management: either for implementation of relevant quality or safety management structures at department level or for application in development projects. Even though the head of train control and monitoring system development is also the project manager, there is still reluctance from other department heads when it comes to standard-compliant development. At this point, his authoritative power in the other departments in the project is limited, which we could assess during several observations of project meetings. We could even sense frustration with his failing attempts to carry over the standard topic to other departments: '*that is how it is in our company. We* [employees developing the train control and monitoring system] *are the only ones with certified testers. We are the only ones with certified requirements engineers*' (project manager, interview). A lack of financial resources and the opposition of the electrical and mechanical engineers result in only a medium transformative impact of the project manager for standard enactment.

7.3.1.2 Quality Manager—Motivated and Frustrated Likewise

The quality manager at MetroEngineers describes his daily tasks:

> *The whole quality management, the processes, the whole document management, the whole versioning management, the whole data management. At the same time, I am the administrator for the SharePoint* [document management system] *and the Team Foundation Server. So, I am administering and advancing the whole data management system. That is all in our responsibility, all those formalities we have to follow.* (Quality manager 1, interview)

The other organizational members clearly identify the quality manager as the person that explicitly deals with standards: '*Stephan, yeah. That is our process guy. That is the one who always comes and asks: "Does it comply with our standards?"*' (software developer 1, interview). Hence, the quality manager possesses the expertise for standard enactment and plays a significant role in the process of standard enactment at MetroEngineers. The project manager points to the importance of the quality manager and his work. He sees his tasks on the same level as the development of the technical solution:

> *Well, on the one hand, it is the functional solution and, on the other hand, it is about compliance with standards. Therefore, we installed a quality manager. Specifically, it is only for our department... and it is about monitoring the standards, the compliance with standards.* (Project manager, interview)

To the project manager, quality management at MetroEngineers equals working with standards. Since the project manager is highly engaged in the enactment of standards and in setting up the relevant organizational structures, he profoundly supports the work of the quality manager in the department. However, higher management did not provide any support for quality management issues. Therein, a misunderstanding of its necessity and advantages becomes evident:

> *Quality* [management] *is really…, well, this is due to our managing director, he doesn't understand it, he doesn't want it. He doesn't consider it as necessary: "That is stupid, why we do it? It costs money. No, no." We have an official quality manager for the whole company… but he is massively overloaded. So, when I entered the company, it all ended up on my desk. And, well, it* [quality] *is definitely neglected here.* (Quality manager 1, interview)

Senior management at MetroEngineers is mainly formed of experienced engineers. Only some of them see the necessity of quality or safety management. Quality management often comes into conflict with the other departments developing the rail vehicle based on functional requirements. Mechanical or electrical engineers consider the work of the quality management as non-functional and not equally important to their own work. Frustration prevails among the quality managers:

> *Sometimes I have the impression that our department is marked by resignation. Everything we* [quality managers] *do—nobody wants it. They* [the other units] *will moan and it is actually totally useless. After those meetings, in which we discussed such basic issues, everybody is discouraged.*
> (Quality manager 2, interview)

As for the project manager, the transformative impact of the quality manager is limited due to the lack of financial resources and the resistance of the engineers. Hence the quality manager only accounts for a medium transformative impact on standard enactment.

7.3.1.3 The Frustrated Safety Manager

With the expansion of its business to full-system development, the employees at MetroEngineers were now in charge of topics such as system safety and compliance with standards. New roles emerged; the safety manager is one of those. He is in charge of reliability, availability, maintainability, and safety: '*So, we, the RAMS people do not develop. We take care of the customers' requirements regarding availability, maintainability, and safety*' (safety manager, interview). The standards for RAMS in the rail industry (EN 50126, 50128, and 50129) provide guidance for RAMS-relevant rail vehicle development. The standard EN 50126 defines RAMS as a process or method set up to avoid failure early in the concept phase of a development project. The three safety standards strictly define the tasks of the safety manager. Hence, the safety manager is strongly aligned with the organizational goal of standard enactment.

In daily development practice, the safety manager often is at odds with the development engineers (e.g. mechanical or electrical engineers) concerning safety requirements conflicting with functional requirements:

> *We are the ones annoying the others* [laughs]. . . . *That is why I am the trouble-maker. But yeah, when you are aware of it, I think it is not that bad* [laughs]. *We are not productive, right?. . . Even among the big companies there is this awareness:. . . They* [the engineers] *construct the thing.*
>
> (Safety manager, interview)

The safety manager even shows signs of frustration and sarcasm when speaking about his standing in the company. The safety manager seems to share the same fate at MetroEngineers as the quality manager: since both are very aligned to processes and standard requirements, they share the same conflicts with the mechanical and electrical engineers. Consequently, they form an alliance at MetroEngineers and follow their principles even together:

> *We keep an eye on the safety management and they keep an eye on us. If you consider it organizationally. . . it is not implemented like this. The safety manager and the quality manager are to be on the same level as the project manager, hierarchically. They both are test authorities for the whole project.*
>
> (Quality manager 1, interview)

The quality manager emphasizes the importance and the responsibilities of both the safety manager and quality manager for rail vehicle development at MetroEngineers. Besides the standard requirements, the safety manager refers to the ethical responsibility of his role. However, his transformative impact for standard enactment lags behind. Again, the medium impact relates to the lack of financial resources and the resistance of the mechanical and electrical engineers.

7.3.1.4 The Diligent Software Developers

Throughout MetroEngineers, the employees acknowledge the train control and monitoring system to be the '*head*' of a rail vehicle—a complex software system handling all the incoming electrical signals from different systems and controlling the train. It therefore seems obvious for the developers that they have an important position in the overall project, since '*the train control and monitoring system developers are the ones that lead the projects because they have the view from above*' (software developer 2, interview).

The software developers share the project manager's vision of processes and standard-compliant development. They speak enthusiastically about standards and their enactment:

> *Since we act in the rail vehicle sector, there is this crucial 50128. And it provides a common thread for a development process. And I have to admit, the standard itself is not too bad... you still have enough freedom to customize to the company's needs... and it provides a whole bunch of documents for your documentation efforts.... It saved us a lot of work. The only issue we have... is to impose it on the company.* (Software developer 2, interview)

Despite these positive aspects, the software developer points out that implementing standard-compliant processes in the company is a difficult task, facing resistance within MetroEngineers. However, the software developers at MetroEngineers fully support the enactment of standards in the organization. Hence, they provide a medium transformative impact regarding standard enactment.

7.3.1.5 Tenacious Engineers

The mechanical and electrical engineers at MetroEngineers design the vehicle body, sub-systems such as doors, seats, stairs, and windows, and the wired connections of the entire vehicle. Among the four sub-projects, there is a single sub-project for electric and mechanical development. During our observations we assessed the collaboration between these sub-projects (see Box 7.1).

Discussions of this provenance regularly emerged especially during the concept phase of the project, where fundamental process and design issues were discussed and determined. Testing procedures are fundamental standard requirements from the functional safety standards for railway vehicle development. During an interview, the quality manager provided an explanation for the resistance of the mechanical and electrical engineers:

> *The problem is that the company first developed from mechanical engineering. As such, the gentlemen sitting above us, the ones that work the longest time for the company, they come from a mechanical engineering corner. And, they learned in*

Box 7.1 Observation protocol: concept meeting, 11 November 2015

At the end of a concept meeting in November 2015, a discussion arises about the testing procedures of the electrical sub-project. While the actual meeting has ended, the project manager incidentally asks the members of the electrics: 'How do you actually test your circuit diagrams?' The sub-project leader of the electrics answers very concisely: 'Not at all. Why?' This triggers a fierce debate on the different testing approaches and efforts of each sub-project. The members of the electrics admit that there is no testing procedure for the circuit diagrams. Thereupon, the project manager declares, frustrated: 'That is not possible, you are the only ones in the company.' Ironically, the electrical engineer adds that the situation is the same in the mechanical sub-project. The discussion continues while the mechanical and electrical engineers question the significance of the testing scenario for a circuit diagram. They further question whether other rail vehicle producers would usually test circuit diagrams. In addition, the engineers argue that testing rather is a software topic since software is more complex and therefore more error-prone. However, the project manager is not satisfied with these answers: 'Bloody circuit diagrams.' The discussion ends with the engineers' conclusion that they subjectively test their diagrams. However, they will consider the idea of a testing approach in the future.

> *the past, that for the mechanical engineering department it also works without* [quality management and processes]. (Quality manager 1, interview)

Since the mechanical and electrical engineers mainly resist the software developers' initiatives of introducing standard-compliant processes in the organization, they largely influence standard enactment in a negative way. They thus provide a low transformative impact for effective standard enactment.

7.3.1.6 The Emerging Requirements Manager

One of the requirements of the functional safety standards is the implementation of a requirements manager. She deals with the functional and non-functional requirements coming from customer requests or from the diverse product and process standards in the railway vehicle sector. A few months after we had begun our inquiry, MetroEngineers finally assigned the role of the long-missing requirements manager:

> *We finally found someone who deals with the requirements in general and especially with the customer requirements. Until now this task still was partly in my responsibility.* (Quality manager 1, interview)

The requirements manager translates the customer and standard requirements into system requirements. These are handed over to the different engineering departments and provide the starting point of the engineers' work. In view of the sheer number of requirements, a software tool, the TFS, is used to manage and trace these requirements. Due to her recent assignment, the requirements manager provides only a low transformative impact, which is expected to grow parallel to her job experience.

7.3.1.7 The TFS Administrator—The Master of Technology

During our inquiries, MetroEngineers was establishing the role of the TFS administrator. His main task is the implementation of processes into the TFS and the technical administration of the software system. Before his employment, these tasks were secondarily accomplished by the quality manager or other employees who felt responsible for it:

> *Now, the team foundation server administration is in the hands of* [another employee] *and me. We set up projects and we customize them. In the past, it was not like this. There were a lot of people involved and there was a mere tohubohu. But, since we are about to migrate, I started cleaning up.*
> (TFS administrator, interview)

Working with the TFS was quite a confusing task without a specific administrator since it often rather hindered the employees in their daily requirements management. While describing his tasks, the new TFS administrator explains that he uses standard requirements for the administration of the TFS and the implemented processes:

> *We worked with the V-model. Before, the mapping was a bit complicated. Therefore, the acceptance was low, so the electrical and the mechanical engineers complained how they should accomplish their tasks. It was not intuitive, and the process was not described. Certainly, there is the V-model and the "wallpaper"* [a printout of the development V-model], *and then you say that there is the*

> *DIN standard* [DIN EN 50128]. *But it only provides directions, it is not exactly written down how you have to do it.* (TFS administrator, interview)

As one of the mediators for standard enactment, the TFS administrator in conjunction with the quality manager interprets the standards and designs standard-compliant processes. His transformative impact for standard enactment is still medium, but it is expected to increase since the TFS is not fully implemented yet.

7.3.1.8 The Powerful Interns

Interns at MetroEngineers accomplish highly critical work regarding the enactment of standards, the change management, and the enactment of new processes or new technologies. A former intern comprehensibly explains the approach to research & development and knowledge acquisition:

> *The business model is based on interns who are employed at the headquarters. It means here at the subsidiary we do not spend a single penny for an intern. Hence, interns are preferably engaged for research topics, especially if they have to write a final thesis.... That is the model; we delegate research topics to our interns. They can work half a year on this topic whereas an engineer would cost 10,000 Euros. And, they* [the interns] *actually cost nothing.*
>
> (Quality manager 1, interview)

Since MetroEngineers is a project-oriented engineering company, financial resources for development activities are scarce. The project managers had to look for alternative resources to accommodate the need for development. Interns are given important process development tasks and are thus also recognized as a meaningful resource for standard enactment. A former intern reports on his Bachelor thesis:

> *Testing was a hot topic at the time. In the project, we were about to finish programming. And according to the standards, testing is next. And at that time, we had nothing, neither processes nor tools. So we started setting up a process, developing the tools, writing specifications for it, validating the tools and all that.* (Software developer 1, interview)

The interns at MetroEngineers develop critical processes which need to follow central standards requirements for functional safety. Another former intern confirms: '*The ones we are now using in the project, I mean, the specific processes, that was my idea. So, they are all developed by myself'* (quality manager 1, interview). Consequently, interns are a powerful and low-cost resource. After they have finalized their theses, MetroEngineers often employs the former interns to preserve their competences for the organization. Interns at MetroEngineers serve as a compensation for the lack of financial resources for standard enactment. As such, they provide a low transformative impact for standard enactment in the organization.

7.3.2 Allocative Resources

7.3.2.1 Financial Resources—Which Resources?

MetroEngineers is a project-oriented engineering service company where financial resources are channelled through project budgets to the specific development activities. In service engineering, financial resources mostly refer to personnel costs. Since 2013, when they expanded their business towards full-system development of entire trains, MetroEngineers has pursued a change in the management process with growth in terms of turnover (2013: €24m, 2014: €36m) and number of employees (2013: 250, 2014: 350). However, as a full-train-system provider with a growing head count, the company did not invest adequately in functions like research & development, quality, and safety management:

> *We recently held those lessons learned meetings and financed it from the new project budget. Normally it would make sense to finance it from a general budget because it is reasonable for every project. But that is a learning process. The company should learn that we are not a service provider for small developments anymore. We are now doing full-system development and we should align the structures in the company adequately. We should not only think project-wise. We should consider a certain development effort.*
>
> (Project manager, interview)

In view of the lack of financial resources, the project manager acted on his own without support from senior management. He had to tap the project budget to implement his ideas of process management and to overcome the paradoxical situation of the poor financial resources:

> *So now, we do full-system development and we would need internal know-how from research and development. However, we still clung to thinking in projects,*

> *and we spend the project budget on specific project tasks. That is a contradiction. It was never solved in our company. It means some departments rather focused on functioning in the classical and expected way and they didn't invest money to advance their processes. We have spent a lot of money and we now realise that we are more efficient. The tools and process we have implemented make us more efficient than the other teams, also seen in financial terms. The last 2 years we had to invest a lot of money. It is not reported officially how much we invested.* (Project manager, interview)

The other department managers did not follow the project manager's approach. They still stick to the old processes and structures—an approach that could be called client-oriented: '*[e]ach official project where there is a client is considered as productive. And everybody who books hours on it is considered productive*' (project manager, interview). The project-oriented approach to budgeting development effort led to a short-term thinking which favoured earlier financial rewards over long-term progress of MetroEngineers.

A lack of financial resources not only triggered the reallocation of budget for topics like research & development, quality, and safety management, but also led to the intensive use of interns for handling research & development topics. Working with interns or tightly limited resources may also lead to disadvantages. A software engineer employed to administer the TFS explains:

> *The other colleagues tried it under the given financial circumstances. It is quite limited and still they tried to implement it* [TFS and standard-compliant processes]. *And that is why there is, I don't want to call it an interim solution, it is rather a pale compromise.* (TFS administrator, interview)

In this situation, a lack of financial support from the senior management for the TFS and the process implementation led to a compromise and later to reworking efforts. In a project-oriented organization, the client-projects are the main source of financial resources for the development of processes and the enactment of standards. However, the client's budget in the BRT project is strictly fixed due to regulations of the Chinese government. In consequence, the employees at MetroEngineers cannot react flexibly according to clients requests:

> *But it usually collides with the client's approach. We reached an agreement about the budget and the client wants to have the most shiny and newest train of the world, which is still up-to-date in 10 to 20 years. But since the budget of our Chinese customer is fixed and the customer wants this and that, we need*

to check whether we have to change or cut out something else to still remain within the budgeted costs. (Software developer 2, interview)

During the BRT project, the customer frequently changed its requests for the design of the metro train. This approach to project management obviously collided with the fixed budget and it resulted in unpaid rework on the train design. In view of scarce financial resources at MetroEngineers, the project manager reacted with claim requests due to project delays:

> *Some claims were already paid because the client was in need to speed up the project. But, generally, we cannot make enough money by claims to compensate our effort in these countless iteration loops.... We are iteratively asking again and again, which consumes an enormous amount of time.*
> (Project manager, interview)

The financial situation at MetroEngineers is quite poor, with massive consequences for the work in the BRT project. The transformative impact of financial resources on standard enactment is low. Senior management provides hardly any additional resources for standard enactment. The requirements from both sides, client and senior management, massively restrict the development work at MetroEngineers. According to the organization's annual report for 2015, MetroEngineers generated substantial losses of nearly €6m. It was attributed to increased receivables due to unpaid customer invoices. Further, the 2015 annual report outlook stated high project risks and it was announced that the company would be put up for sale.

7.3.2.2 The Role Concept of DIN EN 50128

Regarding software development topics, the standard DIN EN 50128 is of specific interest for MetroEngineers. In his Bachelor thesis, the quality manager analysed the role concept of the standard, which soon became the reference for MetroEngineers' processes.

To follow the role concept, MetroEngineers implements roles such as the quality, the safety, and the requirements manager. However, the recruitment of personnel challenges the organization. The recently recruited safety manager is not directly experienced in safety management; the requirements manager joins the project with a 6-month delay, and a new, unexperienced quality manager takes over the BRT project work.

Furthermore, the role concept is difficult to implement and binds a tremendous amount of financial resources, especially regarding personnel. The project manager explains:

The big players secured their market since they set up the standards in such a way that only the big players are able to implement the role concept.... At some point then, they had to realise that even they are not capable of implementing it. (Project manager, interview)

The implementation of the role concept at MetroEngineers is still ongoing and provides a medium transformative impact on standard enactment due to the lack of financial resources.

7.3.2.3 Documents and Document Templates Following DIN EN 50128

We find another remarkable materialization of standard requirements regarding the number of implemented documents and templates for documents at MetroEngineers following the requirements of the standard DIN EN 50128:

The 128 [DIN EN 50128] *makes suggestions for documents and its content. It compiles about 120–130 documents, 64 are essentially necessary. And if you try to compile those 64 documents, you have basically proven to your counterpart* [the assessor] *what you are about to do.* (Software developer 2, interview)

DIN EN 50128 is a powerful reference for documenting the development process. MetroEngineers follows most of these recommendations and is implementing every mandatory document in order to pass a potential future certification process. The employees at MetroEngineers assess the transformative capacity of these documents and templates as very high for their work in the BRT project. However, the actual implementation of each of these required documents falls short due to the lack of financial resources and personnel. The transformative impact of documents and document templates following DIN EN 50128 on standard enactment is thus medium.

7.3.2.4 The V-Model for Software Development

Moreover, DIN EN 50128 also offers a reference model for software development, the V-model. MetroEngineers designed its processes according to the model's guidelines. The project manager points out its relevance for European rail vehicle developers in general:

It means that European authorities and assessors think and function in line with this phase concept. In Europe, we process certain things step by step. The whole V-model is designed in phases in which certain things are to be processed. (Project manager, interview)

During our visits, we could see the manifestation of the MetroEngineers V-model on a huge poster being put up here and there in the offices and meeting rooms. The employees refer to it as the 'wallpaper' since it literally covers an enormous wall area. However, the implementation of the V-model, similar to the role concept, is described as a difficult endeavour, which binds a tremendous amount of financial resources and personnel. In practice, MetroEngineers is not yet able to fully meet the requirements of the V-model, which, vice versa, impacts standard enactment only in a medium way.

7.3.2.5 The TFS—A Never-Ending Story

Tools and technologies play a significant role in the software development practice. Besides several other tools at MetroEngineers, the TFS is the most prominent and most powerful technological resource:

> *Team foundation server is a software tool for the implementation and administration of processes and for the collection of customer requirements. The requirements of the rail standards regarding traceability are fulfilled automatically.* (Quality manager 1, bachelor thesis)

In the eyes of some organizational members, the TFS is *the* central tool for the implementation of new processes which are to be compliant with the European standards for functional safety: '*[w]ith the team foundation server, people have no other choice than living the process since the machine would not allow another process. Full Point!*' (quality manager 1, interview). Implementation and usage of the TFS was a bottom-up innovation initiated by the project manager. Even though there was no financial support from senior management, the project manager found support among quality, requirement, and safety managers in the projects. It was first intended to serve as a management system for the source code only. However, the amount of tasks is constantly growing since the TFS implementation:

> *And Team Foundation Server, the whole requirements management is fully integrated. Test management is complete, change management, claim management, document management. There is an overview of who has to deliver which document when. It is all integrated.... we should be able to work in compliance with the standards.* (Quality manager 1, interview)

With the integration of a plethora of functions into the TFS, it is considered as potent information storage, allowing time–space distance for the knowledge on processes, standards, and the development practice at MetroEngineers. To harvest the potential of this powerful resource, several TFS and process trainings were offered to the organizational members at MetroEngineers. During the process training, the participants were very engaged in giving feedback on the tool and the implemented processes. We interpret their activities as trying to keep control over their own processes in the face of the TFS, a currently emerging powerful resource.

However, while the administration of the tool binds financial and authoritative resources, it will also save significantly through process automation: '*so that the results are uploaded automatically and the like. We will save a huge amount of time*' (quality manager 1, interview). Through its interconnectedness with other tools and its different functions, the implementation of the TFS is a challenging task: '*the technical requirements are the ones that limit us most. We try to adapt our process needs somehow to these technical requirements*' (quality manager 2, interview). However, the different stakeholders at MetroEngineers, the different departments and their employees, do not fully acknowledge the use of the TFS:

> *The actual implementation* [of the processes] *will be difficult since it is a never-ending story. You start all over repeatedly because somebody comes up with a new idea. And then we discuss here and there and then we change it again. For instance, I wrote a user manual at the time. And effectively, I have to change it completely.* (Quality manager 2, interview)

At the time of our inquiry, the TFS was still not fully implemented at MetroEngineers. However, the TFS could be the dominant software tool regarding the engineering processes. For now, however, it only has a medium transformative impact on standard enactment.

7.4 Standards as Social Norms in MetroEngineers' Software Development

7.4.1 Legitimations of Organizational Deviance from Standards

For MetroEngineers we reconstructed six different deviations from standards identified by the employees of the software development unit. We illustrate every deviant practice and the different patterns of legitimizing and classifying these patterns (legitimation frame). The employees at MetroEngineers mostly referred to administrative, business, and regulatory frames when legitimizing deviance from standards (see Table 7.3). The different forms of deviations from standards are summarized in the table and explained in more detail thereafter. Altogether, the findings show a loss enactment of standard-compliant processes at MetroEngineers.

7.4.1.1 Deviation from the Required Role Separation—Omitted Roles

> *Well, there needs to be a safety manager at a certain safety level. Even the TÜV* [German Association for Technical Inspection] *had remarked there should be an additional organizational level, which acts equal to the project manager, someone who could raise the red card and say: "no, that is safety, it is not possible". These are simply the requirements of the standard, that there is this independence between the roles.* (Safety manager, interview)

The safety manager refers to the role separation as required in the European standard DIN EN 50128 and its structural implementation at MetroEngineers. The German Association for Technical Inspection, also responsible for monitoring standard compliance, is referenced here by the safety manager as the relevant evaluator for this form of deviation from standards. The safety manager implies that not only external certifiers have a responsibility to assess and point to deviations. Moreover, the in-house safety managers should have more independence and responsibility as experts to assess deviations from safety-related standards. This is not yet the case for MetroEngineers. The deviation from the standard-required role separation became also evident in the construction of the team for the BRT project (see Box 7.2).

The project manager legitimizes MetroEngineers' deviation from the required role separation as follows:

> *Even the big rail producers have realised that the process model with the ten different roles eventually becomes non-manageable because they structure the roles by own divisions, and when too many divisions work together on a project... this leads to enormous frictional losses. And, in my view, it leads to pushing back and forward of responsibility.... Instead of sitting together to find a productive solution, a requirement is simply refused in an anonymous system, it is sent back to the previous processor along the lines of "it is your turn!" That is why a huge amount of time and effort is lost during the process, which could otherwise be used for a productive solution.* (Project manager, interview)

Table 7.3 Legitimation of deviations from standards at MetroEngineers

Forms of deviation	Legitimation of deviation	Legitimation of which project members	Legitimation frame
Deviation from the required role separation	Role concept is difficult to implement and handle	Project manager	Administrative
	Role concept blurs responsibilities during development	Project manager	Administrative
	Deviance saves costs	Project manager	Business
	Deviance saves efforts	Project manager	Business
	Deviance saves time	Project manager	Business
Deviation from the required development phases	Deviance due to the Chinese client's unstable working approach and non-compliant requirements	Project manager	Business
Deviation from documentation requirements	Lack of compliance requirements for European standards in the Chinese market	Project manager	Regulatory
	Lack of an external assessor or certifier for standard compliance	Project manager	Regulatory
	Deviance saves costs	Quality manager	Business
	Deviance saves efforts	Quality manager	Business
	Deviance saves time	Quality manager	Business
Deviation from quality management requirements	Lack of understanding and willingness of senior management to implement an appropriate quality management	Quality manager	Administrative
	High priorities on cost saving by senior management	Quality manager	Business
Deviation from testing requirements	Lack of resources for the implementation of test procedure for the electrical systems	Electrical engineer, project manager	Business
	Lacking acceptance from other units	Software developer, project manager	Administrative
	Deviance saves costs	Project manager	Business

Deviation from safety integrity levels	The required safety integrity level is inappropriate	Safety manager	Technical
	Deviance saves additional efforts regarding the technical concept and testing	Safety manager	Business
	Deviance saves additional efforts regarding the implementation of roles	Safety manager	Business
	The client deviates: no delivery of required information due to the client's lack of understanding of European standards	Safety manager, project manager	Business
	Lack of an external assessor or certifier for standard compliance	Safety manager	Regulatory
	Deviance saves costs	Safety manager	Business

Box 7.2 Observation protocol: TFS training, 2 March 2016

In a project meeting, specifically set up as a training session for all employees on the TFS, the project manager ironically introduces a new project member as 'the requirements manager'. This role had been newly installed during the development project. The requirements manager instantly resists the ironic introduction and insists that he will take his new job seriously.

Legitimation for deviation from the required role separation is drawn from several reasons: not only is the role concept seen as non-manageable (administrative frame) in the light of a productive solution, but also it is causing additional time and effort constraints (business frame). Moreover, the standard-required role concept is seen as blurring responsibilities during the development work (administrative frame). In sum, MetroEngineers deviates from the required role separation by intentionally omitting standard-required roles. As a result, MetroEngineers set up a tailored and downgraded, and thus deviant, variant of a standard-compliant software development.

7.4.1.2 Deviation from the Required Development Phases—Change in Division and Succession

> *The entire V-model is structured in phases in which I complete certain things. With our client in China, we are forced to make compromises there and to deviate from this development in phases to some extent, which means, in this sense, we deviate from the standards to a certain degree because we have to react relatively flexible to the requirements of the client from China. In the normal case, if you would do this in a European development process, that would not work, I mean, they could not just jump in a previous phase, at least not with justifiable expenditure.* (Project manager, interview)

The second type of deviation also refers to requirements from European standards. The project manager describes the deviation from certain software development phases according to the V-model as required in the DIN EN 50128 standard. This practice shows again deviation as intentional departure from certain standard requirements. The project manager also mentions that leaving out certain standard requirements can lead to additional efforts and expenditures. The Chinese client's working approach forces employees at

MetroEngineers to deviate from European standards. This can also be seen in the following example:

> *We solved it by moving all safety-relevant functions into the electrical part, which means we realise them hard-wired, i.e. not within the control system because it is just not possible. But the client just does not understand that, according to European guidelines, the general path a function relates to has to be under safety-related control, including an evidence of absence of feedback and everything connected. That is the difference.* (Project manager, interview)

The project manager describes a recurring conflict during the development project: the client's requirements are not compliant with European standards or cannot be realised in a standard-compliant manner. European standards require the safety-related design of a functional chain in certain development phases, which is then secured by the evidence of safety integrity levels-certified hardware components. In order to develop as compliantly as possible, the project employees create specific safety-related technical solutions. Here, they transfer all safety-relevant functions from software control to the hardware-related electrical system.

The project manager at MetroEngineers gives several reasons for this form of deviation from standards. First, legitimation for deviance is ascribed to the Chinese client's iterative working approach of constantly changing requirements even in later development phases. Second, the client does not seem to understand the safety-related requirements of the European standard or does not deliver the required information needed for a standard-compliant software development. All in all, the non-compliant requirements of the Chinese client (business frame) are responsible for this deviation.

7.4.1.3 Deviation from Documentation Requirements—Shortened Documentation

> *Well, you can certainly shorten at some point in the field of documentation. Because if there is no certifier who wants to check the documentation in that form and who gives a direct feedback on what is necessary for a certification, then you can certainly downgrade considerably.* (Project manager, interview)

The quality manager further explains:

> *For the Chinese client a contract is not the same as for a German engineer.... Thus some things we can reason along the lines of: well, you actually do not*

> *need this at all, because it is already touched elsewhere, there is something written and here is something written.... Of course, this saves a lot of money. If ten engineers sit here and write a document for a week: that is some thousand Euros down the drain. That is why there always is this attempt here to do as little as possible, so that we can still stand by it and it is still safe and sound.*
> (Quality manager, interview)

The project manager and the quality manager describe a third form of leaving out standard requirements: the less detailed or shortened documentation of the software development process. Regarding the legitimation of deviance, the project manager first points to the lack of compliance requirements for European standards as a reason (regulatory frame). The less strict standard compliance requirements in China and the lack of an external reviewer or certifier (regulatory frame) are mentioned. Second, since the European standard is required by the contract with the Chinese client, the quality manager legitimizes this deviation with his experiences of the different working culture with the Chinese client. Thus, responsibility is partly attributed to the Chinese client's flexibility in interpreting contractual conventions. As well as this, legitimation is gained from the cost argument of saving immense expenditures and time (business frame) by shortening the documentation. Again, this deviation implies an intentional decision for a deviant version of standard-compliant software development depending on the targeted market and its standard compliance requirements and conditions.

7.4.1.4 Deviation from Quality Management Requirements—Superficial Implementation

The quality manager of the software development unit tells the story of the superficial implementation of a general quality manager at MetroEngineers who was instructed rather randomly in compliance with standard requirements.

> *Quality* [management] *is really... well, this is due to our managing director, he doesn't understand it, he doesn't want it. He doesn't consider it as necessary: "That is stupid, why we do it? It costs money. No, no." We have an official quality manager for the whole company. He was once simply condemned to it while passing by coincidently. They sat in the glass case and discussed about it in a meeting: "yes, according to the standard we need somebody there". And he just walked along the corridor and then they said "him!" That is how he got his job. He was not even keen on it; in fact, he is a mechanical designer, and he would rather like to go back to mechanical design again.*

> *Now, he has no time anymore, he is massively overloaded. So, when I entered the company, it all ended up on my desk. And, well, it* [quality] *is definitely neglected here.* (Quality manager 1, interview)

The '*official*' quality manager seemed not to be interested and qualified enough for the spontaneous instruction and thus was unable to cope with this challenge. Unofficially, the quality manager of the software development unit largely took over his quality management tasks. We can regard the superficial implementation of quality management standards by the senior management at MetroEngineers as a form of deviation.

A further example shows how the software development unit tries to overcome deviation from quality management standards by the senior management:

> *We are the only unit that even deals with these topics; we are the only ones who have a quality manager. The company has a quality manager, indeed, but he is only responsible pro forma. That is the way it is in companies. We are the only ones who have certified testers and we are the only ones who have a certified requirements engineer.* (Quality manager, interview)

Legitimation for this deviation is ascribed by the quality manager to the lack of understanding and willingness of the senior management of MetroEngineers (administrative frame). In the view of the chief executive officer, the implementation of an adequate quality management system would not make sense but cause additional costs and efforts. Quality management as a standard requirement is not being paid much attention, which leads to the forced engagement of a decoupled, over-challenged general quality manager. The quality manager of the software development unit is attributing the responsibility for deviation to the senior management and their decisions for low priorities on quality management and high priorities on cost saving (business frame). This deviation from quality management standards is seen as being introduced by management directives, causing a decoupling and pressuring effect on the employees' every-day activities.

A last example describes how the employees at the software development unit at MetroEngineers find themselves a solution in the engagement of Master degree students as interns to cope with the lack of knowledge about standards (see Box 7.3). As legitimation, the quality manager points to the lack of authoritative resources to instruct and monitor other units regarding standard enactment.

Box 7.3 Observation protocol: kick-off meeting, 1 October 2015; concept meeting, 14 October 2015

It appeared that quality management tasks related to standard compliance were given especially to students who worked as interns in the software development unit. The quality manager had started as an intern with the task to compile an overview of standards for software development at MetroEngineers. This resulted in a Bachelor thesis on the standard-compliant software development process at MetroEngineers. Also, a later software developer started as an intern with a Bachelor thesis on standard-compliant software testing. A third Bachelor thesis by an intern provided an overview of relevant Chinese standards.

Box 7.4 Observation protocol: lessons learned meeting, 14 October 2015

In a lesson learned meeting, the software developers voice dissatisfaction towards the electrical engineers for not being compliant with standards, specifically for not testing the electrical systems: 'How do you actually test your circuit diagrams?' (project manager). The electrical engineers reply that electrical systems have not been tested so far due to lack of staff. However, the software engineers persist in arguing that they make immense efforts in testing their software systems according to respective standards. Finally, the project manager challenges them: 'We covered the whole process topic by a structure plan. You have to start some time'.

7.4.1.5 Deviation from Testing Requirements—Omitted Testing

At this time of standard enactment, the members of the software development unit are trying to roll out a standard-compliant process to other functional units in the company, such as the electrical and the mechanical units. However, the electrical engineers have so far not implemented a process for testing the electrical systems (see Box 7.4). Thus, the software engineers label them as deviants.

For the legitimation of the deviation, the electrical engineers point to a lack of resources for sufficient personnel (business frame). On the contrary, the project manager is ascribing responsibility for delaying the standard enactment process to other units. The deviation is seen as a dissatisfactory, preliminary stage to standard compliance. Thus, standard enactment appears as a procedure, which is based on continual efforts to implement standard-compliant processes and structures for all units of the division. The software developers point out the lack of acceptance from other units (administrative frame) as hindrance to a broad standard-compliant development. The process of standard enactment hence is also characterized by conflicts between the units due to their different approaches and allocative as well as authoritative resources for standard compliance.

7.4.1.6 Deviation from Safety Integrity Levels—Lowered Safety Integrity Levels

The field descriptions (Box 7.5 and 7.6) show how the employees tried to renegotiate the safety integrity level as required in the standard DIN EN 50126. The safety integrity level originally required by the Chinese customer was technically inadequate and at the same time far too high to be achieved by MetroEngineers (technical framework). It would have meant immense additional effort in the technical design, testing scope, and implementation of additional roles in the development process (such as verifier or validator) to meet these requirements. Thus, deviation from the safety integrity level framework also implies cost and effort saving intentions (business frame). However, the quality manager in consultation with the safety manager as an expert in the evaluation of possibly neglectable standards shows the limit of

Box 7.5 Observation protocol: first concept meeting, 14 October 2015

During a conceptual project meeting, 2 weeks after the kick-off meeting, the project manager states that 'it is on us to argue the standards' and 'to discuss them away' (project manager). Available knowledge on relevant standards for metro train vehicle development was collected in an Excel document called 'norm tree' containing over eighty single standards. After discussing several strategies for the development work by all participating engineers, the project manager suggests to 'discuss standards away' in future negotiations with the client on the basis of this 'norm tree' and its evaluation by the safety manager.

Box 7.6 Observation protocol: concept meeting, 11 November 2015

In a later concept meeting regarding the filtering of technical requirements from the respective standards, the safety manager presents his analysis and evaluation of thus far received documents from the Chinese client on required standards and safety evaluations. The European standards DIN EN 50126 and 50129 are part of the requirements, combined with a risk analysis in order to assess the security levels for respective safety-critical train components.

From his analysis, the safety manager presents the conclusion that the client's expectations on safety levels of several train components are much higher than expected. A vital discussion on how safety levels are actually assessed emerges among the participants of the project meeting. The project manager problematizes the safety topic by pointing out the fear that, in the case the metro will eventually be sold on the European market, people might say: 'Dear guys, what have you done here?' The safety manager intervenes in a modest manner by explaining the exact calculation of the standardized preliminary risk analysis to everybody in the meeting. The engineers, however, check back several times on the safety manager for possibilities to loosen these calculations and conclude that the required safety levels cannot be realised technically. The project manager eventually suggests renegotiating the standard requirements with the client on the basis of the safety manager's argumentation. However, the safety manager's interpretation of deviance from standards seems rather limited since he strictly keeps to standardized measures and calculations. The engineers in the meeting make several jokes towards the safety manager for having an unpleasant job. The safety manager, however, keeps on touching on serious challenges, such as the renegotiation of the safety integrity level with the Chinese client and the respective severe impacts on the project's organization. At the end of the meeting, the safety manager voices his limits and unwillingness in renegotiating the safety levels all by himself. The project manager thus assures him support: "You do not have to fight on your own".

negotiating deviation from standards: the safety and the reliable composition of the designed product still need to be defendable for MetroEngineers.

The safety manager points out a further line of argumentation when negotiating with the Chinese client on compliance with the safety integrity level framework:

> *Because we do not produce it ourselves but just deliver the design, we pre-suppose that the hardware is certified with safety integrity levels two. Under the presumption that it is a safety integrity level two hardware, we would just have to take care of the compliance of the functional chains. But as I said... there is no certifier so far. So, we are proving it on our own now.*
>
> (Safety manager, interview)

Responsibility for negotiating this deviation is attributed especially to the safety manager as an expert in safety evaluations and to the project manager in negotiations with the client. MetroEngineers takes the responsibility for a safe and appropriate product design as the final service. However, final responsibility for the resulting deviation from European standards is ascribed to the client (business frame) as producer of the train. The employees assess the choice of standards and their enactment is a matter of negotiation with the client under the principles of safety and economic pressures (business frame). As well as this, the safety manager sets a standard in which he expects the client to compile only safety-integrity-level-certified hardware components for the design of the metro. Responsibility for deviation is again ascribed to the client as the final producer of the metro. Even though there seems to be no certifier so far to examine standard compliance (regulatory frame), the safety manager takes on responsibility for the risk analysis and standard-compliant, safety-related functional chains by setting up safety standards for the client.

Moreover, the safety manager points to the ethical responsibility of his role:

> *Ask yourself the question, could you sleep well if something happens?... So, no matter what you do, you have to do it systematically and traceably. And it means documentation effort. That is requested, it is clear.*
>
> (Safety manager, interview)

Overall, responsibility for the general lack of standard compliance is attributed by the software development unit's employees to the senior management at MetroEngineers and to the Chinese client. However, the software development unit is responsible for standard-deviant development.

7.4.2 Expected Sanctions from Deviance

Considering the pressure from expected sanctions at MetroEngineers, it is important to consider that the Chinese client expected compliance with European standards only by contract; compliance with European or Chinese standards is not mandatory for entering the Chinese market. Negative sanctions can thus be expected only from a breach of the contract leading to penalties or the prospective loss of follow-up orders from the Chinese client (business frame). Table 7.4 provides an overview on the expected sanctions from deviations at MetroEngineers.

Business legitimations are most prevalent among the positive and negative sanctions expected from deviance at MetroEngineers. MetroEngineers expects no sanctions from any regulatory authority. The project manager thus explains a standard compliance strategy, which is free of expected negative sanctions:

> *We have once made this decision for us that from now on we will always develop compliant with this standard. In projects in which it is not explicitly required, we intended to lower our aims a little regarding the requirements, which the client does not want to have. We cut them off the process, but we generally use the process to scale with European projects. So that we run the full program in a European project and a downgraded version in a Chinese project.* (Project manager, interview)

Table 7.4 Expected sanctions in the case of standard deviations at MetroEngineers

Sanctioning frame	Expected sanctions on project members in the case of deviations
Business frame	Contractual penalties Loss of follow-up orders Damage to reputation in the European market Saving on development costs Saving efforts on standard implementation and compliance monitoring
Ethical frame	Damage to human life
Regulatory frame	No sanctions expected due to: • lack of internal responsibility for certification • lack of willingness to comply with European standards in China (except software developers) • lack of external reviewer or certifier in China
Technical frame	Not mentioned
Administrative frame	Not mentioned

However, as pointed out in section 7.4.1.6, negative sanctions are also referred to by the safety manager when he points to the ethical responsibility of guaranteeing the safety of human life (ethical frame) and by the project manager when he implies negative consequences for MetroEngineer's reputation on the European market (business frame). However, the software developing unit professes that the newly/during the course of the BRT project negotiated and adjusted safety integrity levels were the appropriate and affordable safety integrity levels for metro trains.

Surprisingly, the employees at MetroEngineers refer to a lot of positive sanctions from deviations. Most prevalent in the argumentation of the employees was the effect of saving costs, time, and efforts by deviation from standards (business frame). This relates to savings not only from a downgraded standard implementation but also from the reduced monitoring of standard compliance. Moreover, since compliance with European standards is not mandatory for entering the markets in China, no direct sanctions are expected when deviating from European as well as Chinese standards (regulatory frame). This is further supported by the employees' impression that there is no external reviewer or certifier (regulatory frame) for standard compliance in China.

7.5 Non-Regulated Deviance from Standards at MetroEngineers: Manipulations Caused by Contradictions

In this section, we provide explanations for why MetroEngineers' standard enactment emerges as non-regulated deviance. To this end, we identify contradictions that appear during the BRT software developing project. As described in Fried and Walgenbach (2020), contradictions occur, first, when standards are not appropriately represented as interpretative schemes, facilities, or social norms in organizational practices. Second, contradictions emerge as inconsistencies *between* standards as interpretative schemes, as facilities, or as social norms. The findings at MetroEngineers represent only a vague enactment of standards and rather a variety of deviant practices which we reconstruct as non-regulated organizational deviance from standards. MetroEngineers' standard enactment as non-regulated deviance from standards is outlined in Figure 7.1.

We can retrace several *asymmetries* and *contradictions* leading MetroEngineers to deviate from standards.

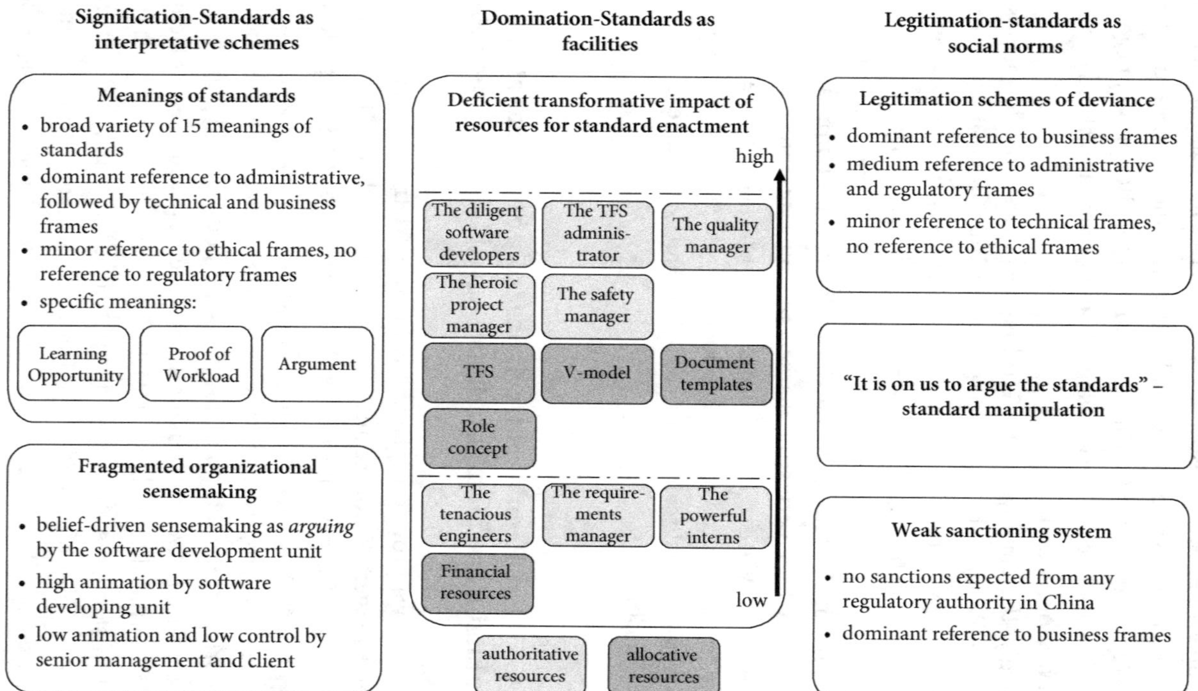

Figure 7.1 Standard enactment in MetroEngineers' software development

7.5.1 Standards as Interpretative Schemes: Fragmented Organizational Sensemaking

During the BRT project, we found a broad variety of fifteen meanings of standards represented by the software developing unit, with equal reference to technical, administrative, and business frames. Project members only sparsely referred to ethical or regulatory frames regarding the signification of standards. The software developing unit relates very positively to the engagement in standard enactment and, hence, implies a strong belief in their importance. However, the high signification of standards for the software developing unit is not shared by MetroEngineer's senior management, the BRT project's mechanical and electrical engineers, or the Chinese client. The ongoing *argumentation* for the proper implementation of standards conflicts with the lack of sensegiving by the BRT project's mechanical and electrical engineers, senior management, and client. The case-specific meanings of *argument*, *proof of workload*, and *learning opportunity* represent the belief-driven sensemaking as *arguing* among the software developing unit. Members of the software developing unit use standards as an argument during discussions on the technical constructions, as evidence in budget negotiations with the client, and as a learning opportunity for process improvements. However, these beliefs are not generally shared at MetroEngineers. We observed that sensemaking for standards at MetroEngineers is *fragmented* (Maitlis 2005): standards do not serve as an organization-wide robust interpretative scheme. Sensemaking for standard enactment is highly animated only by the software developing unit, while senior management and the client neither animate nor control standard enactment.

7.5.2 Standards as Facilities: Deficient Transformative Impact of Resources for Standard Enactment

We can identify a second asymmetry at MetroEngineers: that is, the asymmetry between the transformative capacity of resources and their actual impact in enacting standards efficiently. During the BRT project, we saw an overall deficient availability of authoritative and allocative resources to facilitate a software development process that is compliant with standards. Standards cannot be effectively enacted as a facility, since appropriate financial resources are provided by neither senior management nor the client. Several new resources were established just in the course of the BRT project, such as the requirements manager and the TFS administrator, but they massively lack transformative impact. For instance, in compensation for a lack of resources, MetroEngineers relies on interns as a low-cost resource for generating knowledge on standards or to implement technical solutions such as the TFS. Generally, the immense lack of resources regarding standard enactment leads to ongoing conflicts between the employees of the software developing unit and the electrical as well as mechanical engineers. The senior management focuses on reducing costs due to the financially weak situation of MetroEngineers since the Chinese client does not provide any financial resources for enabling compliance with standard requirements, i.e. for the software development process. The software developing unit's mobilization of resources for standard enactment, i.e. by creating roles such as the requirements manager and the TFS administrator, remains insufficient for compliant standard enactment and overall disintegrated at MetroEngineers.

7.5.3 Standards as Social Norms: Manipulation of Standards and a Weak Sanctioning System

The third asymmetry concerns the aspect of standards as social norms. As originally intended, European standards at MetroEngineers should have generated robust social norms for the software developing unit's work. However, the software developing unit expects no sanctions from any regulatory authority in China, and even if compliance with European standards is mentioned in the contract, compliance with them does not have the same significance. Consequently, standards are not enacted as social norms and do not trigger any regulatory sanctions when deviating from them. Hence, as voiced by the project manager: '*it is on us to argue the standards*'. *Manipulation* of standards by members of the BRT project appears here as deviating from standards to get the software development work done.

Legitimations for deviance from the agreed European standards are predominantly based on *business* frames. We find medium reference to administrative and regulatory frames, minor reference to technical frames, and no reference to ethical frames when legitimizing deviance from standards at MetroEngineers.

Regarding the sanctioning of deviance, we can also see a weak sanctioning system at MetroEngineers. Since the client requires compliance with European standards only by contract, the employees at MetroEngineers expect no sanctions from any regulatory authority. This is further enforced since MetroEngineers is only responsible as designer, not as manufacturer of the ordered rail vehicle. Sanctions at MetroEngineers are mainly of business reference: for instance, saving development costs and reducing standard implementation efforts were the most prominent expected business sanctions. While the damage to human life is voiced as a sanction with an ethical reference, regulatory sanctions are mentioned only as lacking. This is consistent with earlier empirical findings (Tenbrunsel & Messick 1999) that *weak sanctioning systems* promote a focus on the business aspects of decision-making, crowding out other potential frames such as ethical, administrative, or technical reasons for standard compliance.

7.5.4 Contradiction between Standards as Interpretative Schemes and Standards as Social Norms

As Giddens (1984) emphasizes, interpretative schemes deliver the reasons for activities and ideally the normative grounds on which activities are justified. However, at MetroEngineers the interpretative schemes do not provide normative grounds for the software development activities. Subsequently, we see a contradiction between standards as interpretative schemes and standards as social norms: the software developers believe in the ethical, administrative, technical, and regulatory significance of standards. At the same time, they address business reasons and only positive sanctions for deviating from standards in the BRT project. The business interests of software developers are at odds with their positive attitude towards standards. They ultimately undermine the effectiveness of standards at MetroEngineers.

7.5.5 Contradiction between Standards as Interpretative Schemes and Standards as Facilities

Another contradiction becomes apparent between the high significance of standards as interpretive schemes for the software developing unit and the generally low dominance of standards at MetroEngineers by claiming only deficient allocative and authoritative resources for standard enactment. Standards enfold significance among members of the software developing unit, on the one hand; on the other hand, the available resources do not facilitate proper standard enactment, for instance the implementation of the V-model, due to a lack of controlling actions, decisions, events, and developments. The software developers constantly argue for standard compliance by emphasizing the advantages of a standard-compliant development process, but at the same time they experience a *deficient transformative impact of resources.* What is contradictory for the software developing unit appears at the same time as consistent with the *fragmented sensemaking* at MetroEngineers in general: the senior management and the client do not share the same significance of standards; thus, they do not provide sense for standard enactment and consequently no allocative or authoritative resources. The mobilized resources for standard enactment for the BRT project at MetroEngineers were internally relocated from the software developing unit's project budget.

In summary, in the face of the highly contradictory setting for standard enactment at MetroEngineers, the software unit tries ambitiously to comply with European standards. However, they are not succeeding but applying a practice of standard enactment, which we term non-regulated deviance. In the case of MetroEngineers, non-regulated deviance means to answer the various constraining contradictions by manipulative, and eventually deviant standard enactment efforts on-site. As knowledgeable agents of standard enactment, employees of the software development unit take action and try to manage the contradictions, for example by negotiating standards with the client or establishing new authoritative and allocative resources. However, their ambitious efforts remain unheard in the overall organization. The apparent contradictions at MetroEngineers are supporting deviance rather than enabling compliant standard enactment.This gives rise to a risk to the certification approval, access to certain standard-related markets, and possibly even the safety of human life.

References

Fried, A. & Walgenbach, P. 2020. Theoretical framework to explore organizational deviance from standards. *In:* Fried, A. (ed.) *Understanding Deviance in a World of Standards.* Oxford: Oxford University Press.

Fuchs, K. 2011. Zulassungsverfahren ohne Ende? Probleme bei der Zulassung von Schienenfahrzeugen im Eisenbahnverkehr und Ansätze zu ihrer Lösung. *Der Nahverkehr*, 29 (7/8), 16–18.

Giddens, A. 1984. *The Constitution of Society: Outline of the Theory of Structuration.* Cambridge: Polity Press.

Heras-Saizarbitoria, I. & Boiral, O. 2012. Is ISO 9001 really effective for the global supply chain management? A preliminary exploratory analysis on customer–suppliers relationships in China. *In:* Bernardo, M. (ed.) *Quality Management and Beyond: The Current Situation and Future Perspectives.* Girona: Documenta Universitaria.

Li, Y. & Leenen, M. 2012. Der chinesische Bahnmarkt—auch in Zukunft der dynamischste Markt für Bahntechnik? *Eisenbahntechnische Rundschau*, 8, 143–6.

Maitlis, S. 2005. The social processes of organizational sensemaking. *Academy of Management Journal*, 48, 21–49.

Oelsner, J. 2017. Die DIN EN 50126-1 und die komplexe Produkt- und Systemzertifizierung. *EI—Der Eisenbahningenieur*, 01/2017.

Tenbrunsel, A. E. & Messick, D. M. 1999. Sanctioning systems, decision frames, and cooperation. *Administrative Science Quarterly*, 44, 684–707.

PART III

EXPLAINING ORGANIZATIONAL DEVIANCE FROM STANDARDS

In the final part of the book we summarize why organizational deviance from standards happens. We develop a typology for classifying organizational deviance from standards inspired by structuration theory (Fried & Singhal 2020; Fried & Walgenbach 2020; Giddens 1984) and the empirical investigations in part II (Gey et al. 2020a, 2020b; Langer et al. 2020). The typology is based on the analysis of standards as interpretative schemes, facilities, and social norms (Giddens 1979) and the appearing asymmetries and contradictions during standard enactment in organizations. In chapter 8, a cross-case analysis is accomplished that reveals four ideal types of organizational deviance: two commitment-oriented and two manipulation-oriented types of organizational deviance. In chapter 9, we discuss the typology of organizational deviance from standards in terms of their relation to exploratory as well as exploitative organizational processes. Finally, the book is concluded in chapter 10 by a summary of the contributions that are made to the discourse on corporate responsibility and criminal law.

Understanding Deviance in a World of Standards, Andrea Fried, Oxford University Press (2020).

DOI: 10.1093/oso/9780198833888.001.0001

8

Typology of Organizational Deviance from Standards

Andrea Fried and Sarah Langer

In this chapter we reveal four types of organizational deviance from standards—two commitment-oriented types (*attentive deviance* and *over-conformity*) and two manipulation-oriented types (*non-regulated deviance* and *illegitimate deviance*). Attentive deviance, over-conformity, and non-regulated deviance result from empirical findings previously presented in this book (see Gey et al. 2020a, 2020b; Langer et al. 2020). We also suppose a fourth type of organizational deviance that, in comparison to the other types, knowingly violates standards potentially harming societal needs such as human safety or health. We frame this type as illegitimate deviance. Although it is hardly possible for researchers to empirically investigate illegitimate deviance in situ, we however saw the necessity and possibility to outline and discuss also the deliberate violation of standards. Hence, we tried to deduce conditions and features of illegitimate deviance from the aggregated insights of our other empirical cases. Here, we assume cases where strong external sanctions for disclosed deviations from standards exist while the involved stakeholders only show a minimal interest in standard enactment—and prognose what the implications for organizational deviance from standards are.

The two commitment-oriented types and two manipulation-oriented types of organizational deviance we present express two fundamentally different ways of dealing with standards. Commitment-oriented types (attentive deviance and over-conformity) respect standards and acknowledge their business, administrative, ethical, technical, and regulatory contribution. Organizational members following a commitment-oriented type of organizational deviance either monitor standards in a reflexive manner or tightly control standard deviations in a diagnostic way. The way of monitoring (reflexive or diagnostic) has implications on how effective innovation, flexibility, and learning are accomplished in standard-enacting organizations (see also Langer & Fried 2020). In contrast, manipulation-oriented types (non-regulated and illegitimate

Andrea Fried and Sarah Langer, *Typology of Organizational Deviance from Standards* In: *Understanding Deviance in a World of Standards*. Edited by: Andrea Fried, Oxford University Press (2020). © Oxford University Press.
DOI: 10.1093/oso/9780198833888.003.0008

deviance) question standards and contest their business, administrative, ethical, technical, and regulatory contribution fundamentally. Organizational members following a manipulation-oriented type decide either in dependence on organization-specific circumstances to self-monitor deviations according to their own operating procedures, or they hardly monitor deviations from standards at all. The way of standard monitoring (self or inadequate) has implications on how misconduct and organizational wrongdoing in standard-enacting organizations appear, and thus how likely cheating on requirements becomes (see also Langer & Fried 2020).

Inspired by Giddens' concept of the 'duality of structure', we create a typology which is based on the viewpoint that standards are modalities of action (Fried & Walgenbach 2020; Giddens 1984). As depicted also in Figure 3.1, the three structurationist elements—standards as interpretative schemes, as facilities, and as social norms—emerge as organizational dimensions forming organizational deviance from standards. When standards are enacted in organizations, they become modalities of action and as such interpretative schemes of organizational communication. Furthermore, they claim authoritative and allocative resources in power relations. Standards become social norms and thus they legitimate actions and sanction deviations in organizations. Asymmetries and contradictions between and among the appearance of standards as interpretative schemes, facilities, and social norms lead to four different types of organizational deviance. Each of the four types is thus associated with a combination of specifically enacted structurationist elements and asymmetries as well as contradictions. These asymmetries and contradictions provide explanations for the appearance of organizational deviance from standards (see Table 8.1).

In the following, we describe each type of organizational deviance in detail (see Table 8.1) and compare the structurationist elements as well as asymmetries and contradictions in standard enactment (Fried & Walgenbach 2020). Before we introduce the differences among the four types of deviance, we point first to the similarities. At first, the meanings of standards are essentially of an administrative nature for organizational members. If standards are taken seriously, they shape, first and foremost, organizational procedures such as development processes, development roles, management decisions, and further administrative fields in organizations (Power 1997). Furthermore, business reasons are mainly given by organizational members when legitimating deviations from standards. This counts likewise for the expectations organizational members express regarding sanctioning of deviations from standards. Only for one type of deviance, over-conformity, are sanctions from deviance feared not for business reasons but for administrative reasons. Examples of

Table 8.1 Typology of organizational deviance from standards

Structurationist theme	Structurationist elements	Commitment-oriented types of organizational deviance		Manipulation-oriented types of organizational deviance	
		Attentive deviance	**Over-conformity**	**Non-regulated deviance**	**Illegitimate deviance**
Standards as interpretative schemes	Stakeholder interactions on signification	Guided sensemaking (high animation)	Restricted sensemaking (low animation)	Fragmented sensemaking (partly high animation)	Minimal sensemaking (low animation)
	Signification accounts	Argumentation Expectation	Expectation	Argumentation	Expectation
	Main signification frames for standards	Administrative Business	Administrative Technical	Administrative Business Technical	Administrative Technical
Standards as facilities	Transformative impact	Adequate	Adequate	Deficient	Deficient
Standards as social norms	Legitimation accounts	Commitment Manipulation	Commitment	Manipulation	Manipulation
	External sanctioning system	Strong	Strong	Weak	Strong
	Internal sanctioning system	Adequate	Strong	Weak	Weak
	Main legitimation frames for deviance	Business	Business Administrative	Business	Business
	Main sanction frames for deviance	Business	Administrative	Business	Business
Asymmetries	Amongst structurationist elements	Social norms	None	Interpretative schemes Facilities	Social norms
Contradictions	Between structurationist elements	None	None	Interpretative schemes vs social norms Interpretative schemes vs facilities	Interpretative schemes vs social norms Facilities vs social norms

administrative reasons can be the internal disapproval by the quality manager for not meeting standard requirements or delays in the development process. When expecting sanctions from organizational deviance, organizational members often refer to administrative rationales such as the approval of the software quality or the product manager, or the loss of bonus payments.

We believe that these similarities in the signification of standards and in the legitimation of deviance from standards might differ to some extent in non-profit organizations (Drucker 1990). On the one hand, in contrast to non-profit organizations, organizational members of for-profit organizations largely refer to economic reasons for legitimating deviations; they deviate from standards to save costs, efforts, and time in the short run. On the other hand, some also fear business sanctions due to deviations that could affect their profit targets in the longer run. These include, for example, the loss of market share if their products and services are not approved by auditors. In turn, ethical reasons might play a minor role, unlike in non-profit organizations that often pay much attention to these. Thus, we assume that the typology is limited to for-profit organizations and, furthermore, to process standards (Fried & Glaa 2020). The typology, however, demonstrates that the way how standards are enacted as interpretative schemes, facilities, and social norms determines the specific type of organizational deviance. For this reason, we provide a structurationist analysis in the form of a typology in this chapter, as well as an interactional perspective on organizational deviance in the next chapter (Langer & Fried 2020).

8.1 Commitment-Oriented Types of Organizational Deviance

8.1.1 Attentive Deviance from Standards

Attentive deviance, the first commitment-oriented type of organizational deviance from standards, represents deviations that are thoughtfully adjusted for various reasons (see Table 8.1). When organizations follow an approach of attentive deviance, standards serve as interpretative schemes and become a crucial part of organizational communication. They claim enough authoritative and allocative resources to generate substantial impact on maintaining reliant organizational processes. However, these organizations are confronted with asymmetries when standards act as social norms. Here, at least three cases are possible: (1) standards might not fit the organization-specific context, for instance, when the required process model is designated for large organizations, but the standard-enacting organization has only a few units and positions to offer (see also Langer et al. 2020). (2) Standards might hinder, for instance, innovation and learning by relating to an outdated technological or administrative state. (3) Requirements from various standards applicable for the respective product or process might conflict with each other. This is shown in Gey et al. (2020a), where standard requirements from the crane industry conflicted with requirements from special vehicle standards. In general, standards challenge organizational members in such a way that they must reflect on the standards' scope and their enabling or constraining character.

8.1.1.1 Standards as Interpretative Schemes

In the case of attentive deviance, standards provide sufficient meaning for organizational members to engage in standard enactment. Even if there is an emphasis on administrative and business meanings, organizational members are also aware of the technical, ethical, and regulatory significance of standards. For organizational members, it is important to have a far-reaching understanding of the scope of standards and their significance, for instance, for society, but also their enabling or constraining character for innovation and learning. This includes that organizational members use standards requirements as an argument, for instance, not only to accumulate resources for standard enactment but also to take the signification of standards for granted to a certain extent. A balanced sensemaking between a thoughtful, ongoing argumentation on the signification of standards on the one hand, while relying on certain expectations regarding the importance of standards on the other hand, contributes to an attentive deviance from standards (Fried & Walgenbach 2020; Gey et al. 2020a; Weick 1995).

Most significant here is that not only do standards enfold meaning and rich accounts for those whose work is directly affected by them, such as for software developers and their coding activities. The significance of standards is also widely shared among important stakeholders involved in standard enactment. Besides the directly affected organizational members, clients, senior management, and suppliers are also engaged in providing sense for standard enactment. External stakeholders such as assessors and consultants can likewise play an essential role in animating sensemaking for standards. This can happen, for example, by discussing standards in regular consultations and meetings, or establishing a periodic approval process. To summarize, even if sensemaking differs among organizations, high animation and high control of standard enactment is comparably well balanced among the stakeholders involved in standard enactment (Fried & Walgenbach 2020; Maitlis 2005). This form of guided organizational sensemaking during standard enactment is characteristic of attentive deviance (Gey et al. 2020a).

8.1.1.2 Standards as Facilities

Attentive organizational deviance is likely to occur on the basis of a reasonable availability of allocative and authoritative resources for standard enactment. Allocative resources for standard enactment are, for example, financial resources, process models, and software tools for the standard-compliant documentation of processes. Authoritative resources for standard enactment can be incorporated, for instance, by quality, project, or requirements managers, and externals such as process consultants and assessors (Fried & Walgenbach 2020; Gey et al. 2020a; Giddens 1984). We find here a medium to high transformative impact of most allocative and authoritative resources for standard enactment. In comparison to manipulation-oriented types of organizational deviance, efforts for compliant standard enactment are constantly and intensively facilitated by various allocative and authoritative resources, for instance, external consultants and assessors to solve the demanding approval process, or personnel for standard renegotiations with standardizing bodies. Standards thus wield power because organizational members successfully claim investments for their enactment to enable, for instance, stable processes in software development. At the same time, standards do not constrain them by an oversupply of resources and rules, such as too many process milestones or document templates for proving the development process.

8.1.1.3 Standards as Social Norms

Attentive deviance from standards shows a challenged enactment of standards as social norms, since standard requirements are partly conflicting and thus attentive adjustments are necessary. For instance, Gey et al. (2020a) show that some organizations face a situation where standards do not suit their current or prospective products or development processes. For this reason, they might consider ways to negotiate existing standard requirements with assessors or they engage themselves in the creation of standards at the level of involvement in standardization bodies. Organizational members argue on the standards' usefulness and importance and, for context-specific reasons, manipulate them to some extent (Fried & Walgenbach 2020; Weick 1995). However, in general, they commit to standards. Organizations that attentively deviate also accept standards as a source of business sanctions when fearing, for instance, the loss of market shares. By attentively deviating from standards, organizational members do not risk at the same time human life, safety, or the environment.

8.1.1.4 Asymmetries and Contradictions

Asymmetries among standards as social norms are likely to trigger attentive deviance. Besides this, there exist no further substantial asymmetries or contradictions (Fried & Walgenbach 2020; Gey et al. 2020a). They are attentively managed during standard enactment. Organizational members negotiate with assessors to gain approval if not all standard requirements suit their circumstances. Or they might consult external standardization experts, or participate in the standard setting processes of standardization bodies to shape upcoming standard templates adjusted to their needs.

In sum, attentive deviance from standards means that standards are embedded in an organizational discourse, triggering rich rules of interpretation of how organizational processes should look like. Standards wield power by an adequate provision and use of resources supporting their enactment. As social norms, standards are scrutinized in detail, but they are accepted as rules of sanctioning in general. This is accompanied by guided organizational sensemaking for standard enactment where many stakeholders discursively enact standards (Fried & Walgenbach 2020; Giddens 1984). Asymmetries are attentively managed during standard enactment: on the one hand, asymmetries appear as challenges to organizational members; on the other hand, they serve as an opportunity for generally scrutinizing the organizational standard enactment in a reflexive manner (Langer & Fried 2020). Contradictions, however, between standards as interpretative schemes, facilities, and social norms hardly exist within the organization. If they did exist, organizations would tend to follow a manipulation-oriented type of deviance from standards (see section 8.2).

8.1.2 Over-conformity with Standards

Over-conformity with standards is the second commitment-oriented type of organizational deviance (see Table 8.1). It describes a situation in which organizational members deviate by overachieving standard requirements. Additional requirements that are not part of the actual standard requirements are introduced in the daily practice: for instance, additional milestones are integrated in the development processes or templates are added to document the development process. In the case of over-conformity, standards are powerfully enacted as facilities and social norms. As interpretative schemes they are hardly manifest in the discursive consciousness of the organizational members. Standards and their enabling or constraining effects are not scrutinized. As interpretative schemes, facilities, and social norms, they are part of the practical consciousness of organizational members (Fried & Walgenbach 2020; Giddens 1984). Thus, they are taken for granted. Asymmetries and contradictions of standard enactment barely exist.

8.1.2.1 Standards as Interpretative Schemes

Over-conformity with standards is characterized by a restricted sensemaking of standards among those who are regularly involved in standard enactment (Gey et al. 2020b; Maitlis 2005). Meanings of standards are rarely discussed by the stakeholders involved, for example software developers, clients, and top management. Only narrow readings of standard requirements are appreciated. Senior management determines and substantially controls compliance with the prescribed SOPs (Gey et al. 2020b). Discourses on standard interpretations are mainly separated from those who apply standards, for instance, software developers in their daily practice. Furthermore, the restricted sensemaking of standards addresses strong expectations as to what standards should achieve but does not allow argumentations on their limitations or advantages. Thus, the existing organizational rules of interpreting standards are not contested. Alternative attempts to interpret standards are weak or missing.

8.1.2.2 Standards as Facilities

As in the case of attentive deviance, over-conformity with standards occurs in an environment with an adequate availability of allocative and authoritative resources for standard enactment. Most allocative and authoritative resources have a medium to high transformative impact on standard enactment. They facilitate, for instance, the establishment of powerful standard-related roles to monitor the implementation of SOPs. Due to the investment and use of resources for standard enactment, standards can develop power within the organization.

8.1.2.3 Standards as Social Norms

A comparably high commitment to standards is characteristic of this deviance type. Standards are firmly enacted as social norms. Moreover, organizations that show over-conformity to standards add requirements to the already regulatory required ones, for instance, requesting more development milestones or document templates than necessary. They follow the idea that it economically makes sense to have reliable, standard-compliant processes in place in the long term to avoid costly rearrangements in the future. The external sanctions accomplished by auditors, the certification agency, and the like are matched with an internal sanctioning system by the organization. For instance, positive sanctions for fulfilling requirements in SOPs or incentives for successfully completing non-regular audits motivate standard compliance. When over-conforming to standards, this internal sanctioning system gives positive signals to organizational members via performance indicators and ensures a high probability of detection and large fines when not following SOPs (Fried & Walgenbach 2020; Tenbrunsel & Messick 1999).

Thus, commitment to standard compliance is taken-for-granted and supported by a strong internal and external sanctioning system. Administrative reasonings of over-conformity and sanctions support the impression of organizational members that standards become an end in themselves (Gey et al. 2020b).

8.1.2.4 Asymmetries and Contradictions

That standards become an end in themselves is also visible in the fact that neither fundamental asymmetries nor contradictions occur between standards as interpretative schemes, as facilities, and as social norms. Over-conformity with standards means that, on the one hand, standards unleash power by the provision and use of various resources for their enactment and that standards are powerfully referenced as social norms, e.g. when monitoring standard enactment. On the other hand, when organizations over-conform with standards, animated discourses are missing. Thus, standards are part of the practical consciousness of the organizational members (Fried & Walgenbach 2020, Giddens 1984). Organizational members stay in a 'comfort zone'. Unintended consequences of standard enactment and the potentially enabling or constraining character of standards are hardly reflected, at least at an organizational level. Instead, asymmetries or contradictions recognised by single organizational members do not become part of the discursive consciousness, and thus they are hardly part of the organization's reflections on the usefulness of standards. Over-conformity with standards hinders 'out-of-the-box thinking' regarding the enactment of standards.

8.2 Manipulation-Oriented Types of Organizational Deviance

8.2.1 Non-regulated Deviance from Standards

Non-regulated deviance appears as one of the two forms of manipulation-oriented organizational deviance from standards. It comprises deviations from standard requirements that appear in a non-regulated standard environment (see Table 8.1). An empirical example is given in this book: the European company MetroEngineers, active in the transportation sector, hardly faces any comparable regulatory authorities in the Chinese market (Langer et al. 2020).

The fulfilment of societal needs such as human safety, health, or environmental protection remains, for instance, in the hands of software-developing organizations themselves. Both internally and externally, only weak sanctioning systems exist. In the case of non-regulated organizational deviance, standards are referenced in the daily communication of those who are like software developers directly affected by them (Langer et al. 2020). Indirectly affected stakeholders like clients, middle or senior management, and suppliers hardly address the ethical, administrative, technical, economic, or regulatory potential of standards. Furthermore, standards are insufficiently enacted as facilities and social norms. Asymmetries and contradictions among standards as interpretative schemes, facilities, and social norms become apparent (Fried & Walgenbach 2020).

8.2.1.1 Standards as Interpretative Schemes

Non-regulated deviance from standards is characterized by a fragmented organizational sensemaking for standard enactment. Only some organizational members, for instance the software-developing unit, highly animate sensemaking for standards, while senior management and clients neither refer to standards as interpretative schemes nor control standard enactment. Standards thus do not shape organization-wide robust rules of interpretation. Another aspect of this fragmentation is that some organizational members constantly argue that standards have an enabling potential for the organization, whereas others like senior management, clients, and other stakeholders do not. This means, for instance, that only software developers constantly strive to push standard enactment in their organization (Langer et al. 2020). Be it in view of the compliant design of technical constructions, in resource conflicts, or budget negotiations, standards are addressed but have little impact on the results of organizational decision making. They are not part of the practical consciousness (Fried & Walgenbach 2020).

8.2.1.2 Standards as Facilities

Non-regulated organizational deviance is likely to occur on the basis of a deficient transformative impact of resources for standard enactment. For the non-regulated type of deviance, a medium to low transformative impact of allocative and authoritative resources for standard enactment is characteristic. Examples are missing financial resources, the superficial implementation of standard-related positions such as the one of the quality manager, or the accumulation of knowledge on standards by non-professionals like interns (Langer et al. 2020). Hence, standards do not unlock power over resources.

Instead, ongoing conflicts over missing resources and corresponding dissatisfying short-term solutions for standard enactment shape this form of deviance. The resource conflicts for standard enactment might lead to further unintended consequences such as the lowering of the remaining commitment of organizational members to standard enactment.

8.2.1.3 Standards as Social Norms

In contrast to commitment-oriented types, non-regulated deviance aims at the manipulation of standard requirements. Standards are not enacted as social norms, and for the manipulation of standard requirements no regulatory sanctions are expected. Thus, a weak sanctioning system due to a non-regulated standard environment is characteristic here. Mainly sanctions resulting from a business context like losing market shares or customers due to missing standard certifications are feared (Langer et al. 2020). Most likely, an internal sanctioning system is not set up.

8.2.1.4 Asymmetries and Contradictions

In the case of non-regulated deviance, organizations engaging in standard enactment deal with asymmetries on the one hand (see Table 8.1). First, sensemaking for standard enactment is fragmented among the stakeholders involved. Second, even if the need for resources is communicated by some organizational members, the enactment of standards as facilities is not realised; there is an immense lack of resources for standard enactment. In comparison to commitment-oriented types of organizational deviance, efforts on compliant standard enactment are not sufficiently resourced. Additional resources for standard enactment are neither provided by senior management nor calculated by the client.

On the other hand, there are contradictions observable (see Table 8.1): first, the high significance of standards for some organizational members contradicts the lack of resources to enable standard enactment. If no resources for standard enactment are claimed, standards might be part of the discursive consciousness but are not institutionalized and do not become taken for granted (Fried & Walgenbach 2020; Giddens 1984). Second, even if there are some organizational members who argue for standard enactment, they have no other choice but to manipulate to fulfil profit objectives. A troubled working environment and ongoing conflicts around the enactment of standards are the result of these asymmetries and contradictions. Some organizational members try to manage these asymmetries and contradictions, for instance, by negotiating standards with the client or engaging in resource conflicts with senior management, but they are of no avail. Very likely, organizations that accomplish non-regulated deviance from standards do not assure human safety, health, or the protection of the environment sufficiently.

8.2.2 Illegitimate Deviance from Standards

The fourth type of organizational deviance, *illegitimate deviance*, is logically deduced from the aggregated empirical insights of the case studies in this book. As said before, we assume what happens—based on insights from the previous three types of organizational deviance from standards—when organizational members illegitimately violate binding standards and thereby potentially harm societal needs such as human safety or health. This form of organizational deviance could typify, for instance, the case of emission test cheatings by Volkswagen (Nelson 2019). From our insights we assume that illegitimate organizational deviance from standards is likely to occur when standards are barely enacted as interpretative schemes, for example, by the senior or middle management, software developers, and other stakeholders. Here, standards might not provide meaning for the daily practices, they might hardly mobilize resources, and they are rarely accepted internally as a reference for sanctioning misconduct.

8.2.2.1 Standards as Interpretative Schemes

We suppose that in the case of illegitimate deviance, meanings for standards are revealed only minimally. According to Maitlis (2005), minimal organizational sensemaking processes are neither animated nor controlled by stakeholders like senior management, middle managers, clients, or software developers. There are hardly any attempts to discuss and shape an organization-wide understanding of standards. Organizational members make little attempt to promote their meanings of standards or gather the views of other stakeholder groups systematically (Fried & Walgenbach 2020; Maitlis 2005). Standards hardly trigger interpretative schemes.

8.2.2.2 Standards as Facilities

In our view, illegitimate deviance from standards appears furthermore on the basis of a deficient transformative impact of resources for standard enactment. In contrast to commitment-oriented types of organizational deviance, standards are not institutionalized as facilities. Hence, allocative and authoritative resources are barely provided. For instance, financial resources are only deficiently supplied or standard-relevant roles such as the quality manager are only superficially implemented. A transformative impact of resources for standard enactment is very unlikely to enfold since standards are presumably not supported by adequate facilities.

8.2.2.3 Standards as Social Norms

As in the case of attentive deviance and over-conformity, illegitimate deviance from standards is likely to occur in regulative environments with a strong external sanctioning system. In combination with minimal sensemaking for standards and deficient resource allocation for standard enactment, that we expect in the case of illegitimate deviance, organizational members might see it as the only but legitimate option to manipulate standard requirements. They might not engage in the adaption of standard requirements, for instance, by taking part in standard-setting processes or in a serious negotiation of standard requirements with assessors. Decoupling from standards, cheating on standards, and thus misconduct are the ways these organizations possibly go (Fried et al. 2013; Fried & Singhal 2020; Palmer 2017). We assume that, in the case of illegitimate deviance, standards are neither enacted as social norms, nor a reference point for internal sanctions, nor do they serve as interpretative schemes and facilities within the organization. This might only change when misconduct is uncovered.

8.2.2.4 Asymmetries and Contradictions

Illegitimate deviance from standards occurred, for example, in Volkswagen's misconduct during emissions tests (for details see Nelson 2019). The asymmetry between a strong external sanctioning system and the minimal enactment of standards as social norms within the organization we believe to be characteristic of illegitimate deviance. The resulting manipulation of standard requirements leads most likely to failing societal needs such as human safety, health, or environmental protection.

Furthermore, two contradictions shape illegitimate deviance: first, the minimal organizational sensemaking for standards as interpretative schemes contrasts with the strong sanctioning system. Almost all stakeholders who are usually involved in standard enactment do not actively argue for standards even though sanctions for deviance are drastic if discovered. Second, the deficient enactment of standards as facilities contradicts the strong external sanctioning system. Missing investments in allocative and authoritative resources for standard enactment, for instance in software-based documentation tools or in quality managers for software development, are contrary to a strong external sanctioning system that is expected to be grounded on a high probability of detecting standard deviations as well as high fines. These asymmetries and contradictions can lead to misconduct (Palmer 2017).

As revealed by Vaughan (1996, 2004) for the Challenger disaster, deviance can normalize in the long run by shifting the idea of what an acceptable risk is. Deviations might normalize due to a profit-maximising approach, minimal organizational sensemaking for standards, and a deficient transformative impact of resources. Then, organizational members might follow the 'necessary possibility' (Ortmann 2010: 206) of deviating from standards in order to maintain or save the organization's objective, for instance, selling cars in the US market.

8.3 Summary

In this chapter, we have shown that there are two main streams of organizational deviance. First, commitment-oriented types like attentive deviance and over-conformity acknowledge standards and their business, administrative, ethical, technical, and regulatory contribution. Second, manipulation-oriented types like non-regulated deviance and illegitimate deviance question standards and contest their business, administrative, ethical, technical, and regulatory contribution fundamentally. We could furthermore show that structuration theory is a useful theoretical approach to identify these types and clarify the question why organizations deviate from standards. Organizations deviate in different ways because of the different and sometimes unbalanced enactment of standards as interpretative schemes, facilities, and social norms. Hence, they deviate depending on the asymmetries and contradictions the structurationist elements reveal during standard enactment.

References

Drucker, P. F. 1990. *Managing the Non-Profit Organization. Practices and Principles.* London: Routledge.

Fried, A. & Glaa, B. 2020. Introduction to deviance in a world of standards. *In:* Fried, A. (ed.) *Understanding Deviance in a World of Standards.* Oxford: Oxford University Press.

Fried, A. & Singhal, A. 2020. A second order observation of organizational deviance. *In:* Fried, A. (ed.) *Understanding Deviance in a World of Standards.* Oxford: Oxford University Press.

Fried, A. & Walgenbach, P. 2020. Structurationist framework to explore organizational deviance from standards. *In:* Fried, A. (ed.) *Understanding Deviance in a World of Standards.* Oxford: Oxford University Press.

Fried, A., Gey, R., Pretorius, A., & Günther, L. 2013. Decoupling from standards—process management and technical innovation in software development organisations. *International Journal of Innovation Management*, 17 (4).

Gey, R., Langer, S., & Fried, A. 2020a. Attentive deviance from standards at CraneSolutions. *In:* Fried, A. (ed.) *Understanding Deviance in World of Standards*. Oxford: Oxford University Press.

Gey, R., Langer, S., & Fried, A. 2020b. Over-conformity with standards at MedTech. *In:* Fried, A. (ed.) *Understanding Deviance in a World of Standards*. Oxford: Oxford University Press.

Giddens, A. 1979. *Central Problems in Social Theory. Action, Structure and Contradiction in Social Analysis*. Houndmills: Macmillan.

Giddens, A. 1984. *The Constitution of Society. Outline of the Theory of Structuration*. Cambridge: Polity Press.

Langer, S. & Fried, A. 2020. Monitoring of standard enactment: an agency perspective. *In:* Fried, A. (ed.) *Understanding Deviance in a World of Standards*. Oxford: Oxford University Press.

Langer, S., Gey, R., Karadzhova-Beyer, D., & Fried, A. 2020. Deregulated deviance from standards at MetroEngineers. *In:* Fried, A. (ed.) *Understanding Deviance in a World of Standards*. Oxford: Oxford University Press.

Maitlis, S. 2005. The social processes of organizational sensemaking. *Academy of Management Journal*, 48, 21–49.

Nelson, J. 2019. Disclosure driven crime. *UC Davis Law Review*, 52 (3).

Ortmann, G. 2010. On drifting rules and standards. *Scandinavian Journal of Management*, 26, 204–14.

Palmer, D. 2017. Institutions, institutional theory and organizational wrongdoing. *In:* Greenwood, R., Oliver, C., Lawrence, T. B., & Meyer, R. E. (eds) *The SAGE Handbook of Organizational Institutionalism*, 2nd edn. Los Angeles: SAGE.

Power, M. 1997. *The Audit Society. Rituals of Verification*. Oxford: Oxford University Press.

Tenbrunsel, A. E. & Messick, D. M. 1999. Sanctioning systems, decision frames, and cooperation. *Administrative Science Quarterly*, 44, 684–707.

Vaughan, D. 1996. *The Challenger Launch Decision. Risky Technology, Culture and Deviance at NASA*. Chicago: University of Chicago Press.

Vaughan, D. 2004. Theorizing disaster. Analogy, historical ethnography, and the Challenger accident. *Ethnography*, 5, 315–47.

Weick, K. E. 1995. *Sensemaking in Organizations*. Thousand Oaks: SAGE.

9

Monitoring of Standard Enactment for Exploration and Exploitation

Sarah Langer and Andrea Fried

Understanding Deviance in a World of Standards is dedicated to finding explanations for the organizational deviance from standards or, more specifically, from process standards. In this chapter, we ask what knowledgeable agents do when enacting standards and how they control organizational processes, for example, administrative, product, development, distribution, and resource allocation processes (Fried & Walgenbach 2020; Powell 1995). To this end, we discuss the typology of organizational deviances from standards we developed (see chapter 8) in view of the interplay between standards and exploratory as well as exploitative organizational processes.

Standard enactment is defined as a process in which organizational members bring events and structures into existence and swing them into action (see Fried & Glaa 2020, following Weick 1988). In the case of the enactment of process standards, organizational members set up and monitor standard-induced organizational processes. Process standards are enacted in 'contexts that require a firm to be both efficient and innovative, to explore as well as exploit' (Benner & Tushman 2002: 676; see also March 1991).

As Benner and Tushman explain, organizational members monitor organizational processes by means of standards to reduce variance and to 'accentuate incremental, exploitative innovation at the expense of exploratory innovation' (Benner & Tushman 2002: 676, following Sutcliffe et al. 2000; Benner & Tushman 2003). Exploitative processes focus on organizational efficiency. However, these processes may inhibit exploratory activities, and thus innovation, learning, and experimentation. Therefore they 'exacerbate inertia and impede organizational responsiveness to environmental shifts' (Benner & Tushman 2002: 677, following Levinthal 1991; Repenning & Sterman 2002).

The empirical results by Benner and Tushman (2002, 2003, 2015) show a tendency for a *crowding-out effect*, suggesting that exploitation suppresses exploration after standard enactment. Even though Benner and Tushman (2002)

Sarah Langer and Andrea Fried, *Monitoring of Standard Enactment for Exploration and Exploitation* In: *Understanding Deviance in a World of Standards*. Edited by: Andrea Fried, Oxford University Press (2020). © Oxford University Press. DOI: 10.1093/oso/9780198833888.003.0009 see a strong tendency for exploration being crowded out by exploitation, it describes, in our view, only one possible effect. Referring to the typology of organizational deviance from standards developed in chapter 7 (Fried & Langer 2020), we recommend examining the entire range of how organizational members monitor organizational processes and thus enable or constrain exploratory activities. To uncover alternatives to the *crowding-out effect*, we see four approaches of monitoring standard enactment which need more investigation and explication in further research.

As we take a structurationist point of view, we strengthen the role of knowledgeable agents, and thus the role of social agency in standard enactment (Fried & Walgenbach 2020). *Standard agents* are those internal stakeholders who take or whom are given responsibility for standard compliance, including regulatory affairs managers, quality or safety managers, and even software developers themselves. The concept of social agency emphasizes that actors have space for reflexivity to accomplish their own agentic orientation: 'to be a human agent is to have power, to be able to "make a difference" in the world.... The most seemingly "powerless" individuals can mobilize resources whereby they carve out "spaces of control" in respect of their day-to-day lives' (Giddens 1982: 197; see also Abdelnour et al. 2017; Emirbayer & Mische 1998). However, as the four types of monitoring described in this chapter suggest, social agents use in different organizational contexts this space in different ways. They might monitor standard enactment diagnostically, inadequately, in self-monitored ways, or in a reflexive way (see Figure 9.1).

Figure 9.1 shows how we see a connection between the way organizational members monitor deviance from process standards and the exploratory and/or exploitative character of the affected organizational processes. The figure implies that reflexive monitoring and self-monitoring of deviance by standard agents tend to support exploratory organizational processes (upper semi-circle in Figure 9.1), while diagnostic and inadequate monitoring of deviance from standards is likely to enable exploitative organizational processes (lower semi-circle). Beyond this, depending on the type of monitoring, we suggest that exploratory organizational processes are either accomplished in compliance with standards or not. The same counts for exploitative activities where standards either can be manipulated or are followed in compliance with standards. Figure 9.1 depicts accordingly by the inner circle 1 a general commitment of the organizational members to standards, whereas the outer circle 2 represents the organizational members' tendency for standard manipulation. The following sections discuss Figure 9.1 in more detail.

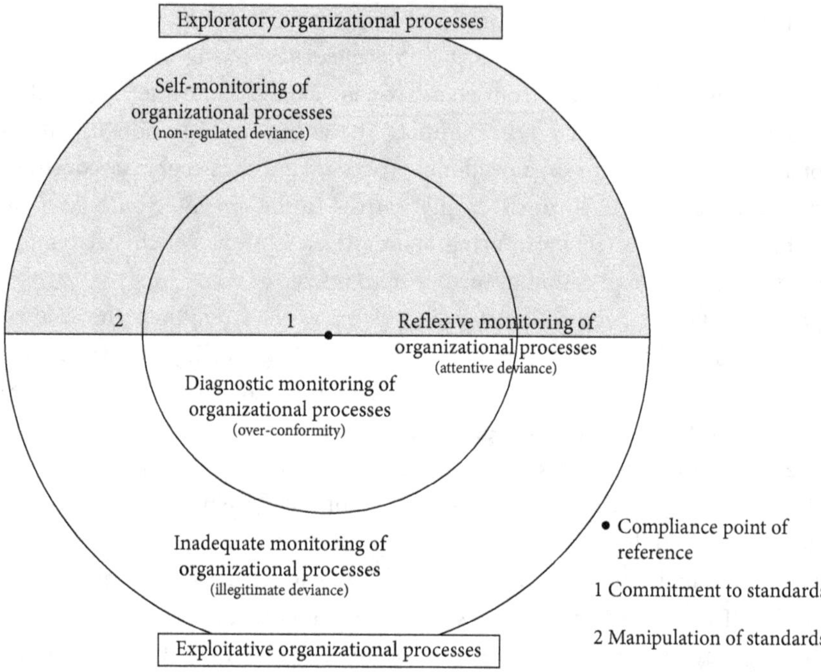

Figure 9.1 Monitoring of standard enactment and deviance for exploration and exploitation

9.1 Exploitation (1): Diagnostic Monitoring of Over-conformity with Standards

'We are living in a comfort zone.'

Over-conformity with standards as described by Fried and Langer (2020) is related to diagnostic monitoring by standard agents who usually control the standard-related activities of other organizational members and aim for an organization-wide commitment to standards (see Figure 9.1). For instance, the software quality managers at MedTech tightly monitor software development processes and seldom consider or encourage critical reflections on standard enactment (Gey et al. 2020b). The software manager at MedTech, on the other hand, critically states 'we are living in a comfort zone' and feels not to have the possibility to think outside the box.

In literature, there are several related discourses on diagnostic monitoring, for instance, the concept of single-loop learning (Argyris & Schön 1978), diagnostic control systems (Simons 1995), and organizational inertia (Gilbert 2005): organizational members show a high commitment to established organizational processes and make sure it stays this way. For instance, Simons identifies three characteristic features of diagnostic monitoring (Simons 1995): standard agents can 'measure the outputs of a process', have standards in place 'against which actual results can be compared', and have 'the ability to correct deviations from standards' (Simons 1995: 59).

To explain why this might be the preferred approach of standard agents monitoring organizational processes, we refer to the typology of organizational deviance from standards (Fried & Langer 2020). In the case of over-conformity, standard agents have the possibility to enact standards in an over-conforming way for several reasons. First, triggered by standards they have strong interpretive schemes available. We assume that standard agents who diagnostically control are convinced of the business, administrative, ethical, technical, and regulatory importance of standards and use their scope of action to emphasize the importance and suitability of standards for organizational processes. They do this by underlining previous positive experiences with standards and refer mainly to advantageous administrative and technical effects of standards. The interpretive schemes are hardly challenged; the discourse on the appropriated standard enactment is restricted by the standard agents (Gey et al. 2020b; Fried & Langer 2020).

Furthermore, we assume that standard agents have decent allocative and authoritative resources at their disposal to carry through their once-created SOPs. The good availability of resources for monitoring organizational processes and for preventing deviations is accompanied by a strong internal and external sanctioning system (e.g. substantial incentives for standard compliance, regular compliance checks by regulatory authorities). Standard agents are concerned that standard-induced interpretative schemes, facilities, and social norms are consistent and complement each other; there are hardly any asymmetries or contradictions appearing in standard enactment. Standard agents are able to correct and sanction deviations from standards and can tightly control organizational processes.

However, as depicted in Figure 9.1, diagnostic monitoring does not address 'the tension between creative innovation and predictable goal achievement' (Simons 1995: 91). If standard enactment is diagnostically controlled, we assume that standards agents might, on the one hand, ensure efficiency of processes. They do not touch existing asymmetries or contradictions of standard enactment, such as inappropriate SOPs for new developments or an overwhelming, time-consuming formalization of development processes (Fried & Langer 2020). On the other hand, diagnostic controlling can crowd out exploration and fundamental innovation in software development, as Benner and Tushman (2002) state. This can potentially lead to frustration among organizational members who are affected by standards in their daily activities and who would acknowledge a more reflexive and flexible handling of standards. For instance, calls for more exploratory activities from some software developers at MedTech were not respected by senior management (Gey et al. 2020b). Instead, the extent of SOPs grew over the years. Diagnostic monitoring of over-conformity with standards describes a situation where standard enactment might become an end in itself, restricting organizational members' aspirations for innovation and learning. Hence, standards tend to ensure mainly process rigidity (Gilbert 2005). By way of contrast, unintended consequences of standard enactment tend to remain unrecognised by standard agents and are hardly perceived as a constraint for learning and innovation (Giddens 1984).

We conclude that communicating the enabling effects of standards as well as having decent resources available for standard enactment and widely sanctioning deviations does not mean that the standard-enacting organization can satisfyingly handle both efficiency and innovation.

9.2 Exploitation (2): Inadequate Monitoring of Illegitimate Deviance from Standards

'There was a tolerance for breaking the rules.'[1]

In the case of illegitimate organizational deviance, we assume that standard enactment is either only ineffectively monitored or even not monitored at all (Kraatz & Zajac 1996; see also Figure 9.1). Considering from our empirical investigations of other cases, we suppose that illegitimate deviance takes place in a regulated environment with high fines and a high probability of detecting deviations from standards (Fried & Langer 2020; Fried & Walgenbach 2020). Organizational members seem to not actively use their capacity to monitor standard enactment and illegitimate deviations from standards. Instead, deviations from standards seem to follow the purpose to get things done in an efficient way. For instance, in the case of Volkswagen's misconduct uncovered

[1] H. D. Pötsch, Head of Volkswagen's Supervisory Board in *The New York Times*, 10 December 2015.

in 2015, we assume that standard enactment is neither animated nor sufficiently internally controlled by internal stakeholders who are affected by standards (Nelson 2019; see also Fried & Langer 2020). Thus, organizational deviance might eventually be covered in functional silence at least for some time, facilitating a 'tolerance for breaking the rules'.

In the literature, illegitimate deviance from standards is understood as breaking established norms and standards in organizations. It is referred to as misbehaviour (Bennett & Robinson 2000), misconduct (Greve et al. 2010), wrongdoing (Palmer 2017), or decoupling (Bromley & Powell 2012). According to Palmer (2017), illegitimate deviance takes place in 'weak institutions' which are characterized by a less robust governance regime. The author suggests to better investigate the micro-foundations of deviance in 'weak institutions'. Illegitimate deviance also relates to discourses on deviance as the 'dirty secret of decoupled organizations', where senior management resists and does not adequately monitor deviations from standards and adjusts organizational processes accordingly (Monahan & Quinn 2006: 377). The pressure for efficiency is said to be the crucial driver for decoupled organizations (Bromley & Powell 2012; Fried et al. 2013; Fried & Langer 2020).

To explain why inadequate monitoring of standard enactment is the preferred approach of some organizations in dealing with standards, we refer to the typology of organizational deviance from standards (Fried & Langer 2020). We assume that there are no standard agents in the case of illegitimate deviance or, if they exist, that they have hardly any influence on standard enactment. There might only be a minimal sensemaking among the stakeholders that supports the engagement in standard enactment. Organizational members hardly have access to allocative and authoritative resources for standard enactment. For instance, SOPs rarely serve as a basis for internal performance measures such as the measurement of process quality. Altogether, we conclude that, in the case of inadequate monitoring, standards do not have sufficient impact on organizational processes. Rather, we find the strong external sanctioning system as contrary to the internal minimal sensemaking, as well as to the low resource allocation for standard enactment and the lack of rules of sanctioning. The dynamic of inadequate monitoring can create a lock-in situation where organizational members reproduce the contradictions of illegitimate deviance in their daily activities.

We assume that organizational members who deviate in an illegitimate way from standards and hardly monitor this deviant standard enactment mainly provide economic reasons as rationale (Fried & Langer 2020). We suppose that inadequate monitoring of standards is related to exploitative organizational processes that—as mentioned above—focus mainly on efficiency. Inadequate monitoring, we suppose, proves to be functional for an exploitative strategy of for-profit organizations in the short run. With the Challenger launch decision, Vaughan provides an example of the normalization of deviance by showing that deviations might become routinized and accepted as standard practice to attain the organization's efficiency goals (Vaughan 1996). We assume that a strong exploitative focus of organizational processes, while standards are hardly effective, can serve economic purposes in the short run, but might risk human safety, human health, or the environment in the long run.

9.3 Exploration (1): Reflexive Monitoring of Attentive Deviance from Standards

'It is like walking on eggshells.'

As depicted in Figure 9.1, we propose that the reflexive monitoring of standard enactment supports organizational members in attentively deviating from standards. Hence, 'walking on eggshells' describes the capability of standard agents to monitor standard enactment in a reflexive manner—continuously equilibrating manipulation of and commitment to standards (Fried & Langer 2020; Gey et al. 2020a). Reflexive monitoring aims at well-balanced organizational processes in terms of both their exploratory and as exploitative elements.

At CraneSolutions, we find standard agents who likewise appreciate and condemn certain standard requirements for organizational processes (Gey et al. 2020a). In their view, not all standard requirements are appropriate for the highly specialized niche products they offer. This inspires them to monitor reflexively for which requirements deviations are needed so as to not constrain but enable software development processes. At CraneSolutions, organizational members only gather, for instance, for milestone meetings and when coordination is necessary. The actual degree of standard compliance and necessary adjustments needed are discussed during these meetings (see also Fried 2017 on 'repair behaviour'). At the same time, external expertise of standard enactment for special development projects is integrated to tailor standard requirements to the project's needs. Since there is no specific regulatory unit as in the case of MedTech, software developers and other stakeholders participate in monitoring. At CraneSolutions, standard agents negotiate, for instance, some standard requirements with auditors and also take part in the creation of standards within standardization bodies (Gey et al. 2020a).

Beside the stratification model that discusses reflexive monitoring, similar discourses can be found in other theoretical approaches (Giddens 1984; see also Fried & Walgenbach 2020). The concept of double-loop learning (Argyris & Schön 1978), concepts on interactive control systems (Simons 1995), and theories on ambidextrous organizations effectively balancing exploration and exploitation (Papachroni et al. 2016) can contribute to the understanding of reflexive monitoring in organizations. All the approaches come to the similar conclusion that organizational members show a commitment to established rules but also change them to some extent when realising that unintended consequences hinder learning and innovation. Hence, they do not necessarily implement organizational rules and standards as originally intended.

Simons (1995) describes this as interactive monitoring: standard agents not only compare results of standard enactment with their expectations on correcting deviations, e.g. from SOPs, but also trigger questioning of the organizational understanding and ask 'what has changed and why' in order to discover deviations and learn from them (Simons 1995: 108; see also Fried 2017). Further, standard agents are not specialized in standards and regulations but are those who are affected by standards in their daily routines. Monitoring in a reflexive way means that standard agents engage in a dialogue to understand the causes and consequences of standard enactment and the resulting deviations in the organizational practice.

In a similar vein, Giddens distinguishes intended and unintended consequences of actions (Giddens 1984; see also Fried & Walgenbach 2020). When organizational members, for instance, propose internal documents referring to standards, and thus, formalize *inter alia* development and production processes, they reach a certain result regarding product and process safety. However, they may also trigger unintended effects such as inferior usability of the product. The intended as well as unintended consequences of the enactment of standards form the basis for prospective actions. According to Simons, the resulting question should be 'what are we going to do about it' (Simons 1995: 109), whereas the answer should impact the SOPs.

To explain why reflexive monitoring is the preferred approach of monitoring organizational processes for some organizations, the typology of organizational deviance from standards suggests an answer (Gey et al. 2020a; Fried &

Langer 2020). In the case of attentive deviance, standard agents attach a high signification for organizational processes to standards in terms of both their business and administrative meaning. On the one hand, they base their arguments for the importance of standards on previous experiences and raise expectations regarding standard enactment in the future. On the other hand, we believe that standard agents who reflexively monitor, considerably control and widely animate the discussion on intended and unintended consequences of standard enactment and deviance throughout the organization. Thus, we suggest that guided organizational sensemaking for standard enactment is part of reflexive monitoring.

We argue that in the case of reflexive monitoring, standard agents find a decent availability of authoritative and allocative resources for standard enactment. Further, we assume that the internal sanctioning system is directed towards not only standard compliance but also creativity, innovative search behaviour, or sharing information for exploring suitable processes and SOPs. External auditors might instead be partners reflecting on the suitability of standards requirements than diagnostic controllers for standard compliance. When asymmetries in standard enactment become apparent, we believe that standard agents explore here unconventional ways of handling these asymmetries, for instance, when social norms are in conflict (e.g. contradictory standard requirements; see also Gey & Fried 2018).

We propose that reflexive monitoring of standard enactment allows both exploratory and exploitative elements of organizational processes to emerge. It enables innovation, as well as opportunity-seeking and stimulates learning. In contrast to diagnostic monitoring, they establish in our view a guided organizational sensemaking regarding standards (Fried & Langer 2020) to encourage critical but also constructive feedback on standard enactment and deviance. Asymmetries in standard enactment are experienced as disturbing. But at the same time, they serve as an occasion to reflect on the appropriateness of standards and enable to attentively deviate, hence ensuring exploratory organizational processes.

As stated earlier, only communicating the importance of standards, providing sufficient resources for standard enactment and sanctioning deviations does not mean that the standard-enacting organization can satisfactorily manage organizational contexts requiring both efficiency and innovation. We believe that it also needs engaged standard agents who constantly monitor the standard enactment regarding its unintended consequences in view of innovation *and* efficiency. In the end, this might be crucial to avoid a crowding-out effect that suppresses exploration (Benner & Tushman 2002).

9.4 Exploration (2): Self-Monitoring of Non-Regulated Deviance from Standards

'It is on us to argue for standards.'

Non-regulated deviance from standards as described by Fried and Langer (2020) is related to the question how standard agents monitor organizational processes when the standard environment is non-regulated (see Figure 9.1). In our view, organizations in this situation tend to self-monitor their processes (Bandura 1991; Baumeister & Heatherton 1996).

In the literature, self-monitoring is discussed in several ways, for instance, in view of corporate social responsibility (Kole & Lehn 1997) or corporate governance deviance (Aguilera et al. 2018), regarding organizational reduction (Mitnick 1978) or self-regulation failures (Baumeister & Heatherton 1996). According to Baumeister and Heatherton (1996), such self-monitoring requires in any event 'three ingredients'. First, organizational members who self-monitor standard enactment need to decide which policies shall become social norms. Considering the immense number of available standards nationally and internationally, this is a challenging step. Second, they need to define for themselves how they control compliance with these requirements, since external regulatory authorities are not responsible or missing. Third, they must control whether the self-chosen monitoring procedures fall short and whether they need to be adjusted in the course of time.

However, without legal regulation there is a tendency that 'people cease to monitor themselves' and 'tend to lose control' (Baumeister & Heatherton 1996: 2). Campbell (2006) argues in the same vein when discussing corporate social responsibility. He states that organizations are more likely to act responsibly under strong sanctioning systems developed by states, collective self-regulation, or other independent organizations. Referring to the case study of MetroEngineers, we can confirm that organizations in non-regulated environments show substantial deviations from standards, and thus manipulate organizational processes (Langer et al. 2020b).

There are several ways in which organizations can act in non-regulated environments (Mitnick 1978): either they can retain existing regulatory bureaucracies, or they start to internally create policies. Further, they can transfer functions of standards to another agency, thus to a different administrative 'umbrella'—e.g. a standardization body like the International Organization for Standardization. Or organizations self-monitor organizational processes, which according to Mitnick does not work well for all industries (Mitnick 1978).

For instance, in the case of MetroEngineers, adequate regulations for the railway sector in China are missing to date (Langer et al. 2020b). Therefore, MetroEngineers had at least two options to act regarding standards in the Chinese market. MetroEngineers could have either referred to railway standards by aiming for European certifications, for example, or started to self-monitor its organizational processes by creating its own, independent standard procedures. The option to retain an existing regulatory bureaucracy was not given, since the software developers of the investigated project had barely any previous experience in standard enactment. This made it more likely that MetroEngineers would start to manipulate organizational processes because it had neither developed its own process policies nor had it worked under another regulatory 'umbrella'. As well as this, only the software developers complained that it is up to them 'to argue for standards' within the organization. However, their efforts for an effective self-monitoring of the whole organization remained unsuccessful.

To explain why this might be the likely approach of monitoring standard enactment in a non-regulated environment, we refer to the non-regulated type of deviance in our typology of organizational deviance from standards (Fried & Langer 2020). When organizations fail to ensure an effective self-monitoring of standard enactment and of deviance from standards, the following institutional conditions might prevail. In contrast to illegitimate deviance, we assume that at least some organizational members act as standard agents. They engage in sensemaking for standards within their specific field (e.g. software development) and try to convince also other organizational members of the significance of standard enactment. Standard agents refer here to manifold administrative, business, and technical arguments. However, we see that the vast majority of potential stakeholders neither share nor support their engagement in standards. Thus, organizational sensemaking remains fragmented. In addition, we believe that a deficient provision of resources and a lack of internal as well as external sanctioning system contribute to a humble standard enactment. Organizational members neither expect high fines for deviations from standards nor see a high probability of detecting these deviations. For these reasons, it becomes rather unlikely that organizational policies serving as adequate social norms for standard enactment are put in place.

Finally, given these insights, we assume that self-monitoring of non-regulated deviance from standards strengthens above all the exploratory character of organizational processes. Since organizational processes are monitored less rigorously compared to organizations in regulated environments, we propose that the focus on the efficiency of organizational processes might be lower in favour of explorative organizational processes. At the same time, human safety and health or the environment might be in danger.

9.5 Implications for Further Research

In this chapter, we formulated assumptions about the relation between exploration and exploitation, organizational deviance, and the monitoring activities of standard agents. Bearing this in mind, we agreed on the observation that standards affect innovation in 'different, sometimes opposing ways; they can both enable and constrain innovation' (Egyedi & Ortt 2017: 105). For this reason, we believe that social agency, and thus standard agents, have a decisive influence on whether standards support not only an exploitative but also an explorative character of organizational processes—standard agents provide sense, allocate resources, and impose sanctions for standard enactment. Also, we underlined that the crowding-out of exploratory processes might be statistically significant for standard-enacting organizations; however, in practice, it is not the reality for all of them (Benner & Tushman 2002).

Hence, we could identify four approaches to monitor standard enactment and their effect on exploratory or exploitative organizational processes. For enacting standards and dealing with deviations from standards, we recommend a reflexive monitoring which allows organizations to attentively deviate from standards. However, reflexive monitoring also means that deviations from standards remain in accordance with the safety of humans and the environment. We believe that reflexive monitoring can enable both commitment to standards and well-balanced exploitative and explorative activities within organizations.

For further research on standard enactment, we suggest the following propositions which are based on the typology of organizational deviance from standards (Fried & Langer 2020):

- Diagnostic monitoring of standard enactment supports exploitative organizational processes *and* the commitment to standards.
- Reflexive monitoring of standard enactment supports balanced organizational processes in terms of both exploratory as well as exploitative activities *and* the commitment to standards.
- Inadequate monitoring of standard enactment supports exploitative organizational processes *and* the manipulation of standards.
- Self-monitoring of standard enactment supports exploratory organizational processes *and* the manipulation of standards.

Based on these propositions, it would be interesting to further explore the standard–innovation nexus by investigating other organizations than software developing companies, non-profit organizations, or standards other than process standards.

References

Abdelnour, S., Hasselbladh, H., & Kallinikos, J. 2017. Agency and institutions in organization studies. *Organization Studies*, 38, 1775–92.

Aguilera, R. V., Judge, W. Q., & Terjesen, S. A. 2018. Corporate governance deviance. *Academy of Management Review*, 43.

Argyris, C. & Schön, D. A. 1978. *Organizational Learning. A Theory of Action Perspective*. Reading, MA: Addison Wesley.

Bandura, A. 1991. Social cognitive theory of self-regulation. *Organizational Behavior and Human Decision Processes*, 50, 248–87.

Baumeister, R. F. & Heatherton, T. F. 1996. Self-regulation failure: an overview. *Psychological Inquiry*, 7, 1–15.

Benner, M. J. & Tushman, M. 2002. Process management and technological innovation: a longitudinal study of the photography and paint industries. *Administrative Science Quarterly*, 47, 676–706.

Benner, M. J. & Tushman, M. 2003. Exploitation, exploration, and process management: the productivity dilemma revisited. *Academy of Management Review*, 28, 238–56.

Benner, M. J. & Tushman, M. 2015. Reflections on the 2013 decade award—'exploitation, exploration, and process management: the productivity dilemma revisited' ten years later. *Academy of Management Review*, 40, 497–514.

Bennett, R. J. & Robinson, S. L. 2000. Development of a measure of workplace deviance. *Journal of Applied Psychology*, 85, 349–60.

Bromley, P. & Powell, W. W. 2012. From smoke and mirrors to walking the talk: decoupling in the contemporary world. *Academy of Management Annals*, 6, 483–530.

Campbell, J. L. 2006. Institutional analysis and the paradox of corporate social responsibility. *American Behavioral Scientist*, 49 (7), 925–38.

Egyedi, T. & Ortt, R. 2017. Towards a functional classification of standards for innovation research. *In:* Hawkins, R., Blind, K., & Page, R. (eds) *Handbook of Innovation and Standards*. Cheltenham: Edward Elgar.

Emirbayer, M. & Mische, A. 1998. What is agency? *American Journal of Sociology*, 103, 962–1023.

Fried, A. 2017. Terminological distinctions of 'control': a review of the implications for management control research in the context of innovation. *Journal of Management Control*, 28, 5–40.

Fried, A. & Glaa, B. 2020. Introduction to deviance in a world of standards. *In:* Fried, A. (ed.) *Understanding Deviance in a World of Standards.* Oxford: Oxford University Press.

Fried, A. & Langer, S. 2020. Typology of organizational deviance from standards. *In:* Fried, A. (ed.) *Understanding Deviance in a World of Standards.* Oxford: Oxford University Press.

Fried, A. & Walgenbach, P. 2020. Structurationist framework to explore organizational deviance from standards. *In:* Fried, A. (ed.) *Understanding Deviance in a World of Standards.* Oxford: Oxford University Press.

Gey, R. & Fried, A. 2018. Metastructuring for standards: how organizations respond to the multiplicity of standards. *In:* Jakobs, K. (ed.) Corporate and Global Standardization Initiatives in Contemporary Society, pp. 252–76. Hershey, PA: IGI Global.

Gey, R., Langer, S., & Fried, A. 2020a. Attentive deviance from standards at CraneSolutions. *In:* Fried, A. (ed.) *Understanding Deviance in World of Standards.* Oxford: Oxford University Press.

Gey, R., Langer, S., & Fried, A. 2020b. Over-conformity with standards at MedTech. *In:* Fried, A. (ed.) *Understanding Deviance in a World of Standards.* Oxford: Oxford University Press.

Giddens, A. 1982. *Profiles and Critiques in Social Theory.* London: Palgrave.

Giddens, A. 1984. The constitution of society. Outline of the theory of structuration. Cambridge: Polity Press.

Gilbert, C. G. 2005. Unbundling the structure of inertia: resource versus routine rigidity. *Academy of Management Journal*, 48, 741–63.

Greve, H. R., Palmer, D., & Pozner, J.-E. 2010. Organizations gone wild: the causes, processes, and consequences of organizational misconduct. *Academy of Management Annals*, 4, 53–107.

Fried, A., Gey, R., Pretorius, A., & Günther, L. 2013. Decoupling from standards—process management and technical innovation in software development organisations. *International Journal of Innovation Management*, 17 (4).

Kole, S. & Lehn, K. 1997. Deregulation, the evolution of corporate governance structure, and survival. *American Economic Review*, 87, 421–5.

Kraatz, M. S. & Zajac, E. J. 1996. Exploring the limits of the new institutionalism: the causes and consequences of illegitimate organizational change. *American Sociological Review*, 61, 812–36.

Langer, S., Gey, R., & Karadzhova-Beyer, D. 2020a. Investigating organizational deviance from standards in depth. *In:* Fried, A. (ed.) *Understanding Deviance in a World of Standards.* Oxford: Oxford University Press.

Langer, S., Gey, R., Karadzhova-Beyer, D., & Fried, A. 2020b. Deregulated deviance from standards at MetroEngineers. *In:* Fried, A. (ed.) *Understanding Deviance in a World of Standards.* Oxford: Oxford University Press.

Levinthal, D. 1991. Organizational adaptation and environmental selection: interrelated processes of change. *Organization Science*, 2, 140–5.

March, J. G. 1991. Exploration and exploitation in organizational learning. *Organization Science, Special Issue: Organizational Learning: Papers in Honor of (and by) James G. March* 2, 71–87.

Mitnick, B. M. 1978. Deregulation as a process of organizational reduction. *Public Administration Review*, 38, 350–7.

Monahan, S. C. & Quinn, B. A. 2006. Beyond 'bad apples' and 'weak leaders'. Toward a neo-institutional explanation of organizational deviance. *Theoretical Criminology*, 10, 361–85.

Nelson, J. 2019. Disclosure driven crime. *UC Davis Law Review*, 52 (3).

Palmer, D. 2017. Institutions, institutional theory and organizational wrongdoing. *In:* Greenwood, R., Oliver, C., Lawrence, T. B., & Meyer, R. E. (eds) *The SAGE Handbook of Organizational Institutionalism*, 2nd edn. Los Angeles: SAGE.

Papachroni, A., Heracleous, L., & Paroutis, S. 2016. In pursuit of ambidexterity: managerial reactions to innovation–efficiency tensions. *Human Relations*, 69, 1791–822.

Powell, T. C. 1995. Total quality management as competitive advantage: a review and empirical study. *Strategic Management Journal*, 16, 15–37.

Repenning, N. P. & Sterman, J. 2002. Capability traps and self-confirming attribution errors in the dynamics of process improvement. *Administrative Science Quarterly*, 47, 265–95.

Simons, R. 1995. *Levers of Control. How Managers Use Innovative Control Systems to Drive Strategic Renewal.* Boston, MA: Harvard Business School Press.

Sutcliffe, K., Sitkin, S., & Browning, L. 2000. Tailoring process management to situational requirements. In: Cole, R. & Scott, W. R. (eds) *The Quality Movement and Qrganization Theory*, pp. 315–30. London: SAGE.

Vaughan, D. 1996. *The Challenger Launch Decision. Risky Technology, Culture and Deviance at NASA.* Chicago: University of Chicago Press.

Weick, K. E. 1988. Enacted sensemaking in crisis situations. *Journal of Management Studies*, 25, 305–17.

10
Understanding Deviance from Standards

Implications for Corporate Responsibility and Criminal Law

Andrea Fried

In this book, we explored the question why organizations deviate from standards. With several theoretical contributions, we broke new theoretical ground in the research areas of not only organizational deviance but also standards and standardization. We also showed how structuration theory (Giddens 1984) can be applied and operationalized for investigating contemporary phenomena in management and organization studies (see Fried & Walgenbach 2020). We proved that uncovering the interplay between structures of signification, domination, and legitimation, together with the resulting contradictions, bears great potential to explain standard-related corporate disasters and scandals as well as success stories from an organization theory point of view (Fried & Glaa 2020).

We applied structuration theory and identified which inherent organizational asymmetries and contradictions trigger which type of organizational deviance, namely attentive deviance from standards, over-conformity with standards, non-regulated deviance, and illegitimate deviance from standards (Fried & Langer 2020; Fried & Walgenbach 2020; Langer et al. 2020b; Gey et al. 2020a, 2020b). In doing so, we went beyond earlier explanations, for instance, given by strain theories. Strain theories state that societies put pressure on individuals to achieve socially accepted goals though they lack the means (e.g. Merton 1938; see also Palmer 2017 for newer attempts). According to strain theories, the lack of means leads to strain followed by criminal behaviour. In this book, we argue that the lack of not only resources but also the rules of sanctioning and the rules of interpretation are of importance in understanding deviations from standards by organizational members. Depending on how

Andrea Fried, *Understanding Deviance from Standards: Implications for Corporate Responsibility and Criminal Law* In: *Understanding Deviance in a World of Standards*. Edited by: Andrea Fried, Oxford University Press (2020).
DOI: 10.1093/oso/9780198833888.003.00010

standard-related rules of interpretation and sanctioning as well as resources are shaped and coordinated, different asymmetries and contradictions occur. Organizational members handle contradictions by deviating from standards not only in illegitimate or non-regulated ways. As knowledgeable agents they can also decide to deviate attentively from standards or to over-conform with standards. In this way, we identify the concept of organizational wrongdoing (e.g. Palmer 2017) as only one possible type of deviance from standards (illegitimate deviance) by identifying one further manipulation-oriented type and two commitment-oriented types of organizational deviance (Fried & Langer 2020).

As mentioned in Fried and Glaa (2020), Volkswagen, Rana Plaza, and Boeing provide examples of corporate manipulations and crimes. These examples lead, on the one hand, to the question of how *manipulation-oriented types of deviance* from standards can be diminished (see chapter 8, Table 8.1). On the other hand, besides standardization bodies, national legislations also address compliance-related duties for companies and clarify that even corporate negligence in stopping or preventing crime can lead to sanctions for companies. Thus, the question arises what should an effective compliance management and standard monitoring of companies include? We hope that the empirical findings and theoretical conceptualizations based on structuration theory about *commitment-oriented types of deviance* from standards help to answer this question (see Table 8.1).

Before I go into detail, some further thoughts about the generalizability of the book's empirical findings shall be voiced. All investigated companies are global actors selling products and services to European, American, and Asian markets. There, they face different external control and sanctioning systems coming from various national legislations, e.g. Germany, the UK, China, and the US. Moreover, these companies are confronted by differing standard environments (see also Gey & Fried 2018). Standards are set, for example, by the US Food and Drug Administration, British Standards, or the German DIN Institute. At the same time, these companies are all engaged in software-developing activities following the same approach of a (software) development process model, even though they are grounded in different industrial sectors. Since human life can be negatively affected by a low functional safety of their products and services, all investigated companies should have had at least an interest to follow state-of-the-art requirements for functional safety provided by existing standard frameworks.

It is for these reasons that I believe some implications for corporate responsibility can be formulated based on the empirical findings and theoretical generalizations of the book. The following five questions mark central aspects of corporate responsibility discussed in view of corporate criminal law and compliance management. Both effective corporate criminal law and appropriate internal compliance management in organizations are important cornerstones for ensuring corporate responsibility.

Is voluntary self-regulation of companies a way of ensuring corporate responsibility?

To answer this question right away, according to the empirical findings presented in this book, voluntary self-regulation is not suggested. Rather, we support arguments that organizations tend to cease efforts on functional safety when a weak external control and sanctioning system exists. Based on the case study MetroEngineers (Langer et al. 2020b), Fried and Langer (2020) describe one manipulation-oriented type of organizational deviance that answers whether organizations should voluntarily decide how to organize their processes: the non-regulated type of deviance from standards. This type of deviance describes a situation in which organizations find themselves confronted with a weak external control and sanctioning system. In the case of the German company MetroEngineers, European standards were not mandatory when selling products and services to China. On the one hand, European standards were part of the contractional conditions. On the other hand, the Chinese client did not insist that this contract condition was fulfilled by its contract partner MetroEngineers. The consequence was an inadequate self-monitoring of standard enactment by MetroEngineers. It contributed to a low animation of functional safety by the majority of stakeholders, including the Chinese client and middle and senior management. Administrative, technical, and business arguments for standard enactment were raised by some organizational members (here the software developers). However, these were not shared by those who are responsible for providing allocative and authoritative resources for standard enactment and those who can implement appropriate control and sanctioning mechanism for standard compliance (such as incentives for standard compliance, effective compliance management, or whistle-blower policies).

Based on our findings, we conclude that a strong external control and sanctioning system would have contributed to more reliable practices of software development in line with requirements for functional safety. An effective external control and sanctioning system gives organizational members, e.g. software developers, arguments to invest in compliant development processes. In this way, standards can provide meaning for functional safety of products and services and can trigger the provision of enough allocative and authoritative resources to ensure safe development processes.

As well as the MetroEngineering case, we can refer to publicly discussed cases like the air disasters of the Boeing Company. This case provides further indications how organizations act in less or non-regulated environments followed by a self-monitoring of organizational processes. In the past decade, the US Federal Aviation Administration (FAA) allowed the Boeing Company to do more self-certification of its products. Subsequently, Boeing started most likely to manipulate, for example, aviation standards for software development and testing (*The Economist*, 23 March 2019; see also Fried & Glaa 2020). In a similar vein, weak external control and sanctioning mechanism played a role in the collapse of the Rana Plaza complex in Bangladesh (*BBC News*, 10 May 2013; see also Fried & Glaa 2020). The non-enforcement of standards for health, fire, and building safety by national legislations, clothing-retail companies, and consumers of textiles was also reflected in a lack of internal control and sanctioning systems such as workers' councils, regulatory affairs, and other institutions to ensure standard compliance. Moreover, deficient allocative and authoritative resources to ensure standard enactment were barely provided to ensure a cost-leadership strategy both for the Bangladeshi garment industry and the clothing-retail companies. One can assume that there was only a fragmented sensemaking among the stakeholders of the supply chain. Many stakeholders such as consumers of textiles and clothing-retail companies have only fragmented information about the supply chain and hardly reflect on their own buying decision. Thus, by only creating new standards without considering regulation of the garment industry with suitable external and internal controls and sanctioning mechanisms, an intense sensemaking process among all stakeholders of the supply chain, and the provision of allocative and authoritative resources for safer production and infrastructure, other disasters of the same kind are likely.

What contributes to a manipulation of standards even if a strong external control and sanctioning system is in place?

A strong external control and sanctioning system contributes but is no guarantee of the commitment of organizational members to standards. Our logical deduction of an fourth, illegitimate type of deviance from standards offers an explanation for this (see Table 8.1). In this case, we propose that the manipulation of standards is caused by a minimal sensemaking among the directly or indirectly involved stakeholders. Organizational members address the conviction that process standards hinder business success in competitive markets. With the illegitimate type of deviance from standards we can provide explanations for what Hans-Dieter Pötsch, head of Volkswagen's supervisory board, most likely meant when pointing out that 'there was a tolerance for breaking the rules' within Volkswagen (*The New York Times*, 10 December 2015; see also Fried & Glaa 2020). The company 'violated the Clean Air Act by the sale of approximately 590,000 model year 2009 to 2016 diesel motor vehicles equipped with "defeat devices" in the form of computer software designed to cheat on federal emissions tests. The major excess pollutant at issue in this case is oxides of nitrogen (NOx), and is a serious health concern' (United States Environmental Protection Agency 2019).

Facing strong competition on the US market, Volkswagen did not resolve the standard-related contradictions—originating presumably from a lack of sense for standard enactment, insufficient internal control and sanctioning mechanisms, and lack of resources for standard enactment (see Table 8.1)—by temporarily circumventing the emissions standards of the US Environmental Protection Agency. The social norms as provided by the Clean Air Act were overruled by Volkswagen by installing 'defeat devices' that 'bypasses, defeats, or renders inoperative a required element of the vehicle's emission control system' (United States Environmental Protection Agency 2019). Most likely, Volkswagen chose to invest in 'defeat devices' instead to achieve a common ground for the importance of emission standards and to provide allocative and authoritative resources to enact the Clean Air Act substantially. To sum up, even if a strong external control and sanctioning system as provided by the Clean Air Act is in place, a deficient provision of allocative and authoritative resources by the organization and a minimal sensemaking among all stakeholders affected by standards can lead nevertheless to 'a tolerance for breaking the rules'.

Should legislative authorities only sanction actual knowledge of and engagement in wrongful acts of standard deviation?

To provide the answer to this question first: our findings support the view that not only should legislative authorities sanction the actual knowledge of and engagement in wrongful acts of standard deviation, but also organizations are responsible for defining the employees' and representatives' scope of employment and authority (Nowak 2016). SOPs shape at least partly the scope of employment and authority for employees and representatives. If the scope of employment and authority is well defined in organizations, it contributes to the likelihood that standard requirements are met, and thus the scope of employment and authority is respected. By applying a structurationist viewpoint, this is ensured when SOPs are meaningful, i.e. they enable business success in the eyes of all stakeholders. This includes that their enabling and constraining effects, for example, on the functional safety of products and services, are constantly reflected. It also means that the SOPs may subsequently be adapted. Furthermore, a well-defined scope of employment and authority is characterized by an appropriate provision of allocative and authoritative resources for standard enactment, such as the position of a quality manager or a safety manager, as well as adequate tools for documenting development processes. Finally, compliance with SOPs must be monitored and, in the case of non-compliance, sanctioned.

An effective compliance management system should contribute to a reflexive monitoring of SOPs, and thus to an attentive way of deviance from standards (see Table 8.1 and Figure 9.1). Consequently, courts should give credit when companies have implemented an effective compliance management system. The effectiveness of a compliance management system is given if not only SOPs are written down as formal rules but also these procedures are likewise enacted as interpretative schemes, facilities, and social norms by organizational members, e.g. in development processes. In turn, if SOPs are not effectively implemented, and thus if the employees' and representatives' scope of employment and authority is not adequately defined, courts might consider punishing wilful blindness and deliberate ignorance. In summary, based on the empirical findings and theoretical generalizations in this book, corporate responsibility goes beyond necessary adequate actions when an engagement in wrongful acts of standard deviation is discovered. It already starts with the responsibility to enact standards as interpretative schemes, facilities, and social norms likewise.

Should legislation stipulate a criminal liability also for companies?

To date, in countries like Finland, Germany, and Sweden, a corporate criminal law does not exist in a sense that companies can commit a criminal act and can be held liable to criminal sanctions. Criminal liability and sanctions can only be applied to representatives and employees of a company. In other words, these legislations only recognise an individual responsibility for criminal acts (Alvesalo-Kuusi et al. 2018; Nowak 2016).

In contrast, a company can be held criminally liable for the crimes of its employees and representatives, for instance, under Brazilian, Mexican, and US federal law. Here, federal law shall 'ensure that corporate entities comply with investigations, enact compliance programs, and continue to follow laws and regulations' (Jimenez 2019: 353). That companies can in general commit a criminal act shall consequently encourage them to comply with standards and to apply a commitment-oriented approach to deviance from standards (see Table 8.1). 'If a corporate culture allowed or encouraged law violation or facilitated law avoidance' (Alvesalo-Kuusi et al. 2018: 226) it is legally possible to punish a corporate criminal act. In this case, punishments can be heavy administrative fines for the companies. Furthermore, companies can also be 'liquidated, forced to forfeit any goods or assets obtained during the violation, and barred from entering into public contracts' (Jimenez 2019: 368).

Our empirical findings and theoretical generalizations specify how a 'corporate culture encouraging standard violation' can look like by providing institutional explanations of manipulation-oriented types of deviance from standards (Fried & Langer 2020). In this way, the book contributes to fundamental questions of corporate law and encourage legislators to enforce—if not existing as in Germany—a corporate criminal law sanctioning organizations and not only individuals for fundamental standard deviations. Furthermore, our findings help to operationalize how companies can create an environment in which compliance with standards becomes meaningful and attractive.

Why should companies allow organizational members to deviate from standards?

Standards as well as SOPs have their limitations in time and scope. They might become invalid when software developers use, for instance, new tools to document their development efforts in a more efficient way or when development work and software tests can be done in virtual and modularized ways. Or SOPs become simply invalid when they are too demanding for organizational members.

Companies should therefore allow organizational members to deviate at least attentively from SOPs (see Table 8.1). At the same time, reasons for deviations should be discussed. In this way, asymmetries in social norms, such as SOPs, become visible and comprehensible. Thereafter, companies possibly seek to adjust or change SOPs to not enforce over-conformity with standards or trigger even manipulations of standards. Institutional solutions such as effective compliance management, incentive systems, or whistle-blowing procedures can support here.

In complex and uncertain environments, companies are challenged to achieve a right 'arm's length' autonomy, e.g. for software developers, when enacting standards. They better control the enactment of standards as well as SOPs in a reflexive and thus dialectical way (Fried et al. 2013; Langer & Fried 2020). The dialectic of control basically builds on the idea that 'to be a human agent is to have power, to be able to "make a difference" in the world.... The most seemingly "powerless" individuals are able to mobilize resources whereby they carve out "spaces of control" in respect of their day-to-day lives' (Giddens 1982: 197–8). The dialectic of control describes how organizational members apply standards not only created by standardizing bodies and/or compliance managers in organizations, but also in foreseen and unforeseen ways. Organizational members enact SOPs by interpreting, modifying, or even manipulating them in (ir)responsible and (un)knowledgeable ways. They may shift the occurrence and meaning of standards to personalize and contextualize them or to cope with their often contradictory requirements. To take the dialectic of control seriously means for organizations, on the one hand, not to insist on stubborn compliance with SOPs and, on the other hand, to systematically examine how the deviant, defiant, and repair behaviour of organizational members is appreciated and reflected in SOPs (Fried 2017).

References

Alvesalo-Kuusi, A., Bittle, S., & Lähteenmäki, L. 2018. Repositioning the corporate criminal: comparing and contrasting corporate criminal liability in Canada and Finland. *International Journal of Comparative and Applied Criminal Justice*, 42, 215–31.

Fried, A. 2017. Terminological distinctions of 'control': a review of the implications for management control research in the context of innovation. *Journal of Management Control*, 28, 5–40.

Fried, A. & Glaa, B. 2020. Introduction to deviance in a world of standards. *In:* Fried, A. (ed.) *Understanding Deviance in a World of Standards.* Oxford: Oxford University Press.

Fried, A. & Langer, S. 2020. Typology of organizational deviance from standards. *In:* Fried, A. (ed.) *Understanding Deviance in a World of Standards.* Oxford: Oxford University Press.

Fried, A. & Walgenbach, P. 2020. Structurationist framework to explore organizational deviance from standards. *In:* Fried, A. (ed.) *Understanding Deviance in a World of Standards.* Oxford: Oxford University Press.

Fried, A., Gey, R., Pretorius, A., & Günther, L. 2013. Decoupling from standards—process management and technical innovation in software development organisations. *International Journal of Innovation Management*, 17 (4).

Gey, R. & Fried, A. 2018. Metastructuring for standards: how organizations respond to the multiplicity of standards. *In:* Jakobs, K. (ed.) *Corporate and Global Standardization Initiatives in Contemporary Society.* Hershey, PA: IGI Global.

Gey, R., Langer, S., & Fried, A. 2020a. Attentive deviance from standards at CraneSolutions. *In:* Fried, A. (ed.) *Understanding Deviance in World of Standards.* Oxford: Oxford University Press.

Gey, R., Langer, S., & Fried, A. 2020b. Over-conformity with standards at MedTech. *In:* Fried, A. (ed.) *Understanding Deviance in a World of Standards.* Oxford: Oxford University Press.

Giddens, A. 1982. *Profiles and Critiques in Social Theory.* London: Palgrave.

Giddens, A. 1984. The Constitution of Society. Outline of the Theory of Structuration. Cambridge: Polity Press.

Jimenez, G. A. 2019. Corporate criminal liability: toward a compliance-orientated approach. *Indiana Journal of Global Legal Studies*, 26, 353–79.

Langer, S. & Fried, A. 2020. Monitoring of standard enactment: an agency perspective. *In:* Fried, A. (ed.) *Understanding Deviance in a World of Standards.* Oxford: Oxford University Press.

Langer, S., Gey, R., Karadzhova-Beyer, D., & Fried, A. 2020b. Non-regulated deviance from standards at MetroEngineers. *In:* Fried, A. (ed.) *Understanding Deviance in a World of Standards.* Oxford: Oxford University Press.

Merton, R. K. 1938. Social structure and anomie. *American Sociological Review*, 3, 672–82.

Nowak, J. 2016. Corporate criminal liability in Germany. *Corporate and Commercial Disputes Review*, 3, 26–7.

Palmer, D. 2017. Institutions, institutional theory and organizational wrongdoing. *In:* Greenwood, R., Oliver, C., Lawrence, T. B., & Meyer, R. E. (eds) *The SAGE Handbook of Organizational Institutionalism*, 2nd edn. Los Angeles: SAGE.

United States Environmental Protection Agency 2019. *Learn about Volkswagen violations.* https://www.epa.gov/vw/learn-about-volkswagen-violations.

Index

Note: Tables, figures, and boxes are indicated by an italic "*t*", "*f*", and "*b*" following the page number.

For the benefit of digital users, indexed terms that span two pages (e.g., 52–53) may, on occasion, appear on only one of those pages.